CAMBRIDGE LIBRARY COLLECTION

Books of enduring scholarly value

History

The books reissued in this series include accounts of historical events and movements by eye-witnesses and contemporaries, as well as landmark studies that assembled significant source materials or developed new historiographical methods. The series includes work in social, political and military history on a wide range of periods and regions, giving modern scholars ready access to influential publications of the past.

American Scenes and Christian Slavery

First published in 1849, American Scenes and Christian Slavery is a description, in epistolary format, of American life, nature, culture, and its slave-trade during the nineteenth century, as observed by a British abolitionist, Ebenezer Davies, during his travels through the United States. Davies had been the minister of Mission Chapel, New Amsterdam, and in this collection of letters, he offers valuable contemporary perspectives on the people and the manners of America as they appeared to him during a journey of over four thousand miles. A favourable reception of a few similar letters that were published in the Patriot magazine paved the way for the preparation of this book. The book's 37 chapters record the author's impressions of Ohio, the river Mississippi and the cities of New Orleans, Cincinnati, Baltimore, Philadelphia, New York, and Boston. Davies' travelogue is a witty account of an English traveller's experiences of nineteenth-century America.

Cambridge University Press has long been a pioneer in the reissuing of out-of-print titles from its own backlist, producing digital reprints of books that are still sought after by scholars and students but could not be reprinted economically using traditional technology. The Cambridge Library Collection extends this activity to a wider range of books which are still of importance to researchers and professionals, either for the source material they contain, or as landmarks in the history of their academic discipline.

Drawing from the world-renowned collections in the Cambridge University Library, and guided by the advice of experts in each subject area, Cambridge University Press is using state-of-the-art scanning machines in its own Printing House to capture the content of each book selected for inclusion. The files are processed to give a consistently clear, crisp image, and the books finished to the high quality standard for which the Press is recognised around the world. The latest print-on-demand technology ensures that the books will remain available indefinitely, and that orders for single or multiple copies can quickly be supplied.

The Cambridge Library Collection will bring back to life books of enduring scholarly value across a wide range of disciplines in the humanities and social sciences and in science and technology.

American Scenes and Christian Slavery

A Recent Tour of Four Thousand Miles in the United States

EBENEZER DAVIES

CAMBRIDGE UNIVERSITY PRESS

Cambridge New York Melbourne Madrid Cape Town Singapore São Paolo Delhi

Published in the United States of America by Cambridge University Press, New York

www.cambridge.org
Information on this title: www.cambridge.org/9781108003872

This edition first published 1849
This digitally printed version 2009

ISBN 978-1-108-00387-2

AMERICAN SCENES,

AND

CHRISTIAN SLAVERY:

A RECENT TOUR OF FOUR THOUSAND MILES IN THE UNITED STATES.

BY

EBENEZER DAVIES,

LATE MINISTER OF MISSION CHAPEL, NEW AMSTERDAM, BERBICE.

LONDON:

JOHN SNOW, 35, PATERNOSTER ROW.

———

MDCCCXLIX.

PREFACE.

Dᴜʀɪɴɢ his recent sojourn in the United States, the
Author did not conceive the intention of writing a book
on the subject. All he contemplated was the publication
of a few letters in a London Journal on which he had
been accustomed to rely for intelligence from Europe
when residing in Berbice. So much he was disposed
to attempt for several reasons.

Having entered the States by their most Southern
port—that of New Orleans, and finding himself at once
in the midst of Slavery, he had opportunities of observing that system not often enjoyed by a British
" Abolitionist." As the Pastor, also, of a large congregation, of whom a great number were but a few years
ago held in cruel bondage, he would naturally look upon
the treatment of the same race in America with keener
eyes and feelings more acute than if he had not stood
in that relation.

Identified, too, with those persons who represent the

principles of the old Puritans and Nonconformists in England, he would survey the growth and spread of those principles in their new soil and climate with a more than common interest. New England, especially, on whose sods the foot-prints of the Pilgrims had been impressed, and on whose rocks their early altars had been reared, would be to him hallowed ground.

Travelling, leisurely, as he did, at his own expense, northward from New Orleans to Boston, and westward as far as Utica,—making a tour of more than four thousand miles, sometimes known and sometimes unknown, just as inclination prompted,—representing no public body, bound to no party, a " Deputation sent by himself,"— he was completely free and independent in thought and action, and enjoyed advantages for observation which do not often meet.

It was natural that he should wish to tell his friends in Great Britain, and in the West Indies, what he had seen and heard. To denounce what is evil and to commend what is good is at all times gratifying; in doing which, he sought to describe the men and the manners of America just as they appeared to him.

Several letters, containing the narrative of a few days spent in New Orleans, appeared in the *Patriot*. Their favourable reception by the readers of that journal led to the preparation of the present volume, in which the letters referred to, having undergone a careful revision, re-appear, followed by nearly thirty others descriptive of the Author's tour.

Our Transatlantic friends are morbidly sensitive as to the strictures of strangers. They hate the whole tribe of Travellers and Tourists, Roamers and Ramblers, Peepers and Proclaimers, and affect to ridicule the idea of men who merely pass through the country, presuming to give opinions on things which it is alleged so cursory a view cannot qualify them fully to understand. Our cousins have, doubtless, had occasional provocations from the detested race in question; but their feeling on this point amounts to a national weakness. It is always worth knowing how we appear to the eyes of others, and what impression the first sight of us is apt to produce; and this knowledge none can communicate but the stranger, the tourist, the passer-by. What faults and failings soever we may have in England, and their " name is legion," by all means let them be unsparingly exposed by every foreign tourist that treads upon our soil. Let us be satirized, ridiculed, laughed at, caricatured, anything, so that we may be shamed out of all that is absurd and vicious in our habits and customs. In the present instance our Western kinsmen are described by one, if they will believe his own testimony, of the most candid and truthful of travellers,— one who has viewed them and all their institutions, except *one*, with the most friendly eye, and who deeply regrets that so much of what is lovely and of good report should be marred and blotted by so much of what is disgraceful to a great and enlightened people.

As to the performance in a literary point of view, the Author will say nothing.   The public will form their own judgment.   If they like it, they will read; if not, the most seductive preface would not tempt them.

E. DAVIES.

LONDON, *January* 1, 1849.

CONTENTS.

LETTER XXII.

LETTER XXIII.

LETTER XXIV.

LETTER XXV.

LETTER XXVI.

LETTER XXVII.

LETTER I.

THE ill health of my wife, occasioned by long residence amid the sultry swamps of Guiana, compelled
me a few months ago to accompany her on a visit to
the United States of America. Having taken our passage in a ship to New Orleans, we found ourselves in
fifteen days on the far-famed Mississippi,—the "father
of waters." On gazing around, our first feeling was
one of awe, to find ourselves actually ascending that
majestic stream, that great artery of the greatest valley
in the world, leading into the very heart of a continent.
The weather was very cold; the trees on the river's bank
were leafless; and the aspect of nature on every hand
told it was winter. What a change! But a fortnight
before we were panting under an almost vertical sun.

We found the Mississippi much narrower than we
had anticipated. In some places it is only about half a
mile wide; while below New Orleans it never, I should
say, exceeds a mile in width. This is remarkable, since
not less than fifty-seven large navigable rivers contri-
bute to swell its waters. It is, however, very deep,

B

and, even at the distance of 500 miles above New Orleans, is navigated by vessels of 300 tons; nay, at 1,364 miles from its mouth, it attains an average depth of fifteen feet. In its course, it waters 2,500 miles of country. Among the rivers that pour themselves into this immense stream are—the Missouri, which has first traversed a space of 2,000 miles; the Arkansas, 1,300 miles; the Red River, 1,000 miles; and the Ohio, 700 miles.

Unfortunately, at the entrance of this noble river, there is a bar called the Balize, so shallow as hitherto to have seriously interfered with the navigation of large and deeply-laden vessels. Even for the cotton trade, a particular construction of ship has been found needful, with a flatter bottom than usual, in order to pass easily over this bar, any effort to remove which the rapidity of the stream would render fruitless. This circumstance, with the want of harbour at the mouth of the Mississippi, has hitherto operated greatly against the trade with New Orleans, which is 110 miles up the river. Recently, however, a magnificent harbour has been discovered between Cat Island and Isle Apitre, within Lake Borgne, and only ten miles from the coast of the mainland. This new harbour, easily accessible from the sea, at all times contains a depth of water varying from thirty to fifty feet, and is so protected on all sides that vessels may ride with the greatest safety in the worst weather. From this harbour to Bayou on the mainland the distance is only twelve miles, and from Bayou to New Orleans forty-six miles,—making altogether only fifty-eight miles from Cat Island Harbour to New Orleans; whereas, by the difficult and dangerous route of the Mississippi, the distance is 110 miles. The importance and value of such a harbour it is difficult to over-estimate. Its beneficial effect on the future destiny of the great valley will be prodigious.

I have said the "great valley," and well it deserves the appellation. It contains as many square miles, with more tillable ground than the whole continent of Europe. It measures about 1,341,649 square miles, and is therefore six times larger than France. And this valley is as rich as it is extensive. It is the "fat" valley. Never did human eye behold a finer soil, or more luxuriant productions. The treasures beneath the surface are as precious as those above. The lead and copper mines are among the best in the world. Iron and coal also abound. Building materials, of beauty and strength, adapted to form cottages for the poor or palaces for the rich, are not wanting. Nature has here furnished in lavish profusion everything necessary for converting the wilderness into smiling fields, studded with populous cities.

But we are not yet within the great valley. We are only at its entrance, sailing up the "father of waters," against the stream, at the rate of four or five miles an hour. It is usual for sailing-vessels to be towed by steam-tugs to their destination; but, having a fair breeze, and no tug at hand, we were indebted to our sails alone. The motion was exceedingly pleasant, after the tossings we had had in the Gulf of Mexico. The vessel glided smoothly along, and new objects presented themselves continually on either hand.

My enjoyment of the scenery, however, was soon marred by an attack of fever and ague, which sent me below. While I was down, several steam-tugs towing vessels down the river met us. Their unearthly groans filled me with terror. Their noise was not that of puff —puff—puff—puff, like all the other steamers that I had ever heard, but something composed of a groan, a grunt, and a growl—deep-drawn, as from the very caverns of Vulcan, and that at awfully-solemn intervals, —grunt—grunt—grunt—grunt !   This peculiarity, I was told, arose from their "high-pressure" engines. The sound, thus explained, brought to my recollection all the dreadful stories of boiler explosions with which the very name of the Mississippi had become associated in my mind.   But (thought I) they have surely learned wisdom from experience, and are become more skilful or more cautious than they used to be !

While I was engaged with these reflections, our captain came down, and handed me a couple of New Orleans papers, which he had just received from the pilot.   Here was a treat; and, feeling a little better, I began with eagerness to open one of them out.   It was the *New Orleans Bee* of January 23; and, *horresco referens*, the first thing that caught my eye was the following paragraph :—

" STEAM-BOAT EXPLOSION.—LOSS OF LIFE.—Captain Haviland, of the steam-ship 'Galveston,' from Galveston, reports that the tow-boat 'Phœnix,' Captain Crowell, burst her boilers when near the head of the South-west Pass [which we had but just passed], killing and wounding about twenty-five in number, seven of whom belonged to the boat, the *balance* to a barque she had alongside; carrying away the foremast of the barque close to her deck, and her mainmast above her cross-trees, together with all her fore-rigging, bulwarks, and injuring her hull considerably. The ship 'Manchester,' which she had also alongside, was seriously injured, having her bulwarks carried away, her long-boat destroyed," &c.

Such was the paragraph, with not a syllable of note or comment on cause or consequences. It was evidently an every-day occurrence. What recklessness was here indicated! and how comforting to a sick and nervous man, now near the very spot of the occurrence, and in a vessel about to be placed in the same pleasant relation to one of those grunting monsters as the unfortunate "barque" had but three days before occupied, with the trifling "balance" of eighteen of her crew "killed and wounded!"

The fever having left me, I ventured on deck. At this moment one of these infernal machines came in sight, towing down three large ships. Instead of having them behind, as on the Thames and Mersey, she (like the "Phœnix") had one on either side, closely lashed to herself, and the other only behind. This terrific monster seemed to be carrying them away arm-in-arm, like two prisoners, to destruction. At all events, it was a position of familiarity and friendship with the "Sprite of Steam" of which I did not at all like the idea; and yet we ourselves were by-and-by to be placed in its perilous embrace!

The dreaded monster gone by, I resumed the perusal of my New Orleans papers. Now (thought I) I am in a slave country! I wonder whether these papers will give any indication of the fact. In a little while my eye, surveying the *Bee* of January 21, caught sight of an advertisement signed "N. St. Martin, Sheriff, Parish of St. Charles," and containing a list of 112 human beings offered for sale! The miserable catalogue was full of instruction. In drawing it up the humane sheriff became quite facetious, telling the public that "Frank, 35 years old, American negro, [was] *good for everything;*" while "Stephen, 46 years old, [was] *fit for nothing at all;*" that "Salinette, 60 years old, hospital-nurse, [was] *a good subject, subject to rheumatisms;*" and that "Peter, American negro-man, 38 years old, [was] *a good cook, having had two fits of madness.*" I will back this against the Dublin *Hue and Cry.*

LETTER II.

THE evening closed upon us, sailing pleasantly up the Mississippi. Having a beautiful moonlight night, we kept on our way. About seven o'clock we overtook a small fishing-boat laden with oysters. In consideration of our allowing them—not the oysters, but the boatmen—to fasten a rope to our vessel, to help them on, they gave us a generous and refreshing supply. But such oysters! In neither size nor shape did they resemble those of the Old World. As to size, they were gigantic,—as to shape, not unlike the human foot. They abound not far from the mouth of the river, and many men obtain a livelihood by carrying them up to the New Orleans market. The mode of cooking adopted in this instance was that of putting them on the fire till the shells opened. To our taste, they were not in flavour to be compared to the London oysters; but we did not venture to tell our American captain so. We had yet, however, to taste the deliciously-cooked oysters of the northern cities.

About 10 p.m., the breeze having in a great measure died away, our captain thought it imprudent to attempt to "go a-head" further that night, and the anchor was cast. We were now fifty miles above the entrance of the river.

Early next day the anchor was raised, the sails were unfurled, and we again moved along. About 8 a.m., through the narrowness of the river, the rapidity of the stream, and other causes, our "smart" captain, who had chuckled vastly on passing all other ships in the river,—and especially British ships,—ran his own vessel right ashore! There we were in a complete "fix," till one of the grunting monsters (coming up with two vessels—one on each arm, as usual,—and letting them go for a few minutes,) came to our rescue. Forbidding as was his aspect, we were very glad to feel a little of his giant power. Of this one I had, of course, a better view than I had had of any other of the species. It had, like the rest, two chimneys in front, like perpendicular tusks, with a ladder between them. The ladder was for the purpose of ascent,—the ascent for the purpose of elevation,—and the elevation for the purpose of "look out." The top of the ladder, in short, rendered the same service as the top of a ship's mast at sea. This "tug" had also, a little further aft, a funnel-like sort of chimney, for the emission of steam. The whole structure was—like a forge below, and a palace above. In the lower story were the boiler, engine, fuel, &c., all exposed to view; while the upper contained splendid apartments for the captain, the engineer, and other officers. The engineer of that vessel, I understood, had a salary of 250 dollars (50 guineas) per month!

Released from our stranded position, we found ourselves in a few minutes lashed to the monster's side, and completely in his power. Here we were, in the same dread position in which the day before we felt horrified to see others! From some of the officers, our captain obtained another newspaper. It was the *New Orleans Daily Picayune* for January 26. Getting hold of it, I found whole columns of slave-sale advertisements. A few specimens will illustrate better than any description the state of things in this "land of liberty!"

" NEGROES FOR SALE. — The subscribers No. 56, Esplanade-street, have just received a lot of valuable Slaves from Virginia and Maryland, consisting of Mechanics, Farm Hands, and House Servants, and have made *arrangements not to be surpassed* in this market for a *regular supply* from the above markets, as also Alabama. We hazard nothing in saying, if our former friends, and others wishing to purchase good servants or hands, will give us a call, they shall not be disappointed.

" N.B. All Negroes sold by the undersigned are fully guaranteed.

" SLATTER & LOCKETT,
" n11—6m." " 56, Esplanade-street."

"For Sale.—A likely Mulatto Negress, aged twenty-two years,—she is a first-rate cook, and a good washer and ironer, besides being a tolerable good seamstress.

"Anderson & Burnet,

" j26."   " 38, Camp-street."

" Slaves for Sale.—I have just received, and offer for sale, a very likely lot of Virginia Negroes.   Those wishing to purchase will do well to give me a call at my office, No. 157, Gravier-street, between Carondelet and Baronne streets.   I will be *constantly receiving* Negroes from Virginia and North Carolina during the winter.

"C. M. Rutherford."

"n13—6m."

" Slaves for Sale.—No. 165, Gravier-street.—The subscriber has always on hand a number of Slaves, consisting of House Servants, Field Hands, and Mechanics, which will be sold low for cash or negotiable paper. Persons desirous of purchasing will find it to their interest to call and examine.   The subscriber will also receive and sell on consignment any Negro that may be intrusted to his care.

" He would also respectfully notify persons engaged in the Slave Trade, that he is prepared to board them and their Slaves on the most reasonable terms.

"Wm. H. Merritt."

"ol—6m."

" References—J. A. Barelli, C. J. Mansoni."

"ONE HUNDRED NEGROES.—For Sale at No. 13, Moreau-street.—All of which have just been received from Maryland and Virginia. My old friends, and others wishing to purchase Slaves, will find it to their interest to call on me before purchasing elsewhere.

Also will receive *large shipments during the season* from the above States.

"R. R. BEASLEY,

"d31—3m."   "13, Moreau-street."

Runaway slaves seem to be constantly advertised, with (as in the case of ship advertisements) a small woodcut figure representing them in the very act of making their escape. Indeed, almost everything advertised is accompanied by its picture,—ships, houses, bonnets, boots, leeches, oysters, and so forth. Even a strayed horse or a strayed cow is advertised with a picture representing the animal in the very act of going astray. On the same principle, and in like manner, human chattels assuming their natural right to go where they please, are advertised with a woodcut representing them as bending forward in the act of running, and carrying with them a small bundle containing their scanty wardrobe,—a pitiable figure! And yet this is done, not to awaken sympathy, but to excite vigilance, as in the following instances, which I have picked out of the *Picayune :*—

"ONE HUNDRED DOLLARS REWARD.—The aforesaid sum will be given to any person who will bring back to the undersigned the negro-girl Eugenia, and her mulatto child aged two years. Said slave has been purloined or enticed away by her former owner, Madame Widow Decaux, who secretly went out of this State on the 12th December, 1846. Said Widow Decaux is well known in New Orleans as a notorious swindler, having been prosecuted for having pawned logs of wood to a merchant of this city instead of dry goods. She has a scar on her forehead, and several others on her neck, and is accompanied by her aged mother, and her boy aged ten years.

"J. B. Dupeire."

" j7—15t*."

" Ran away from the subscriber, on the 20th November last, a negro man named Sandy, about twenty-five years of age, five feet five inches high, very dark complexion, speaks both French and English, *shows the mark of the whip very much.* A liberal reward will be paid for his apprehension, either by confining in any gaol, so that I can secure him, or his delivery to me at Plaquemine, La.

"W. H. Carr."

"j20—3tW."

And yet the editor of this very paper, in his leading article, reviewing the past, (that day being the tenth anniversary of its own existence,) coolly says, "In entering upon our eleventh anniversary, how different the spectacle! Industry in every quarter of the land receives its meet reward; Commerce is remunerated by wholesome gains; *Comfort blesses the toil of the labourer* (!) and Hope encourages the enterprise of all the industrial classes of our citizens."

As the day advanced, my fever returned; and I was obliged to go below. A furious tempest arose, so that even our "monster" could scarcely get along. The lightning flashed, the thunder roared, and the rain fell in torrents. It was a terrific day! As night approached, our captain told us the vessel could not then be got any further,—it was about two miles from the city; and if we particularly wished to go ashore, we must get ready directly, and go with him in the steam-tug. Anxious for a good night's rest, on shore we resolved to go. I had to turn out in that state of profuse perspiration which always succeeds the fever, and my wife hurriedly selected a few necessary things. Poor thing! she was almost overwhelmed with the trying circumstances in which she was placed,—thousands of miles from home—about to enter a place in which she knew not a single soul—her husband ill, and herself an invalid! But there was no help for it. Amidst torrents of rain, we made the fearful transition from the ship to the tug, while both vessels were in violent agitation. It was done. And now we were in the " monster's " own bosom, expecting every moment his bowels to burst, and send us into eternity. The noise of the engine, the grunting of the steam, the raging of the wind, the pelting of the rain, and the roaring of the thunder, made it almost impossible to

hear anything besides; but I managed to shout in my
wife's ear the natural, though not very consolatory
question, "Were we ever in so fearful a position before?" "Never!" (and we had had some experience
of storms by both land and sea) was her awe-stricken
reply.

We detached ourselves from the sailing-vessel;
but, with all the power of steam, we could scarcely
get along.   At last the "monster's" bellowing was
hushed,—the tremor ceased,—we were there! But
how to get ashore was still a difficulty. It was about
100 yards off.   Planks, however, were eventually
placed so as to enable us to descend from our lofty
"tug" into a ship at anchor, from that into another,
from that again into a third, and from that at length
on *terra firma.*

The hour was between 7 and 8 p.m.; and we
were taken to a ship-chandler's store, while our kind
captain went to get a chaise for us. The store was
closed; but the owner and three other gentlemen were
there, seated before a comfortable coal fire, apparently
enjoying themselves after the business of the day.
They received us very courteously, and gave us chairs
by the fireside. The storm of that day they told us
had done much harm to the shipping, and was severer
than any other they had experienced during the last
seven years. While the conversation was going on,
plash made one, *plash* made another, *plash* made a
third, by spurting a certain brownish secretion on the
floor! I had often heard of this as an American habit,

but always thought our cousins in this matter (as in many others) were caricatured. Here, however, was the actual fact, and that in the presence of a lady! Yet these were apparently very respectable men.

Having waited about a quarter of an hour, anxiously listening for the rumbling of the expected wheels, I heard in the distance a strange kind of noise, resembling that of a fire-shovel, a pair of tongs, a poker, and an iron hoop tied loosely together with a string, and drawn over the pavement! "What in the world is that?" said I. "It is the chaise," was the answer. The vehicle was quickly at the door. In we were bundled, and orders given to drive us to the "St. Charles's." We scarcely knew what this "St. Charles's" was; but, as all with whom we had conversed seemed to take it for granted that we should go thither, and as any one *saint* was to us as good as any other, we echoed, "To the St. Charles's." And now began such a course of jolting as we had never before experienced. It seemed as if all the gutters and splash-holes in the universe had been collected together, and we had to drive over the whole. This continued about half an hour, by which we learned that we were at first much further from the "St. Charles's" than we supposed. The machine at last stopped, and we alighted, thankful to have escaped a complete stoppage of our breath.

We were there. A waiter (he was not to be mistaken,—he bore a family resemblance to all the waiters of the world) was instantly at the coach-door, to help us *out* and to help us *in*. He conducted us into a

lobby, up a flight of stairs, and through a long passage, to a large saloon, where about 150 ladies and
gentlemen were assembled,—some sitting, some standing, some talking, some laughing, and some playing
with their fingers. But, no! we shrunk back. Thither
we would not be led, all wet and dirty as we were.
We begged to be shown into a private room. The
waiter stared, and said he had none to take us to,
except I would first go to the "office." But what was
to become of my fellow-traveller in the meantime?
No woman belonging to the establishment made her
appearance, and there my wife was obliged to stand
alone in the passage, whilst I followed the waiter
through aisles and passages, and turnings and twistings, and ups and downs, to a large saloon, where
about 200 gentlemen were smoking cigars! What a
sight! and what a smell! Who can realize the vast
idea of 200 mouths, in one room, pouring forth the
fumes of tobacco? I was directed to the high-priest
of the establishment in the "office," or (as I should
say) at the "bar." Without verbally replying to my
application, he handed me a book in which to record
my name. Having obeyed the hint, I again asked my
taciturn host if myself and wife could be accommodated. He then, with manifest reluctance, took the
cigar out of his mouth, and said he had only one
room to spare, and that was at the top of the house.
It was "Hobson's choice," and I accepted it. And now
for a journey! Talk of ascending the Monument on
Fish-street Hill! what is that compared to ascending

the St. Charles's, at New Orleans? No. 181 was reached at last. The next task was to find my wife, which after another long and circuitous journey was accomplished. In process of time fire was made, and "tea for two" brought up. Let me, therefore, close my letter and enjoy it.

LETTER III.

New Orleans—The Story of Pauline—Adieu to the St. Charles's—
Description of that Establishment—First Sight of Slaves for Sale
—Texts for Southern Divines—Perilous Picture.

FROM No. 181 of the "St. Charles's," we descended, after a good night's rest, to see some of the lions of the place. Here we are (thought I) in New Orleans—the metropolis of a great slave country,—a town in which exist many depôts for the disposal of human beings,—the very city where, a few months ago, poor Pauline was sacrificed as the victim of lust and cruelty! Unhappy girl! What a tragedy! On the 1st of August last, I told the horrid tale to my emancipated people in Berbice. Here it is, as extracted from the *Essex* (United States) *Transcript*. Read it, if you please; and then you will have a notion of the feelings with which I contemplated a city rendered infamous by such a transaction.

"MANY of our readers have probably seen a paragraph stating that a young slave girl was recently hanged at New Orleans for the crime of striking and abusing her mistress. The religious press of the north has not, so far as we are aware, made any comments upon this execution. It is too busy pulling the mote

out of the eye of the heathen, to notice the beam in our
nominal Christianity at home. Yet this case, viewed in
all its aspects, is an atrocity which has (God be thanked)
no parallel in heathen lands. It is a hideous offshoot
of American Republicanism and American Christianity!
It seems that Pauline—a young and beautiful girl—
attracted the admiration of her master, and being (to
use the words of the law) his "chattel personal to all
intents and purposes whatsoever," became the victim of
his lust. So wretched is the condition of the slave
woman, that even the brutal and licentious regard of
her master is looked upon as the highest exaltation of
which her lot is susceptible. The slave girl in this
instance evidently so regarded it; and as a natural
consequence, in her new condition, triumphed over and
insulted her mistress,—in other words, repaid in some
degree the scorn and abuse with which her mistress
had made her painfully familiar. The laws of the
Christian State of Mississippi inflict the punishment of
death upon the slave who lifts his or her hand against
a white person. Pauline was accused of beating her
mistress,—tried, found guilty, and condemned to die!
But it was discovered on the trial that she was in a
condition to become a mother, and her execution was
delayed until the birth of the child. She was conveyed to the prison cell. There, for many weary
months, unchcered by the voice of kindness, alone,
hopeless, desolate, she waited for the advent of the
new and quickening life within her, which was to be
the signal of her own miserable death. And the bells

there called to mass and prayer-meeting, and Methodists sang, and Baptists immersed, and Presbyterians
sprinkled, and young mothers smiled through tears
upon their new-born children,—and maidens and ma-
trons of that great city sat in their cool verandahs, and
talked of love, and household joys, and domestic happiness; while, all that dreary time, the poor slave girl
lay on the scanty straw of her dungeon, waiting—with
what agony the great and pitying God of the white
and black only knows—for the birth of the child of her
adulterous master.   Horrible !   Was ever what George
Sand justly terms 'the great martyrdom of maternity'
—that fearful trial which love alone converts into joy
unspeakable—endured under such conditions ?   What
was her substitute for the kind voices and gentle sooth-
ings of affection ?   The harsh grating of her prison
lock,—the mockings and taunts of unfeeling and brutal
keepers !   What, with the poor Pauline, took the place
of the hopes and joyful anticipations which support and
solace the white mother, and make her couch of torture
happy with sweet dreams ?   The prospect of seeing the
child of her sorrow, of feeling its lips upon her bosom,
of hearing its feeble cry—alone, unvisited of its unna-
tural father ; and then in a few days—just when the
mother's affections are strongest, and the first smile of
her infant compensates for the pangs of the past—the
scaffold and the hangman !   Think of the last terrible
scene,—the tearing of the infant from her arms, the
death-march to the gallows, the rope around her delicate neck, and her long and dreadful struggles, (for,

attenuated and worn by physical suffering and mental sorrow, her slight frame had not sufficient weight left to produce the dislocation of her neck on the falling of the drop,) swinging there alive for nearly half an hour—a spectacle for fiends in the shape of humanity! Mothers of New England! such are the fruits of slavery. Oh! in the name of the blessed God, teach your children to hate it, and to pity its victims. Petty politicians and empty-headed Congress debators are vastly concerned, lest the 'honour of the country' should be compromised in the matter of the Oregon Boundary. Fools! One such horrible atrocity as this murder of poor Pauline 'compromises' us too deeply to warrant any further display of their patriotism. It would compromise Paradise itself! An intelligent and philanthropic European gentleman, who was in New Orleans at the time of the execution, in a letter to a friend in this vicinity, after detailing the circumstances of the revolting affair, exclaims, ' God of goodness! God of justice! There must be a future state to redress the wrongs of this. I am almost tempted to say —there must be a future state, or no God!' "

On Saturday, the 30th, we set off to seek private lodgings. Led by a board having on it in large letters the words "Private Boarding," we "inquired within," found what we wanted, and engaged for eight dollars per week each. We then went to pay our bill at the " St. Charles's," and to bring away our carpet-bag. We had been there two nights, had had one dinner,

two teas, and two breakfasts. These meals, as we did
not like to join the hundreds at the "ordinary," were
served to us (in a very *ordinary* way however) in our
bedroom. In fact, the waiting was miserably done.
And yet for this we had the pleasure of paying eleven
dollars,—say £2. 6s.! We gladly bade adieu to the
"St. Charles's." It suited neither our taste nor our
pocket. Nevertheless, it is a magnificent concern. The
edifice was finished in 1838 by a company, and cost
600,000 dollars. The gentlemen's dining-room is 129
feet by 50, and is 22 feet high; having four ranges of
tables, capable of accommodating 500 persons. The
ladies' dining-room is 52 feet by 36. The house contains 350 rooms, furnishing accommodation for between
600 and 700 guests; and it was quite full when we
were there. The front is adorned with a projecting
portico, supported by six fine Corinthian columns, resting upon a rustic basement. The edifice is crowned
with a large dome, forty-six feet in diameter, having a
beautiful Corinthian turret on the top. This dome is
the most conspicuous object in the city. Viewed from
a distance, it seems to stand in the same relation to
New Orleans as St. Paul's to London. The furniture
of this immense establishment cost 150,000 dollars. A
steam-engine, producing a very disagreeable tremor, is
constantly at work in the culinary department.

While on our way to get the remainder of our baggage from the ship, we came upon a street in which a
long row, or rather several rows, of black and coloured
people were exposed in the open air (and under a smil-

ing sun) for sale ! There must have been from 70 to
100, all young people, varying from 15 to 30 years of
age. All (both men and women) were well dressed, to
set them off to the best advantage, as is always the case
at these sales. Several of the coloured girls—evidently
the daughters of white men—had their sewing-work
with them, as evidence of their skill in that department.
The whole were arranged under a kind of verandah,
having a foot-bench (about six inches high) to stand
upon, and their backs resting against the wall. None
were in any way tied or chained ; but two white men
("soul-drivers," I suppose) were sauntering about in
front of them, each with a cigar in his mouth, a whip
under his arm, and his hands in his pockets, looking
out for purchasers. In its external aspect, the exhibition
was not altogether unlike what I have sometimes seen
in England, when some wandering Italian has ranged
against a wall his bronzed figures of distinguished men,
—Shakspeare, Napoleon, Wellington, Nelson, &c. It
was between twelve and one in the day ; but there was
no crowd, not even a single boy or girl looking on,—so
common and every-day was the character of the scene.
As we moved along in front of this sable row, one of
the white attendants (though my wife had hold of my
arm) said to me, with all the *nonchalance* of a Smith-
field cattle-drover, "Looking out for a few niggers this
morning ?" Never did I feel my manhood so insulted.
My indignation burned for expression. But I endeavoured to affect indifference, and answered in a don't-
care sort of tone, " No, I am not particularly in want

of any to-da—.' I could scarcely finish the sentence.
Emotion choked my utterance. I passed on, gazing at
the troop of degraded human beings, till my eyes
became so filled with tears that I was compelled to
turn my face another way. Though I anticipated such
scenes, and had tried to prepare my mind for them, yet
(now that they were actually before me) I was completely
overcome, and was obliged to seek a place to sit down
while I composed my feelings. With what sentiments
my companion beheld the scene, I will leave you to
conjecture!

It was Saturday morning; and with my professional
habits, I naturally thought of the many divines in that
very city, who were at that moment shut up in their
studies, preparing their discourses for the morrow. I
wished I had them all before me. I could have given
every one of them a text to preach upon. I would
have said, " Gentlemen, see there! and blush for your
fellow-citizens. See there! and never again talk of
American liberty. See there! and lift up your voices
like so many trumpets against this enormity. See
there! and in the face of persecution, poverty, imprisonment, and (if needs be) even death itself, bear your
faithful testimony, and cease not until this foul stain
be wiped away from your national escutcheon. Dr.
S——, to-morrow morning let this be your text,—
' Where is Abel, thy brother?' Dr. H——, let your
discourse be founded on Exod. xxi. 16: 'And he that
stealeth a man, and selleth him, or if he be found in
his hand, he shall surely be put to death.' You, the

Rev. Mr. C——, let your gay and wealthy congregation be edified with a solemn and impressive sermon on Is. lviii. 6: 'Is not this the fast that I have chosen? to loose the bands of wickedness, to undo the heavy burdens, and to let the oppressed go free, and that ye break every yoke?' And you, the Rev. Mr. H——, let your hearers have a full and faithful exposition of that law which is 'fulfilled in one word, even in this, Thou shalt love thy neighbour as thyself.' "

In the afternoon of the same day, as I walked along one of the principal streets, I saw a flag issue from a fine large public building to invite " ladies and gentlemen" to see "the magnificent picture of the departure of the Israelites from Egypt,"—the canvas containing 2,000 square feet, and 2,000,000 of figures! How significant! It would have been still more so, if the number of "figures" had been 3,000,000 instead of 2,000,000. What an "abolition" picture! It must have been worse than "Jacob and his Sons," which was expunged from a catalogue of the American Sunday-School Union, because, in reprehending the sale of Joseph to the merchants, it reflected upon the *internal* slave-trade! Surely such exhibitions will affect the safety of the "peculiar institution!"

LETTER IV.

THINK of a Sabbath in New Orleans! Curious to know how people did really pray and preach, with slavery and slave-trading in their vilest forms around them, I set off in search of the "First Presbyterian Church." It is a beautiful building: seldom, if ever, had I seen a place of worship the exterior of which I liked so much. Being a quarter of an hour too soon, I had opportunity for some preliminary researches. Wishing to see whether there was a "Negro Pew," I went into the gallery, and took a seat on the left side of the organ. The "church" I found as beautiful inside as out. Instead of a pulpit, there was a kind of platform lined with crimson, which looked very nice. Most of the pews below, and some above, were lined with the same material. A splendid chandelier, having many circles of glass brilliants, was suspended from the ceiling. Altogether, the "church" was a very neat and graceful structure,—capable, as I learned, of accommodating about 1,500 people. But the floor— the floor! What a drawback! It was stained all over with tobacco juice! Faugh! Those Southern men are the most filthy people in that respect I ever met with. They are a great "spitting" community. To make it still more revolting to luckless travellers, this nasty habit is generally attended with noises in the throat resembling the united growling of a dozen mastiffs.

While the congregation was assembling, a grey-headed, aristocratic-looking old negro came up into the gallery, walked along "as one having authority," and placed himself in a front pew on the right-hand side of the pulpit. Two black women shortly followed, taking their seats in the same region. Others succeeded, till ultimately there were from forty to fifty of the sable race in that part of the gallery. Not one white was to be seen among the blacks, nor one black among the whites. There, then, was the "Negro Pew!" It was the first time even my West India eyes ever beheld a distinction of colour maintained in the house of God!

At eleven o'clock precisely, a man of tall but stooping figure and dark complexion, about forty years of age, muffled up in a cloak, took his stand at the bottom of the pulpit or platform stairs. It was Dr. S——. He appeared to beckon to some one in the congregation. A tall, lank old gentleman, with a black cravat, and shirt-collar turned over it à l'Américain, stepped forward, and, ascending the steps before the Doctor, occupied one of the two chairs with which the rostrum was furnished, the Doctor taking the other. I supposed him to be one of the elders, going to give out the hymns, or to assist in the devotional exercises. At

this moment the organ—a fine-toned instrument—
struck up, and the choir sang some piece—known, I
presume, only to themselves, for no others joined in it.
This prelude I have since found is universal in America.
In all places of worship provided with an organ, a
"voluntary" on that instrument is the first exercise.
In the present instance the choir had no sooner ceased
than the Doctor stood up, having his cloak still resting
upon his shoulders, and stretched forth his right hand.
At this signal all the people stood up, and he offered a
short prayer. "Where is Abel, thy brother?" thought
I, during this address to the Father of the spirits of
all flesh. He then read the 23rd and 24th Psalms.
"Where is Abel, thy brother?" was still ringing in
my ears. The 33rd Psalm was then sung. "Where
is Abel, thy brother?" was still heard (by me at least)
louder than the swelling tones of the organ. The
singing done, of which the choir still had an entire
monopoly, the Doctor read the 14th chapter of Mark;
and as he read the awful story of our Lord's betrayal,
I could not help thinking that the only difference between some of the Southern slave-dealers and Judas
was, that had they been in his place, they would have
made a "smarter" bargain. The reading, though free
from affectation, was not by any means in the best
style. The chapter finished, the tall elder (as I took
him to be) prayed,—the congregation standing. The
prayer was short and appropriate, and the language
tolerably correct; but the tone and pronunciation were
queer. I supposed them to indicate some provincialism

with which I was not acquainted. Along with that peculiar nasal sound for which nearly all Americans are distinguished, there was in the voice a mixture of coaxing and familiarity which was a little offensive; still, as a "layman's" exercise, it was very good. He prayed for "every grace and Christian virtue." Amen, ejaculated I,—then your slaves will soon be free. He prayed for "our nation and rulers." He prayed that "the great blessings of Civil and Religious Liberty which we enjoy may be handed down to future generations." "Looking out for a few niggers this morning?" thought I. He also prayed for "the army and navy, and our fellow-citizens now on the field of battle," in allusion to the Mexican War.—The prayer ended, Dr. S—— gave out another hymn. During the whole of the service, I may here remark, there was a good deal of going in and out, talking, whispering, spitting, guttural turbulence, &c. At first there were about a dozen white boys in my neighbourhood, who seemed as if they belonged to the Sabbath-school; but, having no teacher to look after them, and enjoying the full swing of liberty, they had before sermon all disappeared.

After the singing, Dr. S—— made several announcements,—amongst others, that the monthly concert to pray for the success of Foreign Missions would be held there to-morrow evening, when several speakers would address the meeting. By all means (said I to myself), and I'll try to be present. He also told his people that the Rev. —. ————, (from some place in Kentucky,—

the particulars I did not catch,) was in the city, as a deputation from the ladies, to solicit subscriptions for the erection of a new church that was greatly needed.

The tall man in the black neckcloth then rose, and, to my surprise and disappointment, read a text. It was 1 Cor. iii. 21 : "For all things are yours." I imagine *he* was the deputation from the Kentuckian ladies.

After a few introductory remarks explanatory of the context, he proposed to inquire what are the things which "enter into" ("constitute," we should say) the inheritance of God's people. Slaves (said I to myself) are a part of the inheritance of "God's people," both here and in Kentucky: I wonder if he will notice that.

The first thing, I observe (said he), that enters into the inheritance of God's people, is the living ministry— "Paul, or Apollos, or Cephas." To illustrate the value of this blessing, he referred to the imaginary Elixir of Life, the Philosopher's Stone, and the Universal Panacea. If such things really existed, what a high value would men set upon them! But here was something of incomparably higher worth. In order to form an estimate of its value, he led his hearers to imagine the entire loss of the living ministry. Secondly, the "world" belongs to God's people. It is sustained for their sake, and therefore sinners are indebted to God's people for the preservation of their lives. To prove this he referred to the words of our Lord, "Ye are the salt of the earth." In speaking of the preserving nature of salt, he supposed the sea to be without salt.

How pestilential then! But as it is, how salubrious
the air that has swept over it! He also referred to
another case. There was once (said he) a ship in a
tremendous storm; the crew and passengers—about
270 in number—were at their wits' end; nothing appeared before them but a watery grave. On board of
that ship was a poor prisoner, bound in chains. He
was deemed to be of the filth of the world, and the off-
scouring of all things. To that poor prisoner the
angel of the Lord came, and told him what must be
done to save the life of every one on board. The angel's
directions were obeyed, and all were preserved. Thus,
for the sake of one of God's people, were 270 lives
spared. He offered another illustration. Three men
came to converse with Abraham, on the plains of
Mamre. They told him that God was about to destroy
five cities. Abraham began to intercede for them.
The preacher recapitulated the wondrous story of this
intercession and its success, as further proving that
ungodly men owe the preservation of their lives to the
presence and prayers of the people of God. The para-
ble of the tares was also cited, as illustrating the same
position. "Let both grow together until the harvest."
Imagine (said he) all the people of God removed from
the face of the earth—no heart to love Him—no tongue
to praise Him,—there would be no reason why the earth
should be continued in existence another moment. In
the light of this subject, see how great a privilege it is
to have pious relatives. "Life" also was, in the third
place, a part of the inheritance of the child of God,

because during it he makes a provision for eternity. He dwelt on the richness of the treasure which God's people are laying up. Suppose (said he) any of you were making money at the rate of fifty dollars an hour, —(I dare say you do so sometimes, reflected I, when you get a good price for your "niggers,")—how rich you would soon be! and how anxious that not a single hour should be lost! But the child of God is laying up treasure at a faster rate than this. Every time he works for God, he is laying it up. The Christian's treasure is also of the right kind, and laid up in the right place. If any of you were going to emigrate to another country, you would be anxious to know what sort of money was current in that country, and to get your's changed into it. The Christian's treasure is the current coin of eternity. It is also in the right place. Where would you like to have your treasure? Why, at home. The Christian's treasure is at home—in his Father's house. Life is his also, because during it he fights the battles of the Lord. Here the preacher made an approving reference to the war against the Mexicans; and I strongly suspect that this view of the Christian's inheritance was dragged in for the very purpose. We fight (said he) under the eye of the General. We fight with a certainty of victory. Death too was, in the fourth place, a portion of the Christian's inheritance. To the people of God curses are made blessings, and to those who are not his people blessings are made curses. So sickness, persecution, and death are made blessings to the saints. Death to the Christian is like an honourable discharge to the soldier after the toil and the danger of the field of strife. But that illustration (said he) is too feeble : I will give you another. Imagine, on a bleak and dreary mountain, the humble dwelling of two old people. They are bending under the weight of years. Amidst destitution and want, they are tottering on the verge of the grave. A messenger comes, and tells them of a relative who has died, and left them a large inheritance,—one by which every want will be supplied, and every desire realized,—one that will, the moment they touch it with the soles of their feet, make them young again : he points, moreover, to the very chariot that is to convey them thither. Would this be bad news to those old people? Now, such is death to the child of God. The cord is cut, and the spirit takes its flight to the abodes of the blest. Or take another illustration. A stage-coach was once upset. Many of the passengers were in great danger. One man snatched a little babe from among the wheels, and laid it down in a place of safety on the roadside. Twenty years after the same man was travelling in a stage, on the same road, and telling those around him about the accident which had taken place a long time before. A young lady, sitting opposite, was listening to the narrative with eager interest, and at last she burst out with rapture, " Is it possible that I have at last found my deliverer ? I was that little babe you rescued !" Something like this will be the disclosures that death will make. Having thus illustrated the inheritance of the people of God, let me ask you (said

c 5

he) who are not his people—what will all these things
be to you, if you die without Christ? The living
ministry? The world? Life? Death? Having spoken
briefly, with power and pathos, on each of these particulars, he very coolly and deliberately turned to
Rev. xxii. 17, and read, "The Spirit and the Bride
say, Come; and let him that heareth say, Come," &c.,
&c., and closed abruptly, with neither an Amen nor
an invocation of any kind.

Such was the first sermon I heard in the United
States. It was thoroughly evangelical and good; but
I listened to it with mingled feelings. It was painful
to think that such a ministry could co-exist with slavery.
The creed it is evident may be evangelical, while there
is a woful neglect of the duties of practical piety.

LETTER V.

First Religious Service in America (continued)—A Collection "taken up"
—Rush out—Evening Service—Sketch of the Sermon—Profanation
of the Sabbath—The Monthly Concert for Prayer.

AFTER sermon Dr. S. gave out a hymn, and told
the congregation that the collection for the support of
the "beneficiaries" of that church would be "taken
up" that morning; adding that, in consequence of this
collection not having been made at the usual time (in
May last), some of the young men who were preparing
for the ministry, and dependent on that congregation
for food and clothing, were now in great want. He
also suggested that, if any present were unprepared
with money, they might put in a slip of paper, with
their name, address, and the amount of their contribution, and some one would call upon them.

The collection was "taken up" during the singing.
At the last verse the congregation stood up. The
benediction was pronounced, with outstretched arm, by
the Doctor; and the moment he uttered the "Amen!"
all rushed out of the place as fast as they could. This
rushing is a characteristic of the Americans. It is seen
in their approach to the dining-table, as well as in a
hundred other instances. I suppose it is what they
call being "smart," and "going a-head."

In the evening I went again to the same "church." The introductory part was shorter and more simple than in the morning. The Doctor's prayer (seven or eight minutes long) was admirable. I wished some dry, prosy petitioners in England could have heard it. It was devout, comprehensive, and to the point. All classes of men—but one—were remembered in it. The slaves were not mentioned,—their freedom was not prayed for!

The Doctor gave us to understand that he was about to deliver the fifth of a series of lectures to young men in great cities. The text was, "The Sabbath was made for man, and not man for the Sabbath;" the subject, "The importance of the Sabbath to young men in great cities."

The text (he observed) involved the principle, that man was not made to observe certain ceremonies and obey certain precepts, but that the observance of rites and laws was enjoined for man's own sake. This principle applied to the institution of the Sabbath. The body, the intellect, the affections—all required the rest which the Sabbath affords. The experiment had been abundantly tried; and it had been invariably found that more could be done, in every department of labour, with the regular observance of the Sabbath as a day of rest than without it. The farmer, the student, the legislator, had all tried it. Man could no more do without the Sabbath than he could do without sleep. Writers on slavery, however they differed on other points, were all agreed on this,—that the withhold-

ing of the Sabbath from the slaves in the West Indies,
together with the other cruelties inflicted upon them,
had materially shortened their lives! (How telescopic,
by the way, are our views with regard to evils at a
distance! West India slavery never wore the hideous
features which slavery presents in the Southern States
of America. Slavery even in Cuba, with all its horrors,
is far milder than in the United States.) France once
presented a fearful example of what a nation would be
without a Sabbath. The testimonies of Drs. Spur-
zheim and Rush were cited in confirmation; also that
of a respectable merchant in New York, well known to
the preacher, who, after the observation and experience
of twenty-five years in that city, declared that of
those who kept their counting-houses open on the
Sabbath not one had escaped insolvency. A poor boy
was apprenticed to an apothecary in a large city. To
increase his wages and encourage his efforts, his master
gave him a recipe and materials for making blacking
on his own account. The blacking was made, and
placed in pots in the shop window; but day after day
passed, and no purchaser appeared. One Sunday
morning, while the shop was open for medicine, before
the hour of public service, a person came in, and asked
for a pot of blacking. The boy was in the very act of
stretching out his hand to reach it, when he reflected
it was the Lord's-day. Falteringly, he told the customer it was the Sabbath, and he could not do it.
After this the boy went to church. The Tempter
there teased him about his folly in losing a customer

for his blacking: the boy held in reply that he had done right, and, were the case to occur again, he would do just the same. On Monday morning, as soon as he had taken down the shutters, a person came in, and bought every pot of blacking there was; and the boy found that, after deducting the cost of materials, he had cleared one dollar. With more faith and fortitude than some of you possess (said the preacher), he went and took that dollar—the first he had ever earned—to the Bible Society. That poor boy is still living, and is now a wealthy man.

The preacher said he knew a man, in his own native State of Tennessee, who on his arrival in America had nothing but a pocket Bible; but he made two resolutions,—1st. That he would honour the Sabbath; 2nd. That he would remember his mother. The first dollar he got he sent to her, and declared that he would never forget the Sabbath and his mother. He also was now a wealthy man.

The punishment of Sabbath-breaking was sure, though not immediate. Like the punishment of intemperance or impurity, it would come. Here the celebrated testimony of Sir Matthew Hale was adduced. Dr. Johnson's rules respecting the Sabbath were read, with the observation that no doubt he owed much of his celebrity to their observance. Wilberforce had declared that, at one period of his life, parliamentary duties were so heavy that he would certainly have sunk under them, had it not been for the rest the Sabbath afforded. But the Sabbath was not merely a day of

rest,—it was a day for improvement. Where there was
no Sabbath, all was bad. The inhabitants of Scotland
and New England were distinguished for industry and
mental vigour; and they were equally distinguished
for observance of the Sabbath. The universal observance of the same day was of great importance. It
guarded against neglect. It told upon the ungodly,
as was shown by an eloquent induction of circumstances,—the shops closed—the sound of the church-
going bell—the throngs of decent worshippers going
to and fro, &c.

Young men in great cities (it was observed) were in
great danger, chiefly from example. They met with
those who were older in sin than themselves—who
prided themselves on knowing where the best oysters
were sold, the cheapest horses to be hired, or the
cheapest boats to be engaged for the Sunday's excursion. Young men were ready to think, "If I don't do
this, I may do something worse." The fallacy and
danger of this mode of reasoning were exposed. It
might be employed to excuse any sin. Public places
of amusement were highways to destruction. Ah! how
those old people in that little cottage— surrounded
with a stone wall—on the hill side—far away—would
weep, if they knew their son was treading on the verge
of these burning craters! Familiarity with Sabbath-
breaking destroyed the sense of guilt. The young
medical student when he first visited the dissecting-
room, and the soldier when he first stood on the field
of battle, were sensible of misgivings, against which

repetition only made them proof,—each gradually losing his first sensations.

The desecration of the Sabbath was a greater evil to society than any tyrant could inflict. How would any infringement of civil rights be resisted! Here was an infringement with consequences infinitely more injurious; and yet the press were dumb dogs, and the pulpit itself was not guiltless!

This masterly discourse was read, but read in such a manner as to lose none of its effect. It occupied upwards of an hour. My irresistible impression as I listened was, *There is a man of God!* Truly a light shining in a dark place; for, as I returned to my lodgings, I found the coffee-houses, oyster-saloons, and theatres all open, just as on any other day, only more thronged with customers. How much such discourses are needed in this place, I leave you to judge from the following extract from the *New Orleans Guide :*—

"The greatest market-day is Sunday. At break of day the gathering commences,—youth and age—beauty and not so beautiful—all colours, nations, and tongues are co-mingled in one heterogeneous mass of delightful confusion. The traveller who leaves the city without visiting one of the popular markets on Sunday morning has suffered a rare treat to escape him."

On the evening of the next day, being the first Monday in the month, I went to the "Concert" for prayer, which had been announced the day before. It was held in a vestry or a school-room under the church. About sixty or seventy persons were in attendance. When I got there, they were singing the last verse of

"O'er the gloomy hills of darkness," &c.

A gentleman then gave an address. His object was to show that extensive fields were open in various parts of the world for the introduction of the Gospel. There was nothing clerical in his appearance, and he boggled a great deal; but, as he said " We, the ministers of the Gospel," I inferred that he was the pastor of some other Presbyterian church in the city. Behind the desk, where sat Dr. S——, was hung up a missionary map of the world, drawn on canvas, and illuminated from behind. It was an excellent device. All missionary prayer-meetings should be furnished with one. Those parts where the Gospel is already preached were light, the realms of Heathenism dark, the lands of Popery red, and so forth.

After the address, the pastor called upon "Brother Franklin" to "lead in prayer." The phrase was new to me, but I liked it,—it was appropriate. The prayer was scriptural and good, as was that also of another brother. The second prayed that the war, in which they were then as a nation engaged, might be over-ruled for good, and " be the means of introducing the Gospel and free institutions to a neighbouring repub-lic." Free institutions, indeed! (I said to myself): if you conquer, I fear it will be the means of introducing slavery where now it is not! After this prayer the pastor, having delivered a very short address, gave out a hymn, and said that while they were singing Brother such-a-one would "take up the collection,"— a phrase which seems to indicate a greater degree of preparation on the part of the people than our "make a collection." The Americans suppose it to be already made, and nothing remains but to take it up. The good brother came round with an old hat to receive contributions for the cause of missions. The pastor then closed with a short prayer and the benediction. Upon the whole, there were indications of a considerable degree of warm-heartedness in reference to the missionary cause, and especially of tender sympathy and affection towards missionaries themselves. As one of the tribe, I found it rather difficult to preserve my *incog*. There were present about half-a-dozen black people, some on the right and some on the left of the pastor—"the place of honour!"

LETTER VI.

"Jack Jones"—A Public Meeting for Ireland—Henry Clay—Other Speakers—American Feeling in reference to the Irish Famine—A Slave-Auction.

On that dreadful day, the 28th of January, on which we arrived in New Orleans, Jack Jones, a Welchman, was drowned in the Mississippi, in a generous effort to save another man from a watery grave. In that effort he succeeded, but at the cost of his own life. On the 2nd of February there was an advertisement in the papers, in which his friends offered a reward for the recovery of the body. Where was the corporation, or some one of the municipalities? for the papers make a continual reference to first, second, and third municipalities. Was there no public body, either civil or humane, to come forward on such an occasion? Had "Jack Jones" gone to the war, and butchered a score or two of harmless Mexicans, he would have been loaded with honours; but he *saved* a human being, close to the metropolis of the South, and his body was left to perish like that of a dog—for aught the citizens cared. I felt proud of my countryman. All honour to "Jack Jones!" May none of Cambria's sons perish in a cause less noble!

On the evening of the 4th of February I attended a

public meeting for the relief of the Irish. It was held in the New Commercial Exchange, and was the first public meeting I had had an opportunity of attending in America. The Commercial Exchange is a fine large building, supported by pillars, and containing an area on the ground floor that would accommodate about 1,500 people. It is but ill-adapted for a public meeting, having no seats or benches. I found about 800 gentlemen present, but no ladies. Nor was that to be wondered at; for out of the 800, about 799 were spitting, 600 smoking cigars, 100 chewing tobacco, and perhaps 200 both chewing and smoking at the same time, for many of those people chew one end of the cigar while burning the other. There was a large platform, and a great number of gentlemen were upon it. Governor Johnson was the president, assisted by lots of vice-presidents. When I entered, a tall old gentleman, with rather high cheek bones, and a voice somewhat tremulous and nasal, was speaking. He descanted, in a second or third rate style, on the horrors of famine in Ireland,—its horrors especially as seen in the family. Coming to a period, he said, "It is under these circumstances that I want you to put your hands into your pockets, and pull out something, and throw it into the lap of starving Ireland!" This caused the most tremendous cheering I ever heard,— "bravo—bravo—bravo,—whoo—hoo—whoo!" The last sound was to me altogether new. Not having learned phonography, I can give you no adequate notion of it; but it was a combination of the owl's screech and the

pig's scream. The favoured orator continued his speech
a little longer, and at the close there was a storm of
applause ten times more terrific than the former. And
who was the speaker? It was none other, as I subsequently ascertained, than the celebrated Henry Clay!
In departing from the tone of eulogy in which it is
fashionable to speak of him, I may be charged with a
want of taste and discrimination. That I cannot help.
My simple object in these letters is to tell how Transatlantic men and manners appeared to my eye or ear.
Before I went to America my respect for Henry Clay
was very great. I am sorry to say it is not so now.
I have closely examined his conduct in reference to
"the peculiar institution," and find it to have been
that—not of a high-minded statesman and true philan-
thropist—but of a trimming, time-serving partisan.
He has been a main pillar of slavery; and as the idol
of the Whig party, a great stumbling-block in the way
of those who sought the overthrow of that system.
The man of whom I have thus freely, yet conscien-
tiously expressed myself, is nevertheless thus spoken of
in the *New Englander,* a quarterly review of high character now open before me:—"We intend to speak in
the praise of Henry Clay. His place among the great
men of our country is permanently fixed. He stands
forth prominent above the politicians of the hour, in
the midst of the chosen few who are perpetual guar-
dians of the interest and of the honour [slavery?]
of the nation. The foundations of his fame are laid
deep and imperishable, and the superstructure is already

erected. It only remains that the mild light of the evening of life be shed around it."

The cheering at the close of Mr. Clay's speech merged into an awful tempest of barking. I could compare it to nothing else,—500 men barking with all their might! I thought it was all up with the meeting—that all was lost in incurable confusion; and yet the gentlemen on the platform looked down upon the raging tempest below with calmness and composure, as a thing of course. Amidst the noise I saw a middle-aged gentleman, rising on the platform, deliberately take off his top-coat, and all was hushed—except at the outskirts of the assembly, where a great trade in talking and tobacco was constantly carried on. This gentleman's name was S. S. Prentiss, Esq.; and the barking, it was now evident, consisted of calling out Prentiss!—Prentiss!—Prentiss! with all their might, on the top of the voice, and with an accent, sharp and rising, on the first syllable.

This gentleman gave us to understand that he was a lawyer—that he had often appeared before his fellow-citizens on former occasions (those occasions he briefly enumerated); but that the present was the most painful of all. He expatiated largely, and with great vehemence of tone and action, on the miseries of famine as experienced in Ireland,—talked much of their own glorious and free country—("Looking out for a few niggers this morning?" occurred to me),—and made some severe reflections—not, I admit, altogether undeserved—on the Government of England. This man was

fluent, though turgid. He seemed resolved to *act* the
orator throughout, and certainly to me appeared in
point of talent far—far a-head of Henry Clay. Bravos
and hoohoos in abundance greeted Mr. Prentiss. He
spoke long; but the noise of the suburbs prevented my
hearing so perfectly as I wished.

The cheering at the close of this speech merged into
barking as before. In this instance it was Hunt!—
Hunt!—Hunt! that they called for. The president
(standing) showed them a sheet of paper, containing
probably a list of subscriptions, and smiled coaxingly
to intimate that he wished that to be read. But it
would not do. Hunt!—Hunt!—Hunt! was still the
cry; and the democracy, as before, carried the day.

By this time the atmosphere of the room had become so poisoned with smoking that I could endure it
no longer. I had not only the general atmosphere
to bear, but special puffs, right in my face, accompany-
ing the questions and remarks which, in that free
meeting, of free citizens, in a free country, were freely
put to me by the free-and-easy gentlemen around.
The meeting resulted in the raising of 15,000 dollars
for the relief of the Irish. The sum was handed by the
American Minister in London to Lord John Russell;
and a note from his Lordship, acknowledging the gift,
has gone the round of the papers on both sides of the
Atlantic. The subject of relief to Ireland was subsequently, in many ways and places, brought under
my notice; and while I have been delighted in many
instances with the display of pure and noble generosity,

it was too evident that much of what was done was done in a spirit of self-glorification over a humbled and afflicted rival. It was a fine opportunity to feed the national vanity, and to deal hard blows to England. Not that I was sorry to see those blows, or to feel them. They drew no blood, and were a hundred times more efficacious than if they had. I felt that there was much in the conduct of England towards her unhappy sister-isle for which she deserved the severest castigation. But I must protest against the form of putting the case, which was very common throughout the United States: "You are shocked at our slavery; and yet you have horrors of ten times greater magnitude, in the Irish famine at your own doors." In this way the Irish famine, was a God-sent sort of a salvo for the slave-holder's conscience, so soothing and grateful to his tortured feelings that he was but too happy to pay for it by a contribution for the relief of Ireland.

In consequence of the following advertisement in the *Picayune*, I screwed up my feelings, and resolved for once at least in my life to see a slave-auction. I was the more disposed to attend this, as it was distinctly stated that they would be sold in families. I should not therefore have to behold the wife torn away from the husband, the husband from the wife, the parent from the child, or the child from the parent, as is so commonly done.

" COTTON-FIELD HANDS.—By Beard, Calhoun, and Co., auctioneers.—Will be sold at auction, on Friday, the 5th inst., at 12 o'clock, at Bank's Arcade, thirty-seven Field Slaves ; comprising eighteen from one plantation, and fourteen from another. All acclimated Negroes. To be sold in Families. Full particulars at sale."   " F. 4."

Setting off a few minutes before 12, after about half-a-dozen inquiries, and as many "guessing" answers, I found "Bank's Arcade." It was very near the Presbyterian church, in which I had heard such excellent sermons on the preceding Sabbath. It was a large open building : one side occupied as a bar for the retail of strong drinks, and the other fitted up for auctioneering purposes,—there being conveniences for three or four of the trade to exercise their vocation at the same time. One end was used for the sale of books and other publications, chiefly novels ; and the other for the exhibition of fancy goods.

As I got in at one end, I heard a voice—with that peculiar, twirling, rapid, nasal twang, which marks the Transatlantic auctioneer—say, " 400 dollars for this fine young woman—only 400 dollars—420, only 420—430 —440, only 440 dollars offered for this fine young woman." By this time I had got in front of the performer, and had a full view of the whole affair. And sure enough she was a "fine young woman," about twenty-three years of age, neatly dressed, not quite —— But the scene shall form the subject of my next letter.

LETTER VII.

The Slave-Auction (continued)—"A Fine Young Woman"—A Man and his Wife—Jim, the Blacksmith—A Family—A Ploughboy—Cornelia—Another Jim—Tom, the House-Boy—Edmund—Tom, and "his reserved rights"—A Carriage Driver—Margaret and her Child.

YES, she *was* a "fine young woman," about 23 years of age, neatly dressed, not black, but slightly coloured. The auctioneer was a sleek-looking fellow, with a face that indicated frequent and familiar intercourse with the brandy-bottle. He stood upon a platform, about four feet high. Behind him was a table, at which a clerk sat to record the sales. High above was a semi-circular board, on which were written in large letters "Beard, Calhoun, and Co." In front, standing upon a chair, exposed to the gaze of a crowd of men, stood the "fine young woman." She had an air of dignity even in that degrading position. Around were twenty or thirty more of the sable race, waiting their turn.

"440 dollars only offered," continued the coarse and heartless auctioneer; "450, thank you; 460, 460 dollars only offered for this excellent young woman—470 only, 470—480, 480 dollars only offered—490—500 dollars offered—going for 500 dollars—once, going for 500 dollars—503 dollars—going for 503 dollars—

going—once—twice—gone for 503 dollars. She is
yours, sir," pointing to the highest bidder. She stepped down, and disappeared in the custody of her new
proprietor.

A man and his wife, both black, were now put up.
They were made to ascend the platform. "Now, how
much for this man and his wife? Who makes an offer?
What say you for the pair? 550 dollars offered—560
dollars only; 560 dollars," &c., &c., till some one bidding 600 dollars—he added, "Really, gentlemen, it
is throwing the people away—going for 600 dollars;
going—once—twice—gone for 600 dollars. They are
yours, sir."

Jim, a blacksmith, about 30 years of age, was the
next. He stood on the chair in front. "Now, who
bids for Jim? He is an excellent blacksmith; can
work on a plantation, and make his own tools; in fact,
can turn his hand to anything. The title is good,"—
(Is it, indeed? breathed I,)—"and he is guaranteed
free from all the vices and maladies provided against
by law. Who bids for him? 600 dollars bid for him
—625 dollars—650 dollars," and so on to 780. "'Pon
my soul, gentlemen, this is throwing the man away;
he is well worth 1,200 dollars of anybody's money;
790 dollars only offered for him—going for 790 dollars;
—going—once—twice—gone for 790 dollars."

The next "lot" was a family, consisting of the husband, a man slightly coloured, about 30 years of age,
the wife about 25, quite black, and reminding me forcibly of an excellent woman in my own congregation,

D 2

a little girl about 4 years of age, and a child in the arms. They were told to mount the platform. As they obeyed, I was attracted by a little incident, which had well nigh caused my feelings to betray me. Never shall I forget it. Parents of England, let me tell it you, and enlist your sympathies on behalf of oppressed and outraged humanity. It was that of a father helping up, by the hand, *his own little girl to be exposed for sale!* "Now, who bids for this family? Title good—guaranteed free from the vices and maladies provided against by law. The man is an excellent shoemaker—can turn his hand to anything,—and his wife is a very good house-servant. Who bids for the lot? 500 dollars bid for them—600 dollars—only 600 dollars—700 dollars offered for them." But the price ultimately mounted up to 1,125 dollars.—"Going for 1,125 dollars—once—twice—gone for 1,125 dollars."

The next was a black boy, 16 years of age. He mounted the chair, not the platform. "Now, gentlemen, here is an excellent ploughboy. Who bids for him? Thank you,—400 dollars bid for him—425," and so on to 550 dollars. "Why, look at him; he is a powerful-limbed boy; he will make a very large strong man." He was knocked down at 625 dollars.

"The next I have to put up, gentlemen, is a young piece of city goods—the girl Cornelia. She is 18 years of age, a good washer and ironer, but not a very good cook. She is well known in the city, and has always belonged to some of the best families." By this time Cornelia was standing upon the chair. "Now, gentlemen, who bids for this girl? She is sold for no fault, but simply for want of money. Who bids for this excellent washer and ironer?" At this moment one of the "gentlemen," standing in front of her, deliberately took his walking-stick, and, with the point of it, lifted up her clothes as high as the knee. I afterwards saw this same man walking arm-in-arm with his white wife in the street. "500 dollars offered for her —530 dollars." She went for 580.

Here let me state, once for all, that I took notes on the spot. Those around me no doubt thought I was deeply interested in the state of the slave-market, and wishful to convey the most accurate information to my slave-breeding and soul-driving correspondents at a distance. Had my real object and character been discovered, I gravely doubt whether I should have left that "great" and "free" city alive!

The next "lot" were Jim, his wife, and two children, one about three, and the other about two years of age,—all on the platform. They were said to be excellent cotton-field hands, title good, and so forth; but, somehow, there were no bidders.

A boy about ten years of age, a fine intelligent-looking little fellow, was now made to mount the chair. "Now, who bids for Tom? an excellent house-boy, a 'smart' young lad; can wait well at table—title good—guaranteed free from all the vices and maladies provided against by law. Who bids for him?" The bidding began at 350 dollars, and ended at 425.

" I have now to put up the boy Edmund, thirty-two years of age, an excellent cotton-field hand. Who bids for the boy Edmund ?" At this moment a gentleman, who, like most of those present, appeared to be a sort of speculator in slaves, stepped forward, and examined with his hands the boy's legs, especially about the ankles, just as I have seen horse-dealers do with those animals at fairs. There were, however, no bidders ; and Edmund was put down again.

The next that mounted the chair was a shrewd-looking negro, about thirty-five years of age. " Now, gentlemen, who bids for Tom ? He is an excellent painter and glazier, and a good cook besides ; title good ; sold for no fault, except that his owner had hired him at 25 dollars a month, and Tom would not work. An excellent painter and glazier, and a good cook besides. His only fault is that he has a great idea of his own reserved rights, to the neglect of those of his master." This was said with a waggish kind of a leer, as if he thought he had said a very smart thing in a very smart way. 300 dollars were first offered for him ; but poor Tom went for 350. " Now, sir," said the man-seller to Tom, with a malicious look, " you 'll go into the country." He was bought by one of the speculators, who no doubt would sell him again for double the amount. Tom, as he descended from the chair, gave a look which seemed to say, " I care not whither I go ; but my own reserved rights shall not be forgotten !"

A girl of seventeen years of age, somewhat coloured,

was the next put up. She was " an excellent washer and getter-up of linen." She was also "a tolerably good cook." But there were no bidders; and the auctioneer said, " Really, gentlemen, I have a great deal of business to do in my office : I cannot lose any more time here, as you are not disposed to bid." And so ended the exhibition.

I was now at leisure to observe that a strange noise which I had heard for some time proceeded from another auctioneer, engaged in the same line of business at the other end of the room. As I approached, I saw him with a young coloured man of about twenty-two years of age, standing on his left hand on the platform. What a sight ! Two men standing together, and the one offering the other for sale to the highest bidder ! In the young man's appearance there was something very good and interesting. He reminded me forcibly of an excellent young man of the same colour in my own congregation. 430 dollars were offered for him ; but, as he was a good carriage driver, and worth a great deal more, only he had not had time to dress himself for the sale, being industrious, sober, and *no runaway* (said with significant emphasis), the bidding ran up to 660 dollars. Here one of the bidders on the auctioneer's right hand asked him something aside ; to which he answered, loudly and emphatically, *" Fully guaranteed in every respect;"* and then said to the young man, "Turn this way, and let the gentleman see you." He was sold for 665 dollars.

The next was a very modest-looking young mulatto girl, of small features and slender frame, with a little child (apparently not more than a year old) in her arms, evidently the daughter of a white man. "Now, who bids for Margaret and her child?" Margaret! my own dear mother's name. "Margaret and her child!" What should I have been this day, if *that* Margaret "and her child" Ebenezer had been so treated? Who can think of his own mother, and not drop a tear of sympathy for this mother—so young, so interesting, and yet so degraded? "Now, gentlemen, who bids for Margaret and her child? She is between sixteen and seventeen years of age, and is six months gone in pregnancy of her second child: I mention the last circumstance, because you would not think it to look at her,—it is right, however, that you should know. She cooks well, sews well, washes well, and irons well. Only 545 dollars! Really, gentlemen, it's throwing the girl away; she is well worth 800 dollars of any man's money. She'll no doubt be the mother of a great many children; and that is a consideration to a purchaser who wants to raise a fine young stock. Only 545 dollars offered for her!" No higher offer being made, she was sent down,—it was no sale. Let us breathe again.

LETTER VIII.

FINDING that another slave-auction was to be held
at noon next day in the St. Louis Exchange, I resolved
to attend. The day was dull and dirty. "Please,
sir," said I to the first man I met, "to tell me where
St. Louis Exchange is?" "Don't know, sir." I
walked on a little further, and tried again. "Please
to direct me to St. Louis Exchange?" "Can't; but
it's somewhere in that direction," pointing with his
finger. "Is this the way to St. Louis Exchange?" I
asked a third. "I guess it is," was the curt and characteristic reply. "How far is it?" "Three blocks
further on; then turn to your right; go a little way
down, and you will find it on your left." I went as
directed, and came to an immense building—a kind
of hotel. There were nearly a dozen entrances, all
leading into one vast saloon, where I found about 200
gentlemen,—some drinking, some eating, some smoking, some reading, some talking, and all spitting.
One end of the saloon was fitted up as a refreshment
place, similar to those on railway stations in England.
But I could see nothing like preparations for a sale.

On looking around I perceived a large door in two halves, with spring hinges, leading as it were further into the building. I pushed one half open, and found myself in a spacious circular hall,—its roof, ending in a dome, supported by a suitable number of massive columns. The floor was tastefully paved with black and white marble, and all the light came from the dome. Some 100 gentlemen were sauntering about, and now and then turning to several groupes of black people to ask them questions. This place was evidently fitted up for auctioneering purposes, and seemed peculiarly adapted for man-selling. At equal distances were a dozen elevated desks for the chief actors, each with a small platform in front for the exhibition of the articles of sale.

It was a quarter to twelve, by the clock that faced the entrance door, when I got in. Anxious to know what kind of questions were put to the slaves, I pushed myself into the knots of intending purchasers, just as if I had been one of them. The inquiries, I found, related to place of birth, subsequent removals, competency for work, and so forth. The answers presented a fearful view of the extent to which the internal slave-trade is carried on. Most of the slaves said they had been "raised" in Virginia and Kentucky. To avoid the suspicion of being a spy, I resolved to put a few questions too. I found myself at the establishment where those named in the advertisement which had drawn me thither were to be disposed of. A pile of handbills—each containing an exact copy of the advertisement, and a French translation—was lying on the platform. Taking one up, I observed the name of "Squires, a carpenter." Assuming all the confidence I could muster, I said, "Which is Squires?" "I'm here, sir." "You are a carpenter, are you not?" "Yes, sir," (with a very polite bow). "And what can you do?" "I can trim a house, sir, from top to bottom." "Can you make a panelled door?" "Yes, sir." "Sash windows?" "Yes, sir." "A staircase?" "Yes, sir." I gave a wise and dignified nod, and passed on to another groupe. In my progress, I found by one of the platforms a middle-aged black woman, and a mulatto girl of perhaps eighteen crouching by her side. "Are you related to each other?" I said. "No, sir." "Have you lived long in the city?" I said to the younger. "About two years, sir; but I was 'raised' in South Carolina." "And why does your owner sell you?" "Because I cannot cut— she wants a cutter—I can only sew." I then returned to the groupe at platform No. 1.

The clock was striking twelve; and, before it had finished, the vast dome reverberated with the noise of half-a-dozen man-sellers bawling at once, disposing of God's images to the highest bidders. . It was a terrible din. But, at our platform, business proceeded rather leisurely. Two gentlemen ascended the desk: the one of a light complexion, about fifty-five years of age, rather fat, whiskers and beard smoothly shaven off; the other, a Frenchified-looking young man, about twenty-five years of age, of dark complexion, with green spectacles to hide some deformity of the eye, no whiskers, but a large quantity of beard on the lower chin. The elderly man, whom I took to be the notary public mentioned in the advertisement, read the terms of sale; then the dark auctioneer, stroking his bearded chin, proceeded to business.

"Now, gentlemen, let me sell you Jacob. He is twenty-six years of age—a first-rate carpenter and wheelwright—*Jacob âgé d'environ 26 ans, charpentier et charron de la première ordre*—guaranteed free from the vices and maladies provided against by law—*garanti exempt des vices et des maladies prévus par la loi.* How much for Jacob? *Combien pour Jacob?*" He was run up from 1,000 dollars, and was going for 1,175, when the fat old gentleman offered 1,200, at which he was knocked down. "Now, gentlemen," said the fat man, with deliberation and emphasis, "the 1,200 dollars was my bid, and therefore Jacob is not sold. He is well worth 1,800 dollars."

At this performance, be it observed, the chief actor uttered everything first in English, and then in French, in the same breath, thereby giving the proceedings a most strange and comical sound.

Abraham, although on the advertisement, was not present.

Sancho, a black man, twenty-seven years of age, was the next in order. He was described as "an excellent carpenter—*excellent charpentier*—can do anything but fine work—fully guaranteed free from the maladies and vices provided against by law;" and, as nobody would

bid higher, he also was bought in by the fat man at
1,025 dollars.

George, a black man, twenty-seven years of age, was
the next to mount the platform. George kept his eyes
fixed upon the dome, as if he felt above looking down
on the grovelling creatures beneath him. He was a
stout-built, thick-set man, who evidently felt to the
very core the degradation to which he was exposed.
" Now, gentlemen, let me sell you George—a first-rate
bricklayer—*excellent poseur de briques*—bears an excellent character—only he absconded once from his. master for a few days. How much do you offer for him ?"
The bidding began at 500 dollars ; but George, like his
predecessors, was bought in at 980 by the fat man,
who protested him to be well worth 1,500.

Squires—whom I questioned about doors, sash-win-
dows, and staircases—was next put up. He was said
to be twenty-eight years of age ; but I think he was
nearer forty. On his forehead was a deep scar, occasioned by some severe cut. He appeared to be a very
good-tempered man, and by his smiling looks seemed
to say, " Buy me, and I'll serve you well." " What
will you offer for Squires, gentlemen ?—an excellent
carpenter—can trim a house—all but the very fine
work —bears an excellent character — is fully guaranteed," &c. &c. " Who bids for Squires ?" Poor
fellow ! he was sold for 900 dollars.

Sancho was put up again, the fat man observing that
he had made a mistake in offering a reserve bid for
him — that he would be sold without reserve. He

was put up at 600 dollars. The biddings gradually ascended to 900, and there stood, till, after a considerable expenditure of the Frenchman's breath and talent, Sancho was knocked down at 900 dollars, though when first put up 1,025 had been offered for him.

John, a black man, twenty-five years of age, "an excellent French and American cook—*excellent cuisinier Français et Américain*," was put up at 600 dollars, and, after the usual quantity of the Frenchman's eloquence, (accompanied, as in all other cases, by the constant rubbing of his tuft of chin-beard with the left hand, while in the right he flourished a fine massive gold pencil-case and a sheet of paper,) fetched 775 dollars, at which price he was knocked down to one Robert Murphy.

Silas also, a black boy, fifteen years of age, a house-servant, with a large scar on the right cheek, was sold for 670 dollars to Robert Murphy; who likewise became the purchaser of Scipio, a black man about twenty-four years of age, "an excellent cook, fully warranted in every respect," for 705 dollars.

"Now, gentlemen," resumed the green-spectacled auctioneer, still stroking his cherished tuft of long black beard,—"now, gentlemen, let me sell you Samson! He is twenty-six years of age — an excellent house-servant—guaranteed free," &c. &c. "What do you offer for Samson?" Poor Samson fell into the hands of the Philistines at 710 dollars.

Sam, the next on the list, was not present. Ben was therefore put up. He was a fine buckish young fellow, about twenty-one. His complexion was lighter than that of a mulatto, and his hair was not at all crisped, but straight, and of a jet black. He was dressed in a good cloth surtout coat, and looked altogether far more respectable and intelligent than most of the bidders. He was evidently a high-minded young man, who felt deeply the insulting position he was made to occupy. Oh! that I could have whispered in his ear a few words of sympathy and comfort. He stood on the platform firm and erect, his eyes apparently fixed on the clock opposite. "Now, gentlemen, what do you offer for Ben?" said the Frenchified salesman; "a first-rate tailor—only twenty-one years of age." 700 dollars proved to be the estimated value of this "excellent tailor."

Charles (not in the catalogue) was now offered. He was a black man, of great muscular power, said to be twenty-eight years of age. He had, it was admitted, absconded once from his master! At this intelligence the countenances of the bidders fell. He had evidently gone down at least 20 per cent. in value. Though offered at 300 dollars, however, he rose to 640, at which price he was sold.

The "ladies" were yet to be exhibited. "Elizabeth" (my own dear sister's name) was the first. But I reserve this part of the scene for another letter.

LETTER IX.

You shall now learn how men buy and sell women in America. "Elizabeth" was the first who was made to mount the platform. She was a very genteel-looking girl, about eighteen years of age, evidently the daughter of a white man, and said to be " a good seamstress and house-servant — *excellente couturière et domestique de maison.*" 600 dollars was the first bid, and 810 the last, at which price (about 170*l.*) Elizabeth—so young and so interesting—was sold !

" Susan," too, was a mulatto—the daughter of a white man. She was short, dumpy, and full-faced, about sixteen years of age, " a plain seamstress and house-servant." She appeared exceedingly modest, and kept her eyes on the floor in front of the platform. On that floor, as usual, the filthy dealers in human flesh were ever and anon pouring forth immense quantities of tobacco juice. For Susan the first bid was 500 dollars, and the highest 700 (nearly 150*l.*), at which she was " knocked down." But the fat old man, as before, in his peculiar drawling nasal tones, said, "The 700 dollars was my bid, and therefore Susan is not sold." Poor Susan was very sad and gloomy.

"Betsy," another "plain seamstress and house-servant," about sixteen years of age, also the daughter of a white man, had a fine intelligent eye, and her effort to restrain her feelings was evidently great. The offers, however, not suiting, the auctioneer closed the exhibition, which had lasted an hour.

The next day being the Sabbath, I took it into my head to find out the Baptist Church. They are all "churches" in America. It was not far from the Presbyterian place of worship. In passing the latter, I saw (as on the previous Sabbath) about forty or fifty boys in the square in front playing at cricket. A number of grave-looking gentlemen were standing under the portico of the church, looking on with apparent complacency,—not one attempting either to check these juvenile Sabbath-breakers, or to allure them to occupations more suitable to the day.

The Baptist Church is a small place, about 60 feet by 30, without galleries, except a little one for the singers. When we arrived, a small Sabbath-school was being conducted in the body of the chapel. About fifty children were present, of whom not one was coloured. One of the teachers kindly led us to a pew. It was the third or fourth from the door. The school, which occupied the part next to the pulpit, was about to be dismissed. The superintendent got into the "table-pew" to address the scholars. It was the first time I had had an opportunity of hearing an address to children in America. In the land of the Todds, the Abbotts, and the Gallaudets, I expected something very lively and interesting. But grievous was my disappointment. The address was dull and lifeless. There was in it neither light nor heat. When the superintendent had done, an elderly gentleman, shrewd and busy-looking, having in his hand a black walking-stick and on his neck a black stock, with shirt-collar turned over it like a white binding (the national fashion of the Americans), came up, and told the school that the proprietor of the splendid picture, "The Departure of the Israelites from Egypt," had requested him to deliver a lecture upon it; that he had engaged to do so on Monday a-week; and that the scholars and teachers of that school would be admitted free. I should like (said I to myself) to hear you: a lecture on the emancipation of those poor slaves can-not fail to be interesting in the slave-holding city of New Orleans. The school was now dismissed, and the scholars left to enjoy their full swing of lawless liberty.

The elderly gentleman descended from his elevation, and walked about the "church," backwards and for-wards, whispering a few words to one, and then to another, in a very bustling manner. As I looked down the aisle, I saw on one side of it, near the pulpit end, a leg projecting about eighteen inches, in a pen-dent position, at an angle of about forty-five degrees. This leg attracted my notice by its strange and solitary appearance. It seemed as if it had got astray from its owner. In America gentlemen's legs do get sometimes most strangely astray, — on the chair arms, on the tables, on the chimney-pieces, and into all sorts of out-of-the-way places. While other people generally try how high they can carry their heads, the ambition of the Americans is to try how high they can carry their heels ! Observing the leg in question a little more attentively, I found that behind it (in the adjoining pew), and in close and intimate connection with it, was a man dressed in black. The bustling old gentleman came by, tapped him on the shoulder, and beckoned him forward, along with himself, to the rostrum. Here they were met by a tall man of grave appearance, about thirty years of age, with a pale face and bald forehead, wearing a white cravat, with corners about ten inches long, stretching out on either side towards the shoulders. He was made to take the central position at the desk; while the man with the leg took the right, and the elderly gentleman the left.

The elderly gentleman (who, from his I'm-at-home kind of air, was evidently the pastor) offered up a short prayer, and then gave out a hymn, which some few friends in the gallery (standing up) sang ; all the rest of the congregation sitting down, and very few joining at all in the psalmody. This exercise over, the central gentleman arose, and, having first read a few verses of Scripture, offered up a very suitable prayer about eight or ten minutes long. The man on the right then gave out another hymn, which was sung as before.

The central gentleman now, in a very low don't-care-whether-you-hear-or-not tone of voice, gave out a text. It was John iii. 7: "Marvel not that I said unto thee, Ye must be born again." I will give you a sketch of his sermon. He observed that of all subjects on which men might be addressed, religious subjects were the most important; and that of all religious subjects, that to which the text referred was the most momentous. Having noticed the context, he proposed to inquire, first, into the necessity of being born again. This change (he observed) was necessary, in order to enjoy heaven. It was a common observation, that "society seeks its level." The Indian, for example, could not be happy amidst the refinements of civilization. The gambler and the swearer could not be happy in the society of the pious and devout. If so in this world, amidst imperfect holiness, how much more so in the pure society of the celestial state!

During these remarks, I was much annoyed by the cracking of nuts not very far off. I looked around, and actually found it was a mother cracking them for her two boys, one of whom might be seven and the other five years of age,—one by her side, and the other in the next pew behind. To the latter she deliberately handed over the kernels in a pocket-handkerchief; and yet, to look at her, you would have thought her a woman of sense and piety!

The preacher noticed, in the second place, the nature of this change. It was spiritual, not physical,— a "revolution" (!) of the mind, rather than a mere change of opinion or of outward deportment. The third observation related to the evidence of the change. Its existence might be ascertained by our own experience, and by the Word of God. The former was not to be trusted without a reference to the latter. This change destroyed the love of the world. It led man to abandon his favourite sins, and to live and labour to do good. It also created in him new desires and enjoyments. These topics were variously and suitably illustrated, and the whole was a very good sermon on the subject.

At the close the man on the right offered an appropriate prayer. The pastor then made several announcements; among them, that a meeting to pray for the success of Sabbath-schools would be held on the morrow evening. In connection with that announcement, he said: "I am a very plain man, and my God is a very plain God. He is so in all his dealings with men. He always acts on the plain common-sense principle, that, if a favour is worth bestowing, it is worth asking for." He also intimated that there would be a Church-meeting immediately after the service, preparatory to the ordinance of the Lord's Supper in the afternoon, inviting at the same time any members of other Baptist Churches who might be present to participate with them in that privilege. This form of invitation led me to understand that they were "close communionists;" and such I have ascertained to be the case, not only with them, but also with all the regular Baptists in America. The influence of Robert

Hall and others was not felt so powerfully on that side of the Atlantic as on this. I suppose that, while this worthy pastor would have freely admitted to the Lord's Supper any immersed slave-holder, he would have sternly refused that privilege to me—a sprinkled missionary from a distant land. You will readily believe, however, that the anti-slavery missionary—the pastor of a large congregation of black and coloured people— was not very ambitious of Christian fellowship with slave-holders.

LETTER X.

THE decided part acted by the Baptist missionaries
in the British Colonies, in reference to slavery, made me
anxious to know the whereabouts of the Baptist minister in New Orleans on that subject; and I therefore
visited his place of worship again in the afternoon.
They were engaged in celebrating the ordinance of the
Lord's Supper. A very clean and neatly-dressed black
woman was standing in the portico, looking in, and
watching the proceedings with deep interest. She evidently wished to enter, but dared not. At the close
I introduced myself to the minister as Davies, from
British Guiana, attached to the ministry of the missionaries of the London Society. He was very kind
and cordial, and pressed my wife and myself to go
home with him to tea. We accepted the invitation.
Among other questions, he asked how our negroes
worked, now that they were free? I told him, "Very
well indeed; and you may very safely venture to eman-
cipate your slaves as soon as you please." This led us

at once *in medias res.* His views I found to be simply
as follows: how pious! how plausible! how convenient! how extensively prevalent in reference to other
evils than slavery! "Slavery is a political institution.
As a Christian minister, I have nothing to do with
politics. My business is to preach the Gospel, and try
to save men's souls. In this course I am sanctioned
by the example of the Apostle Paul. Slavery existed
in his day; but he turned not aside from the great object to attempt its overthrow. He simply told masters
and slaves their duty, without at all interfering with
the relation subsisting between them. Besides, the
opposite of this course would render us and our churches
unpopular, and thereby destroy our usefulness." He
also seemed very sore at the idea of the Christianity of
slave-holders being at all called in question. "People,"
said he, or words to the same effect, "may spare themselves the trouble to pass resolutions of non-fellowship
with us; we wish for no fellowship with those who are
so uncharitable as to question our piety." I began
now to understand why the Abolitionists call the American churches "the bulwark of slavery."

Subsequently, on the same day, I had conversation
with a young man, whom I had that afternoon seen sitting down at the Lord's Table in the Baptist Church.
He told me that there were in New Orleans two Baptist
Churches of coloured people, presided over by faithful
and devoted pastors of their own colour. "And does
your pastor," I inquired, "recognise them, and have
fellowship with them?" "Oh! yes, he has often

preached to them. He feels very anxious, I can assure you, for the conversion of the slaves." "And do those coloured preachers ever occupy your pulpit?" "Oh, dear me, no!" with evident alarm. "Why not? You say they are good men, and sound in doctrine." "Oh! they would not be tolerated. Besides, they are accustomed to speak in broken English, and in very familiar language; otherwise the slaves could not understand them. The slaves, you know, cannot read, and are not allowed to learn." This he said in a tone of voice which indicated an entire acquiescence in that state of things, as if he thought the arrangement perfectly right. But what iniquity! To come between the Word of God and his rational creature! To interpose between the light of Heaven and the soul of man! To withhold the lamp of life from one-sixth of the entire population! Of all the damning features of American slavery, this is the most damning!

"I suppose," continued I, "if any of the black people come to your churches, they have to sit by themselves?"

Young Man. — "Of course: I have never seen it otherwise."

Myself.—"And I have never before seen it so. With us, in British Guiana, blacks and whites mingle together indiscriminately in the worship of our common Father."

Young Man (with amazement).—"There must be a a great change here before it comes to that. It must appear very strange."

Myself.—"Very much like heaven, where they shall come together from the east and from the west, from the north and from the south, &c. Why, we have black deacons, who, at the celebration of the Lord's Supper, carry the bread and wine, and give them even to white people."

Young Man (with more astonishment than ever, and in a tone of offended dignity).—"I don't think I could stand that—I don't! A great change must take place in my feelings before I could. I don't like to mingle Ham and Japhet together for my part—I don't!"

Myself.—"Why, they were mingled together in the ark."

Young Man.—"Yes; but old Noah quarrelled with Ham soon after he came out, and cursed him."

Myself.—"Granted; but you and your pastor profess to be anxious for the slaves' conversion to God, and thereby to roll away the curse." Here the dialogue ended.

In the evening I was desirous of hearing Dr. Hawkes, an Episcopalian minister, of whose talents and popularity I had heard much in New Orleans; but, finding that he did not preach in the evening, I went again to hear Dr. Scott at the Presbyterian Church. Having stood a considerable time at the door inside, and receiving no encouragement to advance, I ventured, along with my wife, to enter the pew next to the door. This proved a most unfortunate position. There was not light enough to take any notes; while the incessant opening and shutting of the door, with its rusty hinges, made it extremely difficult to hear. The discourse, however, which was again addressed to young men in great cities, was characterized by all the power and piety which distinguished the one of the previous Sabbath. I retired deeply impressed with the value of such a ministry in such a place. Dr. Scott was one of the American delegates to the Conference for the formation of the Evangelical Alliance in 1846. He is a Southern man, born and bred amidst the wilds of Tennessee, whose early educational advantages were very small. He is, in a great measure, a self-made man. Brought up in the midst of slavery, he is (I rejoice to hear) a cordial hater of the system. As a minister, he is "thoroughly furnished—a workman that needeth not to be ashamed." His knowledge of the world, as well as of the Word of God and of the human heart, is extensive, and is turned to the best account in his ministrations. In leaving New Orleans I felt no regret, but that I had not called upon this good man.

On Monday morning, the 8th of February, I had a peep at the House of Representatives of the State of Louisiana, then in session at New Orleans. The room, a dark and dingy-looking place, was fitted up with desks and seats in the form of the letter D. A desk and a spittoon were allowed to each honourable member,—the latter article being deemed as necessary as the former. Whether smoking was suffered during the hours of business or not I cannot tell, but the room smelt horribly of stale tobacco. Between fifty and sixty members were present, and never certainly, either in the Old World or in the New, did I see an assemblage of worse-looking men. They seemed fitted for any deeds of robbery, blood, and death. Several distinguished duellists were pointed out to me; among them Colonel Crane, an old man, who had repeatedly fought with Mr. Bowie, the inventor of the "Bowie knife," and had killed several men in personal combat! The motion before the house just at that time was for the release from prison of a Mr. Simms, who a few days before had violently assaulted one of the members in the lobby. He was released accordingly. Who will not pity the 200,000 slaves of this State, who are at the "tender mercies" of these sanguinary men? Nor let it be said, as it often is, that New Orleans and Louisiana are not a fair specimen of things even in the South,—that they are more French than American, &c. This is not the case. Nothing in New Orleans struck me more forcibly than its thoroughly American character. American usages, American influence, American laws, and American religion are there predominant. Things were much better for the black and coloured people when it was not so. The French treated their slaves incomparably kinder than the Americans do. They often married coloured women, and invariably treated their own coloured offspring, whether legitimate or illegitimate, with tenderness and regard. They had them suitably educated and adequately provided for; so that, at the present moment, a large portion of the city of New Orleans is the freehold property of coloured persons. Not so act the Americans. They indulge in the grossest licentiousness with coloured women, but would shudder at the idea of marrying one of them; and, instead of giving any property to their coloured offspring, they do not scruple to sell them as slaves! Had I gone to the Roman Catholic cathedral in that city, which is attended chiefly by the French and their descendants, I should have found no negro pew, but persons of all colours intermingled together in religious observances. The Southerners seem to have no heart—no feeling, except that of love to the almighty dollar.

The population of New Orleans is about 90,000. On this mass of people are brought to bear the labours of at least thirteen ministers of the Methodist Episcopal Church, seven Presbyterians, four Episcopalians, and three Baptists,—all professedly evangelical;—besides a considerable number of Roman Catholics, and other non-evangelical teachers. But Satan has there a large array of synagogues.

I omitted, at the proper time, to describe the scene we witnessed at our "private" lodgings the first day we sat down to dinner. Though it was called a "private" boarding-house, and we had taken the apartments as such, we found ourselves surrounded by about thirty boarders! These were all respectable men, or rather men whom, from their position in society, you would expect to be respectable. Doctors, lieutenants in the army, captains, merchants, editors, clerks of the senate, and so forth, were among them. My wife was the only lady besides the mistress of the house.

We were all waiting in an ante-room for the summons
to dinner. It came. The door of the dining-room was
thrown open; and before you could have said "Jack
Robinson," the whole had rushed through, were seated
at table, and sending forth a forest of forks in the direction of the various dishes! I had often heard of this
wolfish habit, but thought our cousins were caricatured.
Here, however, was the reality. Had I not been an
eye-witness, I could not have believed it. Not a single
seat had been kept vacant for the only lady who had to
be accommodated, and we were both left to console
ourselves in the ante-room! The landlady, however,
having "an eye to business," arranged for our accommodation at the table. There had been on the table
a turkey, a piece of beef, some fish, and pastry,—all
ready carved. Most of these things had instantly disappeared,—the knives and forks had borne them away
in triumph. There was no waiting to be served: every
one stuck his fork in what he liked best, or what was
most within his reach. It was a regular scramble.
The principle seemed to be to *begin* to eat as soon as
possible, no matter what! Some began with nothing
but potatoes, some with a bit of bread, some with a
piece of beef, some with a limb of the turkey. Some,
I noticed, beginning with fowl, then taking roast beef,
then boiled mutton, then fish, and then some pastry,—
all on the same plate, and—faugh!—portions of most
of them there at the same time! No change of plate,
—that would have been extravagant, and would have
savoured of aristocracy. Freedom, it seemed, allowed

every one to help himself; and that with his own knife
and fork, which he had before used for all sorts of
purposes. Such luxuries as salt-spoons and mustard-
spoons are very rare south of the Ohio. My wife
asked the lady of the house for a small slice of the
ham she had before her, when the latter very politely
begged Mrs. Davies to lend her her knife to cut it
with! This was good society in New Orleans. Things
improved as we advanced towards the North; but in
most places, though the Americans provide bountifully,
the cooking is not good, and they make a strange
jumble of things at table. They have the appearance
of a people suddenly raised in the world, and able to
afford themselves nice things, but very ignorant and
awkward in the use of them. With so much hurry
to begin, the time occupied in eating by our company
was very short. We Britishers had scarcely begun,
when one and another got up from table, finishing his
dinner as he walked away. They cannot bear to sit
at table a moment longer than is absolutely necessary.
While we remained seated, they passed before us on
their way out,—one eating, one picking his teeth, one
scraping his throat, one spitting on the floor. Of
course, we seldom made a hearty meal under such circumstances.

LETTER XI.

Farewell to New Orleans—Revolting Bargain—"The Anglo-Saxon" Steam-boat—Moderate Fare—Steam Navigation of the Mississippi —Steam-boat and Railway Literature—Parting View of the "Crescent City"—Slave Advertisements—Baton Rouge—A Sugar Estate —Fellow-Passengers—The Ladies' Cabin—A Baptist Minister— A Reverend Slave-holder.

PREPARING to leave New Orleans, on the evening of the 8th of February, we called for our bill, and found, for the nine days of our stay, a charge of eight dollars more than we had agreed for. Unwilling to be imposed upon, I remonstrated; and we split the difference with our "smart" landlady. We turned our backs upon the city, with a hearty wish that we might never see it again. It is a horrid place. Bowie knives, revolving pistols, and other deadly weapons, are exposed for sale on every side,—a pretty clear proof of an extensive demand.

Shall I tell you of a most revolting abomination, which I know, on good authority, occurred about the time we were there? A large importer of slaves from the "slave-breeding" States, having on board a considerable number of young women, made an offer of the use of their persons to a volunteer regiment of soldiers, then waiting to be conveyed to Mexico. The offer was accepted; and the wretch boasted that he had made 700 dollars, or 150*l.* sterling, by the transaction! The laws of this *great* and *free* country had, however, consigned these helpless young women to his absolute disposal! Alas! for Freedom, had she no holier home than the Southern States of the American Union! And yet of the country in which this licentious bargain was made, even John Todd, the excellent author of "Lectures to Children," thus writes,—"This land is free. The mind is here free,—and the child is to be born—if indeed he ever will be born—whose powers and faculties may not be called out and cultivated. There is no bondage to forms or precedents; but the whole mass may be seasoned, leavened, and moved, and is at liberty to do what is great and good in the way that is most convenient."

Four o'clock in the afternoon found us safely on board the "Anglo-Saxon," a fine new steam-boat, bound for Pittsburgh in Pennsylvania. We booked ourselves for Cincinnati in Ohio, a distance of 1,550 miles. The fare was 12 dollars each; and the captain said we should be from six to ten days in getting to our destination. (We were, however, twelve days.) Twelve dollars, or about 2*l.* 10*s.*, for the occupation of splendid apartments, sitting down at a well-furnished table, and being conveyed 1,550 miles! Scarcely believing that there was not some mistake, I asked a fellow-passenger if the 12 dollars really did include board, and was told that most certainly it did,—it was the regular fare. Travelling at this rate was literally cheaper than stay-

ing at home. It was just one dollar a day each for
food, lodgings, and locomotion ! This "Anglo-Saxon"
—forge below and palace above, as all these boats
appear to be—is a noble vessel. The dimensions, as
given me by the "clerk" or purser, are—length of keel
182 feet, breadth of beam 26 feet, depth of hull 6 feet,
length of cabin 140 feet ; two engines $6\frac{1}{2}$ feet stroke ;
two cylinders $18\frac{1}{2}$ inches in diameter ; height between
decks $9\frac{1}{2}$ feet ; having a fire-engine and hose ; berth
accommodation for 73 cabin-passengers, but often has
more. Unexpectedly, we had got on board the only
temperance vessel on the river—the only one that kept
no "bar." It belonged chiefly to Quakers. The
captain and the clerk, both part-proprietors, had married sisters. The engineer also was connected with
them by marriage. These circumstances encouraged
the hope that we had fallen into good steady hands,
who would do all in their power to avoid explosion.

The number of steam-boats which puff, and groan,
and paddle up and down the Mississippi, is amazing,—
probably not fewer than 1,200. Only in the year
1812 was the *first* seen on these western waters ! The
view of a long range of these splendid vessels lying
against the landing-place is magnificent. Though not
very substantial, they are extremely showy. Lightness
of construction and elegance of accommodation are
chiefly studied. The "Anglo-Saxon" is not by any
means one of the largest class. These vessels are
doubtless well adapted for their purpose as *river* boats ;
in the sea, they could do nothing but capsize and sink.

In no portion of the globe should the invention of steam-boats be more highly appreciated than in the valley of the Mississippi; for nowhere else has the triumph of art over the obstacles of nature been more complete. But for this gigantic application of the power of steam, thousands of boatmen would have been slowly and laboriously *warping*, and rowing, and *poling*, and *cordelling* their boats, in a three months' trip up this mighty stream, which (thanks to Watt) is now ascended in ten days. This "go-a-head" country advances more in five years with steam-boats, than it could have done in fifty without them. The principal points in the Ohio and the Mississippi, which nature had separated by distances and other obstacles more formidable than attend the crossing of the Atlantic, art has brought into practical juxta-position.

On embarking on the "Anglo-Saxon," we found that we could not get off that night, and therefore made ourselves comfortable on board till morning.

February 9.—This morning, while the boat was being got ready, hawkers of light literature flocked on board. Baskets full of trashy novels were continually offered to us. Why should not the same facilities be afforded for obtaining better publications? Truly, "the children of this world are wiser in their generation than the children of light." This reproach is not peculiar to Americans. Why should there not be in England the same facilities for obtaining publications of real value and utility, as for obtaining works of mere amusement, if not something worse?

At noon our engine began to puff, and our paddles to move. The " crescent city" soon vanished in the distance; not, however, till we had enjoyed a striking view of it, and especially of the harbour. An area of many acres, covered with a grotesque variety of flat boats, keel boats, and water craft of every description, that had floated down from the valley above, lined the upper part of the shore. Steam-boats, rounding to, or (like our own) sweeping away, cast their long horizontal streams of smoke behind them; while barques and brigs, schooners and sloops, ranged below each other in order of size, and showing a forest of masts, occupied the wharfs. These and a thousand other objects, seen as they were under a brilliant sun, presented a picture of surpassing splendour; but the curse and blight of slavery were upon it !

Being now fairly under weigh, let me glance at a New Orleans paper of this morning, which I bought from one of the hawkers. How consoling the following paragraph !

" STEAM-BOAT EXPLOSION. — Captain Duncan, of the ' Swan,' reports that the tow-boat, ' Daniel Webster,' burst her larboard boiler on the 6th instant, while towing in a vessel over the South-west Bar. Mr. William Taylor, one of the Balize pilots, and one of the firemen were instantly killed. The rest of the crew of the ' Daniel Webster' were slightly scalded."

These explosions are of daily occurrence; and though we had a fresh boat, and good steady men to manage it, our feeling of security was very small.

The six following advertisements I found in succession in the same paper, besides many more of a like character interspersed throughout the sheet. How *manly* and how *mysterious* is the first !

"To Planters.—For Sale, a splendid Virginia woman-servant, thirty years old, who has been in this country twenty-four years; speaks French and English; good cook, washer, and ironer, and has kept store. She is of a strong constitution; has never been sick, and never had a child. She is for sale for no fault, but on account of domestic trouble. *She is not for sale for any one in this city. No one but a planter need apply.* For particulars apply at No. 189, Common-street.

"F 9—t."

"Mechanics at Private Sale.—We have for sale 3 good Carpenters, 1 good Plasterer, 1 Plantation Blacksmith, 1 excellent Tailor, 1 superior Cabinet-maker. The above slaves are well recommended, and can be sent on trial at their respective trades.

"Beard, Calhoun & Co.,

"8, Bank's Arcade."

"F 3—10t."

"Negroes for Sale.—A young Negro man, first-rate field hand, 19 or 20 years old; also a very likely girl, good house-servant and tolerable seamstress. Apply to

" McMahon & Pearsall,

" 29, Natchez-street."

" F 4—6t."

" Ten Dollars Reward. — Left the steam-boat ' Little Rock,' on Monday morning, the 1st instant, a Mulatto *boy,* named Bob Malane, *about* 40 *years of age,* 5 feet 4 or 5 inches high. Any information respecting *said boy* will be thankfully received at the office of Williams, Phillips & Co., No. 62, Gravier-street.

" William Arnold."

" F 7—3t."

" Fifty Dollars Reward.—Ran away from Mrs. Shall's, in Canal-street, on the 6th instant, at 3 o'clock, p.m., the Negro-girl Eliza, aged 16 years, rather small size, very black, with a handsome face. Had on when she left a dark-coloured calico dress, low quartered shoes, and stockings ; took no other clothing. It is believed she was decoyed away by a free coloured man, well known on several steam-boats, now in the city. Captains · of vessels going to St. Louis are cautioned not to receive the girl on board. The above reward will be given for the apprehension of said slave, if found in the possession of any white or free coloured person, under circumstances that would lead to a conviction at law ; or 10 dollars if delivered at 28, Canal-street,

New Orleans, with any reasonable expenses incurred in so doing.

"RICHARD KING."

"F 7—2t."

"ONE DOLLAR REWARD.—Will be given for the apprehension of the Negro-woman Sarah, aged 31 years, 5 feet 2 inches high, stout built; has good teeth; no scars or blemishes about her face, or marks upon her person. Speaks French, English, and Spanish.

"JOSE ANTONIO LANONDO,

"Corner St. Thomas and Basins Streets."

"F 2—6t."

Against the powerful current of the "father of waters" we advanced at the rate of more than 200 miles a day! It was consequently dark when we passed Baton Rouge, 140 miles from New Orleans. Baton Rouge, now the capital of Louisiana, is situated on the first "bluff," or elevation, to be met with in ascending the river. The United States' Barracks there are built, I am told, in a very fine style.

February 10. — We began to feel the cold very keenly: the thermometer was down at 46. In the middle of the day, we had to stop at an estate to take in a large quantity of sugar and molasses. The upper parts of the valley send down flour and provisions, getting from the lower sugar and molasses in return. This stoppage affording an opportunity of going ashore, I went to see the estate buildings; and though such buildings as existing in Guiana were quite familiar to me, I was interested in observing the difference. Those of Guiana are incomparably superior ;- but *these* are the result of a better policy. Ours are too large and too expensive; these are rude, simple, and cheap, and yet answer the purpose. Seeing slaves at work, I addressed several questions to one of them relative to the cultivation and manufacture of sugar, and received very sensible and even *polite* answers.

By this time we had received an impression of the character of our fellow-passengers. The mass of the "gentlemen" were rude and filthy beyond expression. The promenade or gallery outside, which might be very pleasant, was bespattered all over with vile expectoration. No lady could venture there with safety. The men will persist in spitting on the floor, when it would be quite as convenient to spit into the water. Many of the names of places on the route ending in *ville*,—as Donaldsonville, Francisville, Iberville, Nashville, &c.,—I could not help asking if we had not many passengers from *Spitville*. But this was not the worst feature in the character of our fellow-travellers, who comprised gamblers, fighters, swearers, drunkards, "soul drivers," and everything base and bad. Of these, we had about fifty as cabin passengers; but there were upwards of a hundred deck passengers below— not above,—and they were ten times worse. Among men so much resembling demons I had never before been. However, my wife being with me, I had the *entrée* of the ladies' cabin. This was the abode of quiet and decency, there being but three other ladies besides. Of these, one had her husband with her, a respectable farmer from Pennsylvania, who shipped all his last year's produce in a flat boat, came down in it with his wife, sold his cargo in New Orleans, bought there what he might want during the year, and was now on his way home again by steam. Another lady, who was from Philadelphia, had come all the way to New Orleans in the hope of having a last glance of her husband before he was ordered off to Mexico,—was just too late,—and was returning home alone, with a heavy heart and an anxious mind. The third lady was a German girl from Baden, who had lived in New Orleans for three years, and was now on her way to Cincinnati to see her brother. We had also the boat's washer-woman, an old lady from New England, who sat in the ladies' cabin with as much composure as if she thought herself quite as good as any of the rest. Such is American society! So terribly afraid are they of anything that looks like aristocracy, except towards the coloured people!

I found on board a Baptist minister from the State of Maine, in New England, a thorough anti-slavery man. His testimony against the South on this subject was strong. He had lately been on a visit to a brother minister of his own denomination in North Carolina. At first, whenever the New Englander desired to go into the yard, it was necessary for his reverend brother to accompany him, and introduce him to a number of large dogs; otherwise they would have worried him.

These animals were kept to prevent his reverence's slaves from running away, and to hunt them if they did. And yet, as my travelling companion assured me, this reverend slave-holder gravely and pathetically complained of the reluctance of the slaves to attend family worship!

LETTER XII.

On the 10th of February we passed a great many
sugar estates on both sides of the river, which would
be agreeable objects but for the curse of slavery. For
who can look with pleasure upon the foul abodes of
lust, oppression, and cruelty? At the outer gate, in
front of one of these " patriarchal" establishments,
was a small octagonal building about 6 or 8 feet in mean
diameter. The basement was of brick, pierced by small
air holes, barred with iron, at the height of about 8 feet
from the ground; and the upper part was of wood,
terminating in a pigeon-house. Making a short stay
there to take in fire-wood, we inquired into the use of
the building; but all the answer we could get was, that
it was a " pigeon-house." The Baptist minister from
Maine asked a negro, who was helping to bring wood
on board; and from him he learned the real truth,—
that it was a place of punishment and torture for the
oppressed slave. We have since ascertained that such
buildings are very common, and generally pass under
the euphemistic name of " pigeon-houses."

On the 11th of February—a fine frosty day—we came to Red River, branching on our left in the direction of Texas, with which country it forms an important means of communication. This river, even where it pours its waters into the Mississippi, is not more than from 300 to 500 feet wide, and yet is navigable by steamers for about 1,200 miles. My Baptist friend had recently been on a visit to Elder Wright, a planter and a slave-holder on that river. This Wright was a New-England man, had graduated at Yale College, and boasted that he was "a Northern man with Southern feelings." He was called Elder Wright because he was a preacher,—the Baptists here calling all preachers "elders." Now, this Elder Wright told my friend that a few years ago there was great fear in his district of the slaves rising up against their masters. To this they were supposed to be instigated by the presence and influence of some strangers. Under this apprehension, a secret committee was formed to seize and try every suspected stranger, and, if he could not clear himself to their satisfaction, to "hang him up quietly." Of this secret and murderous committee Elder Wright— an *alumnus* of Yale College, a professor of religion, and a preacher of the gospel—was chosen chairman; and the statement I have just made came in the way described from his own lips! It is notorious that in the South they think nothing of taking away a man's life, if he be even suspected of sympathy with the slave; and a country so thinly inhabited affords abundant opportunities of doing it as "quietly" as can be desired. America is indeed a land of "liberty!"

At night we came to Natchez, a town beautifully situated on the top of a hill, about 300 feet above the level of the river, and for this reason called "Natchez-on-the-Hill." Its population is about 5,000; and it is the largest town in the State of Mississippi. Its distance from New Orleans is 300 miles. Darkness had set in when we approached it; yet the numerous lights on shore, rising row above row. to a great elevation, gave it a lively and interesting appearance. But, alas! Natchez also is a great slave market; and I can never think of it without remembering the sufferings of poor Mary Brown. Let me narrate her painful story. It may waken in some breast a feeling of sympathy for the American slave.

Mary Brown, a coloured girl, was the daughter of *free* parents in Washington city—the capital of the freest nation under heaven! She lived with her parents till the death of her mother. One day, when she was near the Potomac Bridge, the sheriff overtook her, and told her that she must go with him. She inquired what for? He made no reply, but told her to come along, and took her immediately to a slave-auction. Mary told him she was free; but he contradicted her, and the sale proceeded. The auctioneer soon sold her for 350 dollars to a Mississippi trader. She was first taken to jail; and after a few hours was handcuffed, chained to a *man-slave*, and started in a drove of about forty for New Orleans. Her handcuffs made her wrists swell so much that at night they were obliged to take them off, and put fetters round her ankles. In the morning the handcuffs were again put on. Thus they travelled for two weeks, wading rivers, whipped up all day, and beaten at night if they had not performed the prescribed distance. She frequently waded rivers in her chains, with water up to her waist. The month was October, and the air cold and frosty. After she had travelled thus twelve or fifteen days, her arms and ankles had become so swollen that she felt as if she could go no further. They had no beds, usually sleeping in barns, sometimes out on the naked ground; and such were her misery and pain that she could only lie and cry all night. Still she was driven on for another week; and every time the trader caught her crying he beat her, uttering fearful curses. If he caught her praying, he said, he would " give her *hell*." Mary was a member of the Methodist Church in Washington. There were several pious people in the company; and at night, when the driver found them melancholy and disposed to pray, he had a fiddle brought, and made them dance in their chains, whipping them till they complied. Mary at length became so weak that she really could travel on foot no further. Her feeble frame was exhausted, and sank beneath accumulated sufferings. She was seized with a burning fever; and the diabolical trader—not moved with pity, but only fearing he should lose her—placed her for the remainder of the way in a waggon. Arriving at Natchez, they were all offered for sale. Mary, being still sick, begged she might be sold to a kind master. Sometimes she made this request in the hearing of purchasers, but was always insulted for it, and afterwards punished by her cruel master for her presumption. On one occasion he tied her up by the hands so that she could barely touch the floor with her toes. He kept her thus suspended a whole day, whipping her at intervals. In any other country this inhuman beast would have been tried for the greatest crime, short of murder, that man can commit against woman, and transported for life. Poor Mary Brown was at length sold, at 450 dollars, as a house-servant to a wealthy man of Vicksburgh, who compelled her to cohabit with him, and had children by her,—most probably filling up the measure of his iniquity by selling his own flesh. Wrongs like these must have inspired our poet when he exclaimed,—

> " To think that man—thou just and gentle God—
> Should stand before Thee with a tyrant's rod
> O'er creatures like himself, with souls from Thee,
> Yet dare to boast of perfect liberty !
> Away ! away ! I 'd rather hold my neck
> In doubtful tenure from a sultan's beck,
> In climes where Liberty has scarce been named,
> Nor any right but that of ruling claimed,
> Than thus to live where bastard Freedom waves
> Her fustian flag in mockery over slaves ! "

As we advanced, we continually met with flat boats, laden with produce, and floating sluggishly down. In the vernacular phrase, these boats are called " Kentucky flats," or " broad-horns." They are curiously constructed. At a distance, they appear like large chests or trunks afloat. They are from 50 to 100 feet long, and generally about 15 or 20 feet wide. The timbers of the bottom are massive beams. The sides are

boarded up square to the height of 6 feet above the
water; the roof being slightly curved, like a trunk lid,
to throw off rain.   They are adapted to carry from 200
to 400 barrels.   Great numbers of cattle, hogs, and
horses are conveyed to market in them.   Coals, too,
are thus brought down from the upper parts of the
valley.   Some of these barges have apartments fitted
up for the accommodation of a family, with a stove,
beds, tables, &c.   You may sometimes see in them
ladies, servants, cows, horses, sheep, dogs, and poultry,
—all floating on the same bottom.   It was precisely in
this fashion that the Pennsylvanian farmer and his
wife had reached New Orleans.   Indeed, most of our
fellow-passengers had come as captains or crews of flat
boats.   Of course, no attempt is made to get these
unwieldy boats back against the current.   It would
be impracticable.   The flat boat makes but one trip
during its individual existence.   Arrived at New Orleans, it is sold for "lumber," and taken to pieces.
In short, by this arrangement timber and produce are
brought to market at the same time, the "stuff" of
which the float is composed being but little injured.
One cannot look at these temporary structures without
being impressed with the vast importance of those
water-powers which the Americans, with a wonderful
tact, bring to bear in the way of saw-mills on the ex-
haustless resources of the forest.   The very first thing
looked for in settling a new district is water-power.

These flats, though destined for but a single voyage,
sometimes do not reach their port,—seldom without

more or less of danger,—and never without infinite toil·
They usually carry but three or four hands. Their
form and gravity render them very unmanageable.
Lying flat and dead in the water, with square timbers
below their bottom planks, they often run on a sand-
bank with a strong head-way, and bury their timbers
in the soil. To get them afloat again is a great labour.
Sometimes they run upon a " snag," and are instantly
swallowed up with all their crew and all their cargo.
Sometimes a steamer runs into one of them, and produces a catastrophe equally fatal to both. But all the
toils, and dangers, and exposures connected with the
long and perilous voyage of a flat boat, do not appear
to the passer-by. As you cut along by the power of
steam, the flat boat seems anything but a place of toil
or care. One of the hands scrapes a violin, while the
others dance. Affectionate greetings, or rude defiances,
or trials of wit, or proffers of love to the girls on shore,
or saucy messages pass between them and the spectators along the bank, or on the steam-boat. Yet,
knowing the dangers to which they were really exposed,
the sight of them often brought to my remembrance
an appropriate verse of Dr. Watts :—

> " Your streams were floating me along
>   Down to the gulf of black despair ;
> And, whilst I listened to your song,
>   Your streams had e'en conveyed me there."

These boats, however, do not venture to travel by
night ; consequently, at any good landing-place on the
Mississippi, you may see towards evening a large num-

F

ber of them assembled. They have come from regions thousands of miles apart. They have never met before,—they will probably never meet again. The fleet of flats covers, perhaps, a surface of several acres. " Fowls are fluttering over the roofs as invariable appendages. The piercing note of the chanticleer is heard. The cattle low. The horses trample as in their stables. The swine scream, and fight with each other. The turkeys jobble. The dogs of a hundred regions become acquainted. The boatmen travel about from boat to boat, to make inquiries and form acquaintances." It is a world in miniature.

LETTER XIII.

WE came on the 12th of February to the Grand Gulph and " Big Black River." The former is situated at the base of a bold and solitary " bluff." Here, a few years ago, " a negro man was condemned by the *mob* to be *burned alive over a slow fire,* which was put into execution, for murdering a black woman and her master Mr. Green, a respectable citizen of that place, who attempted to save her from the clutches of this monster." Such is the newspaper version of the affair. Had the real truth been stated, it would have appeared that this Green was the " *monster,*" who had seduced the wretched negro's wife !

The " Big Black River" is not so very " big" after all. It is extremely narrow, although navigable for some hundreds of miles.

Besides the danger of explosion—which, I apprehend, arises from " racing" and carelessness more than from any other cause — steam-boats on the " father of waters" are exposed to " snags." These snags are trunks of large trees that have become fastened in the bed of the river, and are often found lying against the stream at angles of from 30 to 40 degrees. As the river varies much with regard to the quantity of water in its channel,—frequently rising or falling from 6 to 12 feet in a few hours,—these snags are sometimes so deep in the water that they can be passed over with safety; at other times, however, they are but just covered. If a boat coming—especially down the stream — with high pressure and at full speed, making between twenty and thirty miles an hour, runs against one of these firmly-fixed, immoveable snags, it sustains a fearful shock. Not unfrequently a large hole is thus made in the bottom; and boat, cargo, crew, passengers, and all, sink in an instant. The danger is greatly increased by fogs, often so dense that the helmsman, though situated on the hurricane-deck and over the fore part of the vessel, can see nothing before him. In such a case, wise and cautious men " lie to," and wait till the mist has cleared off.

May not these " snags" serve to remind us of certain characters and circumstances with which we meet on the voyage of life? Who cannot call to mind many snags—men, rugged, stubborn, and contentious, —snags by all means to be avoided? D'Israeli was the snag of Peel—Russia was the snag of Napoleon— Slavery is the snag of the Evangelical Alliance.

On board our steamer was a fine black young man, who acted as barber, waiter, and man-of-all-work. Curious to know whether he was a slave or not, I requested my friend from Maine to sound him. "To whom do you belong?" said the Baptist. "I belong to myself, sir," was the prompt and dignified reply. "That's right," I involuntarily exclaimed; "he is free!" In answer to further questions, he told us that he was from New Orleans, and had bought himself about two years before for 600 dollars. He could therefore truly say, "I belong to myself, sir!" Oh! that every slave in America could say the same! But how monstrous, that a man should have to pay to one of his fellow-men upwards of 120*l.* sterling in order to "own himself!" Land of liberty, forsooth!

In the evening we reached Vicksburg. This place, like nearly all other places in this region, is deeply stained with deeds of violence and blood. A few years ago, a set of thieves and gamblers were here put to death by Lynch law. "Gentlemen of property and standing laughed the law (the constitutional law) to scorn, rushed to the gamblers' house, put ropes round their necks, dragged them through the streets, hanged them in the public square, and thus saved the sum they had not yet paid. Thousands witnessed this wholesale murder; yet of the scores of legal officers present, not a soul raised a finger to prevent it: the whole city consented to it, and thus aided and abetted it. How many hundreds of them helped to commit the murders with their own hands does not appear; but not one of them has been indicted for it, and no one made the least effort to bring them to trial. Thus, up to the present hour, the blood of those murdered men rests on that whole city; and it will continue to be a CITY OF MURDERERS so long as its citizens agree together to shield those felons from punishment."

Darkness had covered the city of blood when we arrived, and therefore we could not see it. One of the passengers, in stepping on a plank to go ashore, fell into the water. It was a frightful sight to see the dark figure of a fellow-man splattering and holloing in so perilous a position. Seldom can a person be saved who falls into the Mississippi, so rapid is the current; and, moreover, the banks are so steep that, though he be a good swimmer, he cannot get up. The knowledge of these facts generally destroys in the person who falls in all hope and self-command. Fortunately, however, in the present instance a rope was instantly thrown out, and the individual was saved. He assured us, afterwards, that some one had designedly pushed him from the plank into the water.

On the 13th of February we breasted a small settlement on our left, called Providence, in Louisiana. We observed on the river's bank what a man at my elbow (a professor of religion, who had discovered a great propensity to talk about his religious experience before gamblers) coolly designated "a drove of horses, mules, and niggers." Observe the order of his enumeration! Of the "niggers" there were about 100, small and great, young and old, and of both sexes. The whole "drove" were waiting to be shipped for the New Orleans market, and were jealously guarded by several large dogs. From individual instances like this, one may form a clearer notion of the internal slave-trade of America. Thousands every year are thus brought down the Mississippi to supply the Natchez and New Orleans markets. " Those who are trans-ported down the Mississippi," says a manual of American slavery, " are stowed away on the decks of steam-boats, males and females, old and young, usually chained, subject to the jeers and taunts of the passengers and navigators, and often by bribes or threats, or by the lash, made subject to abominations not to be named." On the same deck, you may see horses and human beings tenants of the same apartments, and going to supply the same market. The *dumb* beasts, being less manageable, are allowed the first place; while the *human* are forced into spare corners and vacant places. My informant saw one trader who was taking down to New Orleans 100 horses, some sheep, and between fifty and sixty slaves. The sheep and the slaves occupied the same deck. Many interesting and intelligent women were of the number. I could relate facts concerning the brutal treatment of these defenceless females, while on the downward passage, which would kindle the hot indignation of every mother, and daughter, and sister in Old England. The slaves are carried down in com-panies, varying in number from 20 to 500. Men of considerable capital are engaged in the traffic. Go into the principal towns on the Mississippi, and you will find these negro traders in the bar-rooms boasting of their adroitness in driving human flesh, and describing the process by which they succeed in " *taming down* the

spirit of a *refractory* negro." Here, then, were human
beings, children of our common Father, bone of our
bone, and flesh of our flesh, classed with the brutes
that perish,—nay, degraded below them, and placed
under the surveillance of dogs. The horrors of such
a system it is impossible to exaggerate.

The majority of our fellow-passengers did nothing but
gamble, eat, drink, smoke, and spit, from morning till
night. In the afternoon a dispute arose between two
of them about ten dollars, which the one maintained he
had won from the other. One of the two quickly drew
out his Bowie knife, and would certainly have stabbed
the other but for the intervention of the boat's officers.
When the whites have so little hesitation in shedding
each other's blood, we cannot be surprised at the indifference with which negro life is put an end to. "A
rencontre took place last week," says the *New Orleans
Delta*, "between the overseer of Mr. A. Collins (a
planter in our vicinity) and one of the negroes. It
seems the overseer wished to chastise the negro for
some offence, and the negro resisted and struck the
overseer with a spade. The overseer grappled with
him, and called some of the negroes to his assistance;
but, perceiving that the negroes were not willing to
assist him, he drew his knife, and stabbed the negro to
the heart. A coroner's inquest has been held, and a
verdict given in accordance with the circumstances,
declaring the overseer justifiable."

The 14th of February was Sunday. My Baptist
friend, when engaging his passage, had given the cap-

tain a hint that, when the Sabbath came, he should like to have divine service on board. Nothing, however, was now said about it. Not, I think, that the officers of the boat would have disliked it; but, considering the general character of their passengers, they perhaps thought it would have been only " casting pearls before swine." One passenger indeed, who *said* he was a Congregationalist, expressed to my friend a wish to have worship; but he was playing at cards every day, and was in other respects no great credit to Congregationalism. The Baptist assured me that his countrymen too generally, when they travel, leave their religion behind !

The Baptist related to me an awful story respecting a captain with whom he had sailed from New England to Guadaloupe, and thence to New Orleans. This man belonged to my friend's congregation, and professed to have been " converted" under his ministry. His pastor had frequent occasion to reprove him for his disregard of the Sabbath at sea. In New Orleans he engaged to take a cargo of Government stores to Tampico, for the supply of the army. He had to sign a bond to take in the cargo, and sail before a certain day, or forfeit the sum of 500 dollars. The Sabbath came. The pastor was at that time absent, on his visit to " Elder Wright" before mentioned, on the Red River. An agent of the " Bethel Union," who was going round to invite seamen to the "Bethel" worship, invited the said captain and his men. He excused himself and his crew on the plea that they had no time—were under contract—had signed a bond—and might forfeit 500 dollars, &c. "What!" said the agent, "not afford time to attend the worship of God" on his own day! "No, I really cannot—very sorry—what I have never done before—should like to go"—was the faltering reply. "Well," replied the agent with great solemnity, "God will soon call you to account for this." "I know He will," rejoined the captain with a downcast eye. The interview ended. The agent proceeded on his pious mission, and the captain to take in his cargo. The next morning, as he was looking over the side of the vessel to see how deep she was in the water, he fell overboard. His body was never found. His watch, which had been left in the cabin, and a few other personal articles, the pastor was now taking with him to the afflicted widow and family.

LETTER XIV.

Voyage up the Mississippi (continued)—The Arkansas—Treatment of the Indians—M. de Tocqueville—" Napoleon " and Lynch Law—Memphis, and its Advertisements—A Scene witnessed there—The Ohio —Nashville, and Amos Dresser.

AT 4 o'clock P.M. of February the 14th, we reached the mouth of the Arkansas. This is a noble river, navigable for 2,000 miles ! Not twenty years ago, the remnants of the four great Indian nations of the southern part of what is now the United States, amounting to about 75,000 souls, were urged to remove to the banks of this river, with an assurance of an undisturbed and permanent home. These four nations were the Choctaws, the Chickasaws, the Creeks, and the Cherokees. They were established upon a territory, which they occupied before the settlement of any Europeans in their vicinity, and which had been confirmed to them by solemn treaties again and again. The Anglo-Americans of the States of Georgia, Alabama, and Mississippi were however annoyed at their proximity, because it was unfavourable to the " peculiar institution " of America. Slaves occasionally made their escape to these children of the forest, and found sympathy and succour. This would not do. The Indians must be removed. But how was it to be ac-

complished ?   Annoy them; harass them; wrong them
in every possible way, so that they may be sickened
with the place. Georgia, accordingly, first attempted to
establish a division line for the purpose of limiting the
boundaries of the Cherokees.   Then, in 1829, the
State of Alabama divided the Creek territory into
counties, and subjected the Indian population to the
power of white magistrates. And, in 1830, the State of
Mississippi assimilated the Chocktaws and Chickasaws
to the white population, and declared that any one who
should take the title of Chief should be punished with a
fine of 1,000 dollars and a year's imprisonment.
Under these accumulated annoyances, the Cherokees,
on the 18th of December, 1829, addressed to Congress
the following powerful and touching appeal :—

" By the will of our Father in heaven, the Governor
of the whole world, the red man of America has become small, and the white man great and renowned.
When the ancestors of the people of the United States
first came to the shores of America, they found the red
man strong, though he was ignorant and savage; yet
he received them kindly, and gave them dry land to
rest their weary feet. They met in peace, and shook
hands in token of friendship. Whatever the white
man wanted and asked of the Indian, the latter wil-
lingly gave. At that time the Indian was the lord,
and the white man the suppliant. But now the scene
has changed. The strength of the red man has become weakness. As his neighbours increased in numbers, his power became less and less; and now, of the

many and powerful tribes who once covered the United States, only a few are to be seen,—a few whom a sweeping pestilence has left. The northern tribes, who were once so numerous and powerful, are now nearly extinct. Thus it has happened to the red man of America. Shall we, who are remnants, share the same fate?"

"Oh, no!" was the response. "Beyond the great river Mississippi," said the President to them in 1829, "where a part of your nation has gone, your Father has provided a country large enough for all of you; and he advises you to remove to it. There your white brothers will not trouble you : they will have no claim to the land, and you can live upon it, you and your children, as long as the grass grows or the water runs, in peace and plenty. *It will be yours for ever.*"

With this assurance, many left the land of their birth and the homes of their childhood, travelled hundreds of miles, crossed the Mississippi, and settled on the banks of the Arkansas. M. de Tocqueville was "assured, towards the end of the year 1831, that 10,000 Indians had already gone to the shores of the Arkansas, and fresh detachments were constantly following them." Many, however, were unwilling to be thus expatriated. "The Indians readily discover," says M. de Tocqueville, "that the settlement which is proposed to them is merely a temporary expedient. Who can assure them that they will at length be allowed to dwell in peace in their new retreat? The United States pledge themselves to the observance of the obligation; but the territory which they at present occupy was formerly secured to them by the most solemn oaths of Anglo-American faith. The American Government does not, indeed, rob them of their land, but it allows perpetual incursions to be made upon them. In a few years the same white population which now flocks around them, will track them to the solitudes of the Arkansas : they will then be exposed to the same evils, without the same remedies ; and as the limits of the earth will at last fail them, their only refuge is the grave."

The views of this keen French philosopher were prophetic. In vain did I strain my eyes, as we passed along, to discover any trace of these Indians. Not one representative of those noble aborigines was to be seen. In 1836 Arkansas was constituted a State, and admitted into the Union ; and, if you look at a recent map of the United States, you will see the "location" of these Indians marked, not in the State of Arkansas at all, but far—far beyond, towards the setting sun, in what is called the "Western Territory," where, indeed, the river Arkansas has its source. Nor will ten years pass away before they will be again disturbed, and pushed further back.

At the mouth of the Arkansas is a village called Napoleon, of which I received, on authority not to be disputed, the following horrible account. A few years ago it was the head quarters of lawless and bloody men. They fabricated base coin, gambled, robbed, murdered. To such a pitch of wickedness had they

arrived, and such a terror were they to the whole country, that a party of men from Memphis (a city on the
eastern side of the Mississippi, 180 miles up) took the
law into their own hands, armed themselves with
deadly weapons, came down, scoured the country
around, caught about fifty of the ringleaders, and put
them to death. Some they shot,—some they hanged,—
and some they threw, tied hand and foot, into the
river. Of this dreadful tragedy no judicial notice was
ever taken !

February 15.—I had an attack of intermittent fever,
and consequently saw nothing of the scenery around.
At night the fog was so dense that the officers deemed
it prudent to "lie to."

February 16. — At 9 a.m. we were abreast of the
city of Memphis, on the Tennessee side of the river.
Higher up there is Cairo. These slave-holders, who
retain their fellow-men in worse than Egyptian bondage, seem to have a great partiality for Egyptian names.
Memphis is pleasantly situated on high "bluffs," and
is a great point for the shipping of cotton. It does
not, however, thrive by *honest* industry. I obtained a
copy of the *Daily Inquirer* of that day, where—among
advertisements of pianos, music, bonnets, shawls, &c.,
for the ladies—I found the following :—

"ONE HUNDRED DOLLARS REWARD.—Ran away
from the subscriber, on the 20th of October last, two
Negro Fellows of the following description.—To wit,—
Evan, 25 years of age, about 5 feet 11 inches high,

complexion black, thick bristly beard, low soft voice, and apt to look down when spoken to ; has a large scar on the calf of one of his legs, caused by the bite of a dog when he was 8 or 10 years old ; some of his jaw-teeth missing or decayed.   Ellis, 22 years of age, about 5 feet 11 inches high ; complexion dark mulatto, tinged with Indian blood ; beard thin and light.   From information derived from a brother of these boys, who was caught in Washington County, Miss., it appears they intended to apply for employment as wood-choppers in the upper part of this State, until they could raise money enough to dress fine, then set off for the State of Illinois.   It is highly probable they will resort to fictitious names, for the purpose of baffling pursuit.

" The above reward will be paid to any person confining them in any jail, so that I can get them again ; or fifty dollars for either of them.

"DUNCAN M'ALPIN."

" SLAVE MARKET.—The subscribers have now, and will continue to keep on hand throughout the season, a large supply of choice Negroes, suited to every capacity, which they offer at the lowest market rates.   They have agents abroad engaged in purchasing for them, which enables them to bid defiance to competition.

" Depôt on Adams-street, between Main and Second Streets.

" BOLTON & DICKINS."

"JAILOR'S NOTICE.—Was committed to the jail of Shelby County, on 25th January, a Negro Boy named Silas. He says he belongs to William Wise, of Fayette, County Tenne. He is about 30 years old, black complexion, about 5 feet 11 inches high; weighs about 165 lbs. The owner of said Negro is requested to come and prove property, and pay charges, or he will be dealt with according to law.

"E. W. HARREL,

"Feb. 13.—3tW."   "*Jailor.*"

In connection with Memphis, M. de Tocqueville narrates the following touching incident, relative to the expatriation of the Indians, to which I have already referred. "At the end of the year 1831, while I was on the left bank of the Mississippi, at a place named by Europeans Memphis, there arrived a numerous band of Choctaws. These *savages* [so his American translator renders it] had left their country, and were endeavouring to gain the right bank of the Mississippi, where they hoped to find an asylum which had been promised them by the American Government. It was the middle of winter, and the cold was unusually severe : the snow had frozen hard upon the ground, and the river was drifting huge masses of ice. The Indians had their families with them; and they brought in their train the wounded and the sick, with children newly born, and old men upon the verge of death. They possessed neither tents nor waggons, but only their arms and some provisions. I saw them embark to pass the mighty river, and never will that solemn spectacle fade from my remembrance! No cry, no sob was heard among the assembled crowd : all were silent. Their calamities were of ancient date, and they knew them to be irremediable. The Indians had all stepped into the bark that was to carry them across, but their dogs remained upon the bank. As soon as these animals perceived that their masters were finally leaving the shore, they set up a dismal howl, and, plunging all together into the icy waters of the Mississippi, they swam after the boat." So much for Memphis and its associations!

February 18th, at 5 A. M., we entered the Ohio River, and at 1 P. M. the mouth of the Tennessee ; coming shortly afterwards to Smithland, at the mouth of the Cumberland River, which runs parallel with the Tennessee, and communicates directly with Nashville, the capital of that State. This city also has its association of ideas. I cannot think of it without at the same time thinking of Amos Dresser. He was a student at Lane Seminary (Dr. Beecher's), and subsequently a missionary to Jamaica. In the vacation of 1835 he undertook to sell Bibles in the State of Tennessee, with a view to raise the means of continuing his studies for the ministry. Under suspicion of being an Abolitionist, he was arrested by the " Vigilance Committee" (a Lynch-law institution), while attending a religious meeting in the neighbourhood of Nashville. After an afternoon and evening's inquisition, he was condemned to receive twenty lashes with the cow-hide on his naked body. Between 11 and 12 on Saturday night the sentence was executed upon him, in the presence of most of the committee, and of an infuriated and blaspheming mob. The Vigilance Committee consisted of sixty persons. Of these, twenty-seven were members of churches: one was a religious teacher, and others were *elders* of the Presbyterian Church,—one of whom had a few days before offered Mr. Dresser the bread and wine at the Lord's Supper. But let Amos Dresser himself describe the scene and the circumstances.

"I knelt down," says he, "to receive the punishment, which was inflicted by Mr. Braughton, the city officer, with a HEAVY COW-SKIN. When the infliction ceased, an involuntary thanksgiving to God, for the fortitude with which I had been enabled to endure it, arose in my soul, to which I began aloud to give utterance. The death-like silence that prevailed for a moment was suddenly broken with loud exclamations,—'G—d d——n him! Stop his praying!' I was raised to my feet by Mr. Braughton, and conducted by him to my lodgings, where it was thought safe for me to remain but a few moments.

"Among my triers was a great portion of the respectability of Nashville; nearly half of the whole number professors of Christianity, the reputed stay of the Church, supporters of the cause of benevolence in the form of tract and missionary societies and Sabbath-schools; several members and *most* of the elders of the Presbyterian Church, from whose hands but a few days before I had received the emblems of the broken body and shed blood of our blessed Saviour!"

In relating this shameful circumstance, the editor of the *Georgia Chronicle*, a professor of religion, said that Dresser "should have been hung up as high as Haman, to rot upon the gibbet until the wind whistled through his bones. The cry of the whole South should be death, *instant death*, to the Abolitionist, wherever he is caught." What a great and free country!

LETTER XV.

THE Ohio, the " beautiful river," is a magnificent stream formed by the confluence at Pittsburg of the Allegany and Monongahela Rivers, and is 1,008 miles long, constituting the boundary of six States: Ohio, Indiana, and Illinois on the north,—all free States; and Virginia, Kentucky, and Tennessee on the south,— all slave States. A trip on this river, therefore, affords a fine opportunity for observing the contrast between slavery and freedom.

The Ohio is the great artery through which the inland commerce of the Eastern States flows into the valley of the Mississippi. In ascending this river, we had first on our left the State of Illinois. This territory, which contains an area of 60,000 square miles, was settled by the French in 1720, and was admitted into the Union in 1818. Its population in 1810 was 12,300; in 1840, 476,180. It is now, probably, not far short of 1,000,000!

On the 19th of February, about noon, we arrived at Evansville, on the Indiana side of the river. This was the prettiest place we had yet seen; and its charms were enhanced by the assurance that it was free from the taint of slavery. The rise of this little town has been rapid. Its population is about 3,000. Three " churches," with their neat and graceful spires, rising above the other buildings, were conspicuous in the distance.

At 5 P. M. we passed Owensborough, on the Kentucky side of the river. This, too, is a neat little town, with a proportionate number of places of worship. Indeed, on every hand, places of worship appear to rise simultaneously with the young settlement. The free and efficient working of the voluntary principle is the glory of America. In reference to "church" accommodation, it everywhere appears to decided advantage compared to the most favoured parts of England. On this subject Dr. Baird's book on Religion in America is very truthful.

The fever left me on entering the Ohio, and returned no more,—a clear proof that this river is healthier than the Mississippi. The latter has much fog and malaria, which tell quickly upon a constitution like mine, already predisposed by residence among the swamps of Guiana to fever and ague.

As I have already intimated, we had now Indiana, a free State, on our left. This State is rapidly advancing in wealth and population. It was settled by the French in 1730, and became an independent State in 1816. It has an area of 36,840 square miles, being by two-fifths less than its neighbour Illinois. Its population at the beginning of this century was only 5,640; in 1840 it was 685,860. It is now above a million! In 1840 it produced upwards of four millions of bushels of wheat, and twenty-eight millions of corn!

February 20.—The scenery was diversified. Hills covered with trees rose on either side. In the summer, when all is fresh and green, there must be here scenes of loveliness and grandeur unsurpassed. At present the country had a cold and winterly aspect. It rained, too, the whole day. At 3 P.M. we approached New Albany, on the Indiana side. It is a flourishing place, with from 5,000 to 6,000 inhabitants. Just above this town are some falls in the Ohio, that can seldom be ascended by steamers, which therefore pass through a side canal, with locks, formed (through the superior influence of the slave-power) on the Kentucky or slave bank of the river. We had to pass through three locks, which have been very foolishly made too small to receive steamers of the largest class in the navigation of the Ohio. Ours fortunately, not being of that class, could " go a-head."

At 5 P.M. we got to Louisville, a city of about 30,000 or 40,000 inhabitants, on the Kentucky side. This city is a great depôt for slaves, whence they are shipped for the New Orleans market. By this means it has acquired a detestable notoriety.

" A trader was about to start from Louisville, Kentucky," says the *Anti-Slavery Record*, " with one hundred slaves for New Orleans. Among them were two women, with infants at the breast. Knowing that these infants would depreciate the value of the mothers, the trader sold them for *one dollar each.* Another mother was separated from her sick child about four or five years old. Her anguish was so great that she sickened and died before reaching her destination."

Take another instance, on the same authority:—

" Not very long ago, in Lincoln County, Kentucky, a female slave was sold to a Southern slaver under most afflicting circumstances. She had at her breast an infant boy three months old. The slaver did not want the child on any terms. The master sold the mother, and retained the child. She was hurried away immediately to the depôt at Louisville, to be sent down the river to the Southern market. The last news my informant had of her was that she was lying *sick,* in the most miserable condition, her breast having risen, inflamed, and *burst !* "

Let another case, testified by the Rev. C. S. Renshaw, add to the fame of this *infamous* city.

" Hughes and Neil traded in slaves down the river : they had bought up a part of their stock in the upper counties of Kentucky, and brought them down to Louisville, where the remainder of their drove was in jail waiting their arrival. Just before the steam-boat put off for the lower country, two negro women were offered for sale, each of them having a child at the breast. The traders bought them, took their babes from their arms, and offered them to the highest bidder ; and they were sold for one dollar a piece, whilst the stricken parents were driven on board the boats, and in an hour were on their way to the New Orleans market. You are aware that a young babe diminishes the value of a field hand in the lower country, while it enhances her value in the breeding States."

February 21.—Another dreary Sabbath on board. The principal objects of interest pointed out to us on that day were the residence and the tomb of the late President Harrison. The latter is a plain brick erection, in the midst of a field on the top of a hill, about half a mile in the rear of the former. The recollection of that man, so highly elevated, and so quickly cut down, could hardly fail to suggest a train of not unprofitable reflections. He was, I suppose, a moral and well-meaning man, distinguished for qualities not often to be found in high places; but I was sorry to be obliged to infer that much of what I had heard respecting the *religiousness* of his character wanted confirmation.

At half-past 4 P.M. we arrived at the long-wished-for Cincinnati — the "Queen of the West." Our voyage from New Orleans had thus occupied twelve days, during which time we had been boarded and lodged, as well as conveyed over a space of 1,550 miles, for 12 dollars each, or one dollar per diem! It was the cheapest, and (apart from the companionships) the most pleasant mode of travelling we had ever experienced. As the boat stayed but a couple of hours at Cincinnati, we had to land without delay. Being a stranger in a strange land, I inquired for the Congregational minister, and was told that his name was Boynton. In perambulating the streets in search of his house, I was pleased to see but one shop open. It was a tailor's, and, as I afterwards learned, belonged to a Jew, who closed it on Saturdays, the law of the State compelling all to close their shops one day in the week. In every street, we were struck with the glorious liberty enjoyed by the pigs. On all hands, the swinish multitude were seen luxuriating in unrestricted freedom. Mr. Boynton, who received us kindly, did not know of any place where we could be accommodated with private board and lodging, but promised to make inquiry that evening. He was a man of about forty years of age, wearing on the Sabbath, and even in the pulpit (as most American ministers do), a black neckerchief, and shirt-collar turned down over it. That night we had to go to an hotel, and were recommended to the Denison House, which we found pretty cheap and comfortable. But the American hotels are not, in point of comfort, to be compared for a moment to those of Old England. My wife was too tired to go out in the evening; and unwilling for my own part to close the Sabbath without going to some place of public worship, I thought I would try to find the sanctuary of "my brethren—my kinsmen according to the flesh"—the Welsh. Following the directions I had received, I arrived at the top of a certain street, when I heard the sound of sacred song ; but I could not tell whether it was Welsh or not, nor exactly

whence it came. As I stood listening, an overgrown
boy came by, of whom I inquired, "Where does that
singing come from ?" — "I *guess* it comes from a
church down below there." "Is it a Welsh Church ?"
—"I can't tell, but I *guess* it is." "Well, then," I rejoined, "I *guess* I will go and see." I turned, and
the youth "guessed" he would follow me. I got to
the door. The singing had not ceased. It *was* Welsh—
the language in which I had first heard "*Am Geidwad
i'r Colledig !*"* How interesting in the "Far West" to
hear sounds so sweet and so familiar to my childhood !
None but those who have experienced can tell the
charm of such an incident. The minister was in the
pulpit. His dress and hair were very plain, and his
complexion was extremely dark. He was evidently a
Welshman : there was no mistake about it : his gravity,
plainness, attitude—all told the fact. I ventured forward, and walked along to the stove, which to me was
an object of agreeable attraction. Around the stove
were two or three chairs. A big aristocratic-looking
Welshman, a sort of a "Blaenor," who occupied one of
these chairs, invited me to take another that was vacant.
The eyes of all in the synagogue were upon me. My
"guessing" informant had followed me even there,
though he evidently understood not a word of Welsh.
The building was about 40 feet by 35, without galleries, and was about two-thirds full. The pulpit was
fitted up in the platform style—the "genuine" American mode. The text was, "How shall we escape, if

* Literally, "Of a Saviour for the lost."

we neglect so great a salvation?" The sermon was
good and faithful. The audience—the men on one
side of the chapel, and the women on the other—did
not excite much interest. The men, especially, were
among the worst hearers I had ever seen. I felt
ashamed of my countrymen. The spitting was incessant, and attended with certain unmentionable circumstances which render it most disgusting and offensive.
What a contrast to my own clean and comely congregation of black and coloured people in New Amsterdam! In about twenty minutes after the preacher had
begun his sermon, one-half of the men had their heads
down, resting on both arms folded on the tops of the
pews before them. Whether they were asleep or not,
the attitude was that of deep sleep. This behaviour
was grossly rude,—to say nothing of the apathetic state
of mind which it indicated. I wondered how the
preacher could get on at all, with such hearers before
him. I am sorry to say that the Welsh too frequently
manifest a great want of-decorum and devotion in their
religious assemblies. This is telling, and will tell,
against dissent in the Principality.

LETTER XVI.

THE Welsh service being ended, my big friend on the next chair asked me, in the same language, if I was a *llafarwr* (preacher). I answered him in the usual Welsh phrase, " *Byddaf yn dweyd ychydig weithiau,*" which means that I did a little in that way. On learning this, he desired my " *cyhoeddiad* " (publication—another Welsh phrase) to preach there some night during the coming week; and he wished it to be announced there and then, to which I would not consent. He introduced me to Mr. Jones, the minister. After most of the congregation were gone, a groupe, including my big friend and Mr. Jones, collected around me, and most earnestly pressed for my " publication." I told them I had never been a Welsh preacher, that it was nearly five-and-twenty years since I had left the Principality, and that, moreover, *I could not* preach at all to men who put down their heads in the sluggish and sleepy manner in which most of their men had done that night. " Oh ! but they won't do so when you, a

stranger, preach," was the reply. "Then," I said,
"there must be a great want of true devotion among
them, if that would make all the difference." However, being much pressed, I promised at last to give
them, before I left the city, a little missionary information in Welsh.

The name of my big friend was Bebb, a near relative,
as I subsequently learned, of His Excellency W. Bebb,
the present Governor of the State of Ohio. The history of this Governor deserves a passing notice. He is
the nephew of the late Rev. John Roberts, of Llanbrynmair, a man of great worth and usefulness, whose
praise is in all the Congregational Churches of North
Wales. Mr. Roberts, when a young man, joined the
Church at Llanbrynmair, began to preach under its
sanction, became its pastor, sustained that office for
thirty-six years, and is succeeded by his two excellent
sons, Samuel and John, as co-pastors! Towards the
close of last century, Mr. Roberts's sister, married to a
Mr. Bebb, emigrated to America; as did also his brother George, who still survives, and of whom Dr.
Matheson gives an interesting account in the seventh
letter of the second volume of "Reed and Matheson's
Narrative," calling him "*Judge* Roberts, the *Pastor* of
the Congregational Church!" at Ebensburg, in Pennsylvania.

Mrs. Bebb was soon left a widow, with two sons,
William and Evan. But "the Judge of the widow"
and "the Father of the fatherless" did not forsake her.
She is a woman of a strong mind and great piety, and

a thorough hater of slavery and oppression in all their forms. Her own principles she endeavoured to instil into the minds of her sons, sparing no efforts to fit them for acting a useful and honourable part in society. William was brought up to the law, and Evan to commerce. And now, in the evening of her days, the pious old Welsh-woman has the gratification of seeing Evan an enterprising and successful merchant in New York, while William enjoys the highest honour that his fellow-citizens of Ohio can confer upon him! He is the Governor of a territory of nearly 40,000 square miles, and a population of 2,000,000. Mr. Jones, the minister, is intimately acquainted with Mrs. Bebb, who carefully instructed her distinguished son in the good old language of Wales, so that, at the time of his recent canvass for office, he was able to address the Cambrian portion of his constituency in their mother tongue.

On entering into office, he declared his determined opposition to the " black laws " of Ohio. Those "black laws" are black indeed. They are the foul blot of this otherwise honoured State. One of them is intended to prevent the coloured citizens of other States from removing to Ohio. It was enacted in 1807, and is to this effect,—that within twenty days after the entrance of an emigrant into the State, he is to find two freehold sureties in the sum of 500 dollars for his *good behaviour*, and likewise for his *maintenance*, should he, at any future period, be unable to maintain himself. The Legislature well knew that it would be utterly impossible, generally speaking, for a *black* or *coloured* stranger to find such securities.   In 1800 there were only 337 free blacks in the territory; but in 1830, notwithstanding the "black laws," there were 9,500.   A large portion of them entered in entire ignorance of this iniquitous law, and some perhaps in bold defiance of it.   But it has by no means remained a dead letter.   In 1829 a very general effort was made to enforce it,—about 1,000 free blacks being driven from the State, to take refuge in the more free and Christian country of Canada.   Sir J. Colebrook, the Governor of Upper Canada, said to the coloured deputation that waited upon him, "Tell the *Republicans* on your side of the line that we Royalists do not know men by their colour.   Should you come to us, you will be entitled to all the privileges of the rest of His Majesty's subjects."   A noble sentiment! and one calculated to make a "*Britisher*" proud of his country, particularly since the abolition of slavery in our other colonies.   At the time these people were thus driven away, the State of Ohio contained but 23 inhabitants to one square mile!

In 1838 official notice was given to the inhabitants of the town of Fairfield, in Ohio, that all "black or mulatto persons" residing there were to comply with the requirements of the law of 1807 within twenty days, or it would be enforced against them.   The proclamation addresses the *white* inhabitants in the following remarkable terms: "Whites, look out!   If any person or persons *employing* any black or mulatto person, contrary to the 3rd section of this law, you may look out for the breakers!"

At the very time I was in Ohio an attempt was made, in Mercer County, to eject by force a number of inoffensive black people. Originally slaves in Virginia, they had been liberated by the will of their late master, and located on a suitable quantity of land which he had secured for them. But the magnanimous and liberty-boasting Americans would not allow them to enjoy their little settlement unmolested; and it was extremely doubtful whether the Governor would be able to protect them from outrage.

In 1839 a number of coloured inhabitants of Ohio addressed a respectful petition to the Legislature, praying for the removal of certain legal disabilities under which they were labouring. The answer was a denial, not merely of the *prayer* of the petition, but of the very *right* of petition! " Resolved, that the blacks and mulattoes who may be residents within this State have no constitutional right to present their petitions to the General Assembly for any purpose whatsoever; and that any reception of such petitions on the part of the General Assembly is a mere act of privilege or policy, and not imposed by any expressed or implied power of the Constitution!"

But the *blackest* of these black laws is the following: " That no black or mulatto person or persons shall hereafter be permitted to be sworn, or give evidence in any court of record or elsewhere in this State, in any cause depending, or matter of controversy, when either party to the same is a *white* person; or in any prosecution of the State against any *white* person!"

Under such a law a white man may with perfect impunity defraud or abuse a negro to any extent, provided that he is careful to avoid the presence of any of his own caste at the execution of his contract, or the commission of his crime!

To these "black laws" Governor Bebb has avowed an uncompromising hostility; but the first session of the State Legislature after his election had just closed, and the black laws were still in force. Mr. Bebb was not sufficiently supported in his just and humane intentions to enable him to carry those intentions out. I was assured, however, by those who knew him well, that he was only "biding his time," being as determined as ever to wipe away from the statute-book every remnant of these foul enactments. If he succeed, the poor old Welsh-woman, in her obscurity and widowhood, will have rendered an important service to the cause of humanity and justice. Let mothers think of this, and be encouraged!

The day after our arrival in Cincinnati, being the 22nd of February, we obtained, by the aid of Dr. Weed (one of Mr. Boynton's deacons), a suitable private lodging. Dr. Weed in early life studied for the medical profession, and graduated in physic. Afterwards he spent some years as a missionary among the Indians. Now he is a bookseller, publisher, and stationer in Cincinnati, affording an illustration of that versatility for which the Americans are distinguished. "Men are to be met with," says M. de Tocqueville, (and the present writer has himself seen many instances,) "who have successively been barristers, farmers, merchants, ministers of the Gospel, and physicians. If the American be less perfect in each craft than the European, at least there is scarcely any trade with which he is utterly unacquainted." I have heard of a man in New York, who, having tried the ministry and completely failed, wisely judged that that was not the way in which he could best serve God, and turned to commerce. He is now a substantial merchant, and supports five other men to preach the Gospel; each of whom, he is wont to say, does it much better than he could ever have done.

The lodging which Dr. Weed kindly found us was at the house of the Misses M'Pherson, five Quaker sisters, living together. It was clean and respectable,— the cheapest and most comfortable lodging we had hitherto met with. The table was bountifully supplied with excellent and well-cooked provisions; for which the charge was only 4 dollars each per week, and half-a-dollar for fuel, making altogether only 9 dollars for us both. Of the kindness and hospitality of these ladies we shall always retain a grateful remembrance.

In the afternoon I had the honour of being introduced to Dr. Beecher, Dr. Stowe, Professor Allen, and several other Presbyterian ministers of the New School. They were assembled for fraternal intercourse in the vestry of one of the " churches." I was struck with the sallowness of their complexions, and the want of polish in their manners. Dr. Beecher invited me to go up some day to see Lane Seminary, about two miles

off. To this invitation I readily acceded. I was greatly
interested in this veteran, of whose fame I had so often
heard.

February 23rd.—In the evening, I went to a meeting
of the Democratic party in the town-hall, thinking
it would afford me a good opportunity for observing
American manners. The place was full; and when I
arrived, a gentleman was addressing the meeting with
great vehemence of tone and gesture. His speech consisted of innumerable changes rung on the sentiment
—" There must be a vigorous prosecution of the war
against Mexico." But I must reserve any further
account of this meeting for my next letter.

LETTER XVII.

IN resuming my notice of the Democratic meeting, let me observe that the Democratic party in America is not very reputable. It is the war party, the pro-slavery party, the mob party, and, at present, the dominant party,—the party, in fine, of President Polk. It had just been aroused to the highest pitch of indignation, by a telling speech delivered in Congress against the Mexican War by Thomas Corwin, Esq., one of the Ohio senators. This meeting, then, was intended as a demonstration in favour of Polk and his policy; but it turned out a miserable failure.

When the blustering speaker who "had the floor" when I entered sat down, the "president" (for they do not say the chairman) rose, amidst a tremendous storm of favourite names, uttered simultaneously by all present at the top of their voices, and, as soon as he could be heard, said it had been moved and seconded that So-and-so, Esq., be requested to address the meeting: those who were in favour of that motion were to say "Ay,"—those against it, "No." One great "Ay" was then uttered by the mass, and a few "Noes" were

heard. The "Ayes" had it. But an unforeseen difficulty occurred. So-and-so, Esq., either was not there,
or would not speak. Amidst deafening noise again,
the president rose, and said it had been moved and
seconded that John Brough, Esq., be requested to address the meeting. "Ay"—"No;" but the "Ayes"
had it. "Now, John Brough," said a droll-looking
Irishman, apparently a hod-carrier, who was at my
elbow,—

> "Now, John Brough,
> Out with the stuff."

Here was Paddy on the western side of the Allegany
Mountains, with his native accent and native wit as
fresh and unimpaired as if he had but just left his
green isle, and landed on one of the quays at Liverpool.
But John Brough again declined the honour conferred
upon him! Then it was moved and seconded and
"ayed" that So-and-so, Esq., be requested to address
the meeting; but *he* also was not forthcoming! *Nil
desperandum.* It was moved and seconded and "ayed"
that — Callaghan, Esq., be requested to address the
meeting. After some hesitation, and a reference to
his own "proverbial modesty," he proceeded to foam,
and stamp, and thump, and bluster for "the vigorous
prosecution of the war," till the American eagle should
"stretch his wings over the halls of the Montezumas."
At this stage of the proceedings, the spitting and smoke
had become so offensive that I was compelled to retire;
and I did so with no very high notions of the intelligence and respectability of the American democrats.

The next day being fine and frosty, and the roads hard, I set off in the morning to pay my intended visit to Lane Seminary. I found it a long two miles, all up hill. The seminary itself, the building in which the students are accommodated, is a large plain brick edifice, four stories high, besides the basement-story, and has very much the appearance of a small Lancashire factory. It is 100 feet long by about 40 feet wide, and contains 84 rooms for students. The situation is pleasant, and at a nice distance from the roadside. A large bell was being tolled awkwardly when I arrived. It was 11 o'clock A.M. I found the front door thrown wide open, with every indication of its being entered by all comers without the least ceremony—not even that of wiping the shoes. There was neither door-bell nor knocker, scraper nor mat; and the floor of the lobby seemed but slightly acquainted with the broom,—to say nothing of the scrubbing-brush. It looked like the floor of a corn or provision warehouse. I had no alternative but to venture in. Immediately after, there entered a young man with a fowling-piece, whom before I had seen at a little distance watching the movements of a flock of wild pigeons. I took him for a sportsman; but he was a young divine! I asked him if Dr. Beecher was about. He replied that he guessed not, but he would be at the lecture-room in a few minutes, for the bell that had just tolled was a summons to that room. " Does the Doctor, then," said I, " deliver a lecture this morning?"—" No, it is *declamation* this morning." " Is it such an exercise," I continued, " as a stranger

may attend?"—" Oh, yes!" he replied; "it is *public*
declamation." He then directed me to the lecture-
room. It was across the yard, and under the chapel
belonging to the institution. This chapel is a very
neat building, after the model of a Grecian temple,
having the roof in front carried out and supported by
six well-proportioned columns in the form of a portico.
In a part of the basement-story was the lecture-room
in question. The students were mustering. By-and-
by Dr. Stowe entered. He invited me to take a chair
by his side, on a kind of platform. Professor Allen
then came in, and after him Dr. Beecher. The exercise began with a short prayer by Mr. Allen. He then
called upon a Mr. Armstrong, one of the students, to
ascend the platform. The young man obeyed; and,
somewhat abruptly and vehemently, rehearsed from
memory a Poem on War. Suiting the action to the
words, he began—

" *On*—to the glorious conflict—ON !'"

It quite startled me! Soon afterwards I heard,—

" And Montezuma's halls shall *ring*."

What! (reasoned I) is this the sequel to the Democratic
meeting of last night? Has Mars, who presided at
the town-hall, a seat in the lecture-room of this
Theological Seminary? As the young man proceeded,
however, I perceived that his poem was, in fact, a
denunciation of the horrors of war,—not, as I had supposed, the composition of another person committed to
memory, and now rehearsed as an exercise in elocution,

but entirely his own. It was altogether a creditable performance. The Professors at the close made their criticisms upon it, which were all highly favourable. Dr. Beecher said, " My only criticism is, *Print it, print it.*" The venerable Doctor, with the natural partiality of a tutor, afterwards observed to me he had never heard anything against war that took so strong a hold of his feelings as that poem. Dr. Stowe also told me that Mr. Armstrong was considered a young man of fine talents and great devotion; and that some of the students had facetiously said, " Brother Armstrong was so pious that even the dogs would not bark at him !"

Mr. Armstrong was not at all disposed to take his tutor's advice. But he favoured me with a copy of his poem, on condition that I would not cause it to be printed in America,—in England I might. It contains some turgid expressions, some halting and prosaic lines, and might be improved by a severe revision; but, besides its interest as a Transatlantic college-exercise, I feel it possesses sufficient merit to relieve the tediousness of my own prose.

> " ' *On*—to the glorious conflict—ON !'—
>   Is heard throughout the land,
>   While flashing columns, thick and strong,
>   Sweep by with swelling band.
> ' Our country, right or wrong,' they shout,
>   ' Shall still our motto be:
>   With *this* we are prepared to rout
>   Our foes from sea to sea.
>   Our own right arms to us shall bring
>   The victory and the spoils;
>   And Montezuma's halls shall ring,
>   When there we end our toils.'

On, then, ye brave! like tigers rage,
　That you may win your crown;
Mowing both infancy and age
　In ruthless carnage down.
Where flows the tide of life and light,
　Amid the city's hum,
There let the cry, at dead of night,
　Be heard, 'They come, they come!'
Mid scenes of sweet domestic bliss,
　Pour shells of livid fire;
While red-hot balls among them hiss,
　To make the work entire.
And when the scream of agony
　Is heard above the din,
Then ply your guns with energy,
　And throw your columns in:
Thro' street and lane, thro' house and church,
　The sword and faggot bear,
And every inmost recess search,
　To fill with shrieks the air.
Where waving fields and smiling homes
　Now deck the sunny plain,
And laughter-loving childhood roams
　Unmoved by care or pain;
Let famine gaunt and grim despair
　Behind you stalk along,
And pestilence taint all the air
　With victims from the strong.
Let dogs from mangled beauty's cheeks
　The flesh and sinews tear,
And craunch the bones around for weeks,
　And gnaw the skulls till bare.
Let vultures gather round the heaps
　Made up of man and beast,
And, while the widowed mother weeps,
　Indulge their horrid feast;
Till, startled by wild piteous groans,
　On dreary wings they rise,
To come again, mid dying moans,
　And tear out glazing eyes.

Tho' widows' tears, and orphans' cries,
 When starving round the spot
Where much-loved forms once met their eyes
 Which now are left to rot,
With trumpet-tongue, for vengeance call
 Upon each guilty head
That drowns, mid revelry and brawls,
 Remembrance of the dead.
Tho' faint from fighting—wounded—wan,
 To camp you'll turn your feet,
And no sweet, smiling, happy home,
 Your saddened hearts will greet:
No hands of love—no eyes of light—
 Will make your wants their care,
Or soothe you thro' the dreary night,
 Or smooth your clotted hair.
But crushed by sickness, famine, thirst,
 You'll strive in vain to sleep,
Mid corpses mangled, blackened, burst,
 And blood and mire deep;
While horrid groans, and fiendish yells,
 And every loathsome stench,
Will kindle images of hell
 You'll strive in vain to quench.
Yet *on!*—press on, in all your might,
 With banners to the field,
And mingle in the glorious fight,
 With Satan for your shield:
For marble columns, if you die,
 May on them bear your name;
While papers, tho' they sometimes lie,
 Will praise you, or will blame.
Yet woe! to those who build a house,
 Or kingdom, not by right,—
Who in their feebleness propose
 Against the Lord to fight.
For when the Archangel's trumpet sounds,
 And all the dead shall hear,
And haste from earth's remotest bounds
 In judgment to appear,—

When every work, and word, and *thought*,
　Well known or hid from sight,
Before the Universe is brought
　To blaze in lines of light,—
When by the test of *perfect* law
　Your '*glorious*' course is tried,
On what resources will you draw?—
　In what will you confide?
For know that eyes of awful light
　Burn on you from above,
Where nought but kindness meets the sight,
　And all the air is love.
When all unused to such employ
　As charms the angelic bands,
How can you hope to share their joy
　Who dwell in heavenly lands?"

Such was the poem of Frederick Alexander Armstrong. After its rehearsal, a young gentleman *read* a prose Essay on Education. It was clever, and indicated a mind of a high order, but was too playful; and the performance was severely criticised. Here ended the "public declamation."

LETTER XVIII.

THE "public declamation" ended, Dr. Beecher asked me to accompany him to his house. It was about an eighth of a mile from the institution, over a very bad road, or rather over no road at all. He conducted me into a snug little sitting-room, having no grate; but a wood fire on the floor under the chimney. It looked primitive and homely. This style of fire is not uncommon in America. The logs of wood lie across two horizontal bars of iron, by which they are raised four or six inches from the floor. The Doctor's first care was to replenish the fire with a few sturdy pieces of wood. All through the States, I have observed that the task of feeding the fire generally devolves on the head of the family. In this little room I was introduced to Mrs. Beecher. She is, I believe, the third lady on whom the Doctor has conferred his name. In one corner of this apartment was a gun, and on the sofa a heap of shot. Thousands of wild pigeons were flying about. The visit of these birds made the Doctor very uneasy. He was ever and anon snatching up his gun, and going out to have a pop at them. Though upwards of seventy years of age, he is an excellent marksman. It was to me a little odd to see a venerable D.D., a Professor of Theology, handling a fowling-piece! The Americans, have by circumstances been trained to great skill in the use of fire-arms. The gun, however, proved a fatal instrument in the hands of one of the Doctor's sons, a young man of great promise, who was killed by the accidental explosion of one. Nevertheless, Dr. Beecher has five sons, all (like himself) in the ministry! He has a maiden daughter, who has distinguished herself by her literary attainments and active benevolence. The excellent and accomplished wife of Dr. Stowe was also a Miss Beecher.

At 1 o'clock P.M. we dined. The Professors never dine, or take any other meal, with the assembled students. This is a disadvantage. But in America eating, under any circumstances, is not so sociable a matter as in England.

After dinner, I took my leave of Dr. Beecher, and went to see the library of the institution. This is over the chapel, but so arranged as not at all to detract from the just proportions of the building. Indeed, no one would suspect that there was a story above. This library was collected with great care and judgment by Dr. Stowe, in England and on the continent of Europe, and contains 10,000 volumes! The library-room is capable of receiving 30,000 volumes. But even now it is the largest library on this side the Allegany Mountains. It comprises not only the standard works in all the departments of a theological course, but also a very rich variety of authors in general literature and science. The books are arranged in alcoves according to their character,—Theology—Biblical Literature—Classics—History—Philosophy; and so forth.

There is a " Society of Inquiry" in connection with the seminary, which has a distinct library of 326 volumes. " The Reading Room and Athenæum" is furnished with 21 newspapers, and several of the best literary and theological periodicals.

From the library, my guide (one of the students) led me down into the lecture-room, where Professor Stowe was engaged with a Hebrew class. They were reading in the Song of Solomon. The exhibition did not strike me as much superior to what we used to have at Rotherham College ten or twelve years ago. In point of domestic *comfort*, the latter is incomparably before Lane Seminary, and in literary advantages not far behind. Professor Stowe kindly drove me back to Cincinnati in his buggy, or waggon, or phaeton.

Lane Seminary is an institution devoted entirely to theological education, in connection with the New-School Presbyterians. The building, including chapel and library, cost about 50,000 dollars, or 10,000*l.*, and must have been very cheap at that. In 1828–30, Ebenezer Lane, Esq., and his brother Andrew Lane, Esq., made a donation of 4,000 dollars for the purpose of establishing the seminary, whereupon it was incorporated under the name of "Lane Seminary," and trustees were appointed. To these trustees the Rev. Mr. Kemper and his sons made over, for the benefit of the institution, 60 acres of land, including the site on which the buildings stand. In 1832 Arthur Tappan, Esq., of New York, subscribed 20,000 dollars for the Professorship of Theology. In the same year 15,000 dollars were raised for the Professorship of Ecclesiastical History; the largest contributor to which was Ambrose White, Esq., of Philadelphia: and an equal sum was contributed for the Professorship of Biblical Literature,—Stephen Van Rennselaer, Esq., of Albany, being the chief contributor. In 1835, a fund of 20,000 dollars was raised for the Professorship of Sacred Rhetoric, of which a large portion was given by John Tappan, Esq., of Boston. A literary department was organized in 1829, which was discontinued in 1834; at which period the institution, in its full operation as a Theological Seminary, may be said to have commenced. Since then it has sent forth about 250 ministers!

Candidates for admission must produce satisfactory testimonials, that they are members, in good standing, of some Christian Church; that they possess competent talents; and that they have regularly graduated at some college or university, or have pursued a course of study equivalent to the common college course.

The course of study occupies three years; and every student is expected to enter with the intention of completing the full course. So far as practicable, the different branches are pursued simultaneously. Thus the department of Biblical Literature, during the first year, occupies three days in the week; during the second, two; and during the third, one: Church History, one day in the week : Sacred Rhetoric and Pastoral Theology, one day in the week during the` first year, two the second, and three the third. The object of this arrangement is to afford a pleasant variety in study, and to keep up a proper interest in all the departments through the whole course. " Hitherto," it is stated, "the plan has been pursued with results highly satisfactory to the Faculty." Theological students may be glad to learn the following particulars of the whole course.

I. BIBLICAL LITERATURE.—This department embraces—1. Biblical Geography and Antiquities. 2. Principles of Biblical Interpretation. 3. General Introduction to the Old and New Testaments, and Particular Introduction to the Pentateuch, Gospels, and Acts. 4. Interpretation of the Gospels in Harmony and of the Acts. 5. Interpretation of the Historical Writings of Moses. 6. Particular Introduction to the several Books of the Old and New Testaments. 7. Hebrew Poetry, including Figurative and Symbolical Language of Scripture. 8. Interpretation of Psalms, Proverbs, and Ecclesiastes. 9. Epistles to Romans, Corinthians, Timothy, and 1 Peter. 10. Nature and Fulfilment of Prophecy, particularly in reference to the Messiah. 11. Interpretation of Isaiah, Zechariah, and Nahum. 12. The Revelation, in connection with Daniel.

H

II. Church History and Polity.—In this department a regular course of lectures is given on the History of Doctrines to all the classes, and on Church Polity to the senior classes.

III. Systematic Theology.—In this department are included—1. Cause and Effect. 2. Mental Philosophy. 3. Atheism, its History and Hypothesis, Arguments, Objections, and Folly. 4. The Being, Character, and Attributes of God. 5. Reason, Light of Nature, Necessity of Revelation. 6. The Truth and Inspiration of the Bible. 7. Doctrine of Revelation.

IV. Sacred Rhetoric and Pastoral Theology. *First Year.* — Lectures on Rhetoric and Elocution. Exercises in Reading and Elocution. *Second Year.*— Written Discussions, with Public Criticism in the class. *Third Year.* — Exercises in criticising Skeletons continued. Public and Private Criticism of Sermons. Lectures on Preaching and on Pastoral Duties.

The annual term of study begins on the second Wednesday in September, and closes on the second Wednesday in June, which is the Anniversary. The term closes with a public examination.

Dr. Andrew Reed, who visited Lane Seminary in 1834, refers to it as a *model* manual-labour institution. With the advancement of society around, it has lost in a great measure that peculiarity. There is now but little done in that way, though it is still recorded in italics among its regulations, that "every student is expected to labour three hours a day at some agricultural or mechanical business." "While the leading aim of this regulation," it is added, "is to promote health and vigour of both body and mind, compensation is received according to the value of the labour."

No charge is made for tuition. Rooms are fully furnished and rented at 5 dollars a year from each student. The incidental expenses, including fuel and light for public rooms, ringing the bell, and sweeping, are 5 dollars more. The room-rent and incidental bill are paid in advance. For the aid of indigent students funds are collected annually, by means of which board is furnished to such gratuitously. To those who receive no assistance from the funds, the price of board is about 90 cents a week. The cost of fuel and lights for each student, in his own room, will average from 8 to 12 dollars a year. Thus the entire expense to a young man for a whole term of nine months is only from 50 to 60 dollars, or from 10 to 12 guineas of our money.

"The results of these thirteen years of labour," say the trustees in a document recently issued, "considering the difficulties attending the establishment of such an institution in a new country, amid a population as yet unassimilated in feelings and habits, and whose schools, academies, and colleges are of comparatively recent origin, are indeed highly encouraging. The friends of the institution, and of religion and learning generally, thankful for what has already been accomplished, will feel encouraged to do whatever may be necessary for the highest efficiency of the seminary; and will give their prayers that the labours of the 300 young men, who have enjoyed or now enjoy its advantages," (there being about 50 then in the house,) "may be abundantly blessed by the Head of the Church."

Lane Seminary is a valuable and catholic institution. At their entrance, the students have to subscribe to no confession of faith; and, when they have completed their curriculum, they are at perfect liberty to exercise their ministry among whatever denomination they please. Congregational as well as Presbyterial Churches obtain pastors from this " school of the prophets."

The "Faculty" at present consists of the Rev. Lyman Beecher, D.D., President, and Professor of Theology; the Rev. Calvin E. Stowe, D.D., Professor of Biblical Literature, and Lecturer on Church History; and the Rev. D. Howe Allen, Professor of Sacred Rhetoric and Pastoral Theology, and Lecturer on Church Polity.

Nothing struck me more than the feeling of equality that seemed to subsist between students and professors. The latter, in speaking to or of any of the former, would generally say " Brother " So-and-so. The students also, in their bearing towards the professors, seemed each to say, " I am as good a man as you are." This is the genius of America. You meet it everywhere. There man is man (except his skin be black), and he expects to be treated as such. Respect to superiors is not among the maxims of our Transatlantic brethren. The organ of veneration is, perhaps, imperfectly developed.

LETTER XIX.

A Sabbath at Cincinnati—The Second Presbyterian Church—Mutilation
of a Popular Hymn—The Rushing Habit—A wrong " Guess "—A
German Sunday-School—Visit to a Church of Coloured People—
Engagement at the Welsh " Church " — Monthly Concert — The
Medical College of Ohio—Tea at the House of a Coloured Minister.

On the previous Friday, Professor Allen called to
request me to preach in his stead at the Second Presbyterian Church on Sunday morning, the 28th of
February, as he had to go some twenty miles into the
country to " assist at a revival." I agreed to do so.
Sunday morning was excessively cold, with a heavy fall
of snow. On arriving at the " church," I found there
was no vestry. Indeed, a vestry, as a private room for
the minister, is seldom found in America. The places
are exceedingly neat and comfortable, but they want
that convenience. I had therefore to go with my hat
and top-coat, covered with snow, right into the pulpit.
This church outside is a noble-looking building, with
massive pillars in front, and a bell-tower containing a
town-clock ; but the interior seemed comparatively
small. It had a gallery at one end, which held only
the singers and the organ. The seats below were not
more than one-third full. Dr. Beecher ministered in
this place for about ten years. It was now without a

pastor, but was temporarily supplied by Professor
Allen.   The congregation was far more decorous and
attentive than those in New Orleans.   After the introductory service, and while the hymn before sermon was
being sung, a man came trudging down the aisle,
bearing an immense scuttle full of coals to supply the
stoves.   How easy it would have been before service
to place a box of fuel in the vicinity of each stove, and
thereby avoid this unseemly bustle!   But in the singing of the hymn, I found something to surprise and
offend me even more than the coal-scuttle.   The hymn
was—

> " O'er the gloomy hills of darkness," &c.

I had selected it myself; but when I got to the second
verse, where I had expected to find

> " Let the Indian, let the negro,
>   Let the rude barbarian see," &c.,

lo! "the Indian" and "the negro" had vanished,
and

> " Let the dark benighted pagan "

was substituted.   A wretched alteration, — as feeble
and tautological in effect as it is suspicious in design.
The altered reading, I learned, prevails universally in
America, except in the *original* version used by the
Welsh congregations.   Slave-holders, and the abettors
of that horrid system which makes it a crime to teach
a negro to read the Word of God, felt perhaps that
they could not devoutly and consistently sing

> " Let the Indian, let the negro," &c.

This church, I heard, was more polluted with a pro-slavery feeling than any other in Cincinnati of the same denomination,—a circumstance which, I believe, had something to do with Dr. Beecher's resignation of the pastorate.

At the close of the sermon, having pronounced the benediction, I engaged, according to our English custom, in a short act of private devotion. When I raised my head and opened my eyes, the very last man of the congregation was actually making his exit through the doorway; and it was quite as much as I could manage to put on my top-coat and gloves and reach the door before the sexton closed it. This rushing habit in the House of God strikes a stranger as rude and irreverent. You meet with no indications of private devotion, either preceding or following public worship. A man marches into his pew, or his pulpit, sits down, wipes his nose, and stares at all about him ; and at the close, the moment the "Amen" is uttered, he is off with as much speed as if the house were on fire. In this instance, the service had not exceeded an hour and a half; and yet they hurried out as if they thought the beef was all burnt, and the pudding all spoiled. Of course, there were no thanks to the stranger for his services,—to say nothing of the *quiddam honorarium*, which to a man travelling for health, at his own expense, with an invalid wife, might have been supposed not unacceptable.

When, however, I got to the portico outside, a gentleman, with his wife, was waiting to see me before they stepped into their carriage. Here was some token

of politeness and hospitality,—an invitation to dinner,
no doubt.—"Thank you, sir, I am very much obliged
to you; but I left my wife very ill at our lodgings this
morning, and therefore I cannot have the pleasure to
dine with you to-day," was the civil excuse I was preparing.   Never was expectation more beside the mark.
My "guess" was altogether wrong.   "What are you
going to do with yourself this afternoon?" was the
gentleman's blunt salutation.   "What have *you* to
propose, sir?" was my reply.   "I am the superintendent," he said, " of a German Sunday-school in the
upper part of the city, and I should like you to come
and address the children this afternoon."   I promised
to go, and he to send to my "lodgings" for me.   We
both kept our appointment.   The number of scholars
was about 100.   This effort to bring the Germans
under a right religious influence is very laudable; for
there are about 10,000 of that people in Cincinnati.
One quarter of the city is entirely German.   You see
nothing else on the sign-boards; you hear nothing else
in the streets.   Of these Germans the greater part are
Roman Catholics.

After visiting the school, I found myself in time to
attend one of the chapels of the coloured people at
3 P.M.   A medical student, whom I had met in the
morning, and again at the German school, accompanied
me.   He was a New Englander, and a thorough anti-
slavery man.   When we got to the chapel—a Baptist
one—they were at prayer.   Walking in softly, we entered a pew right in the midst of them.   The minister—

a mulatto of about thirty years of age, with a fine intelligent eye—was very simple in dress, and unostentatious in manner. His language, too, was appropriate and correct. He was evidently a man of good common sense. His text was Psalm li. 12, 13. He referred very properly to the occasion on which the Psalm was composed, and drew from the text a large mass of sound practical instruction. The chapel (capable of containing about 150 people) was only half-full. Before the sermon, I had observed a very old negro, in a large shabby camlet cloak and a black cap, ascending the pulpit-stairs. I supposed that, being dull of hearing, he had taken that position that he might better listen to the service. However, when the sermon was over, this patriarchal-looking black man rose to pray; and he prayed "like a bishop," with astonishing correctness and fluency! He was formerly a slave in Kentucky, and was at this time about eighty years of age. They call him "Father Watkins." At the close I introduced myself to him and to the minister. They both expressed regret that they had not had me up in the pulpit, to tell them something, as "Father Watkins" said, about their "brothers and sisters on the other side of the water." The minister gave me his card, and invited me and my wife to take tea with him on Tuesday afternoon. This was the first invitation I received within the city of Cincinnati to take a meal anywhere; and it was the more interesting to me as coming from a coloured man.

In the evening I went, according to appointment, to

the Welsh Chapel. There I met a Mr. Bushnel, an American missionary from the Gaboon River, on the western coast of Africa. He first spoke in English, and I afterwards a little in Welsh; gladly embracing the opportunity to exhort my countrymen in that "Far West" to feel kindly and tenderly towards the coloured race among them; asking them how they would themselves feel if, as Welshmen, they were branded and despised wherever they went! I was grieved to see the excess to which they carried the filthy habit of spitting. The coloured people in *their* chapel were incomparably cleaner in that respect.

In the morning a notice had been put into my hand at the Presbyterian Church for announcement, to the effect that Mr. Bushnel and myself would address the " monthly concert at the church in Sixth-street " on the morrow evening. Of this arrangement not a syllable had been said to me beforehand. This was American liberty, and I quietly submitted to it. The attendance was not large; and we two missionaries had it all to ourselves. No other ministers were present, —not even the minister of the church in which we were assembled. The people, however, seemed heartily interested in the subject of missions. At the close, a lady from Manchester, who had seen me there in 1845 at the missionary meeting, came forward full of affection to shake hands. She was a member of Mr. Griffin's church in that city, and had removed to America a few months before, with her husband (who is a member of the " Society of Friends ") and children.

I was glad to find that they were likely to be comfortable in their adopted country.

Next morning I went with Dr. Reuben D. Mussey, a New Englander, to see the Medical College of Ohio. Dr. Mussey is the Professor of Surgery and Dean of the Faculty, and is highly esteemed for his professional skill and general character. He and his son, who was my guide on the Sunday, very kindly showed and explained to me everything of interest in the institution. The cabinet belonging to the anatomical department is supplied with all the materials necessary for acquiring a minute and perfect knowledge of the human frame. These consist of detached bones, of wired natural skeletons, and of dried preparations to exhibit the muscles, bloodvessels, nerves, &c. The cabinet of comparative anatomy is supposed to be more extensively supplied than any other in the United States. Besides perfect skeletons of American and foreign birds and other animals, there is an immense number of detached *crania,* from the elephant and hippopotamus down to the minuter orders. The cabinet in the surgical department has been formed at great expense, chiefly by Dr. Mussey himself, during the labour of more than forty years. It contains a large number of rare specimens,—600 specimens of diseased bones alone. Other departments are equally well furnished. The Faculty is composed of six Professorships,—Surgery, Anatomy and Physiology, Chemistry and Pharmacy, Materia Medica, Obstetrics and Diseases of Women and Children, and the Theory and

Practice of Medicine. The fees of tuition are only 15 dollars, or 3 guineas, to each professor, making an aggregate of 90 dollars. There were 190 students. It will probably be admitted that this institution, formed in a new country, has arrived at an astonishing degree of vigour and maturity. It is only one of many instances in which the Americans are before us in the facilities afforded for professional education.

In the afternoon my wife and myself went to take tea with the coloured minister. His dwelling, though small and humble, was neat and clean. With his intelligence and general information we were quite delighted. He spoke with feeling of the gross insults to which the coloured people, even in this free State, are exposed. When they travel by railway, though they pay the same fare as other people, they are generally put in the luggage-van! He had himself, when on board of steam-boats, often been sent to the " pantry " to eat his food. Nor will the white people employ them but in the most menial offices; so that it is nearly impossible for them to rise to affluence and horse-and-gig respectability. The consequence is that they are deeply and justly disaffected towards the American people and the American laws. They clearly understand that England is their friend. For one month all the free coloured people wore crape as mourning for Thomas Clarkson.

LETTER XX.

A LADY, belonging to the Presbyterian Church at
which I preached, kindly sent her carriage to take us
about to see the city. We visited the new Roman
Catholic Cathedral, one of the principal " lions." It
was begun in 1841, and, though used for public worship, is not yet finished. The building is a parallelo-
gram of 200 feet long by 80 feet wide, and is 58 feet
from the floor to the ceiling. The roof is partly supported by the side walls, and partly by two rows of
freestone columns — nine in each row — at a distance
of about 11 feet from the wall inside. These columns
are of the Corinthian Order, and are 35 feet high, and
3 feet 6 inches in diameter. There is no gallery,
except at one end, for the organ, which cost 5,400
dollars, or about 1,100*l.* sterling. The floor of the
building is furnished with a centre aisle of 6 feet wide,
and two other aisles, each 11 feet wide, along the side
walls, for processional purposes. The remainder of
the area is formed into 140 pews, 10 feet deep. Each
pew will accommodate with comfort only six persons ;
so that this immense edifice affords sitting room for

no more than 840 people! It is a magnificent structure, displaying in all its proportions a remarkable
degree of elegance and taste. The tower, when
finished, will present an elevation of 200 feet, with a
portico of twelve Corinthian columns, six in front and
three on either side, on the model of the Tower of
the Wind at Athens. The entire building will be Grecian in all its parts. One-fourth of the population
of Cincinnati are Roman Catholics. They have lately
discontinued the use of public government-schools for
their children, and have established some of their own.
I am not so much alarmed at the progress of Popery
in America as I was before I visited that country. Its
proselytes are exceedingly few. Its supporters consist
chiefly of the thousands of Europeans, already Roman
Catholic, who flock to the New World. The real *progress* of Popery is greater in Britain than in America.

In the evening I preached for Mr. Boynton in the
" Sixth-street Church." Mr. Boynton and his Church,
heretofore Presbyterians, have recently become Con-
gregationalists. This has given great umbrage to the
Presbyterians. Congregationalism is rapidly gaining
ground in the Western World, and seems destined
there, as in England since Cromwell's time, to swallow
up Presbyterianism. I make no invidious comparison
between the two systems : I merely look at facts. And
it does appear to me that Congregationalism—so simple,
so free, so unsectarian, and so catholic—is nevertheless a
powerful absorbent. It *has* absorbed all that was orthodox in the old Presbyterian Churches of England; and it

is absorbing the Calvinistic Methodists and the churches named after the Countess of Huntingdon. It has all along exerted a powerful influence on the Presbyterianism of America. The Congregational element diffused among those churches occasioned the division of the Presbyterian Church into Old School and New School.

Mr. Boynton is what a friend of mine called "intensely American." He has lately published, under the title of "Our Country the Herald of a New Era," a lecture delivered before the "Young Men's Mercantile Library Association." To show the magnificent ideas the Americans entertain of themselves and their country, I will transcribe a few passages.

"This nation is an enigma, whose import no man as yet may fully know. She is a germ of boundless things. The unfolded bud excites the hope of one-half the human race, while it stirs the remainder with both anger and alarm. Who shall now paint the beauty and attraction of the expanded flower? Our Eagle is scarcely fledged; but one wing stretches over Massachusetts Bay, and the other touches the mouth of the Columbia. Who shall say, then, what lands shall be overshadowed by the full-grown pinion? Who shall point to any spot of the northern continent, and say, with certainty, Here the starry banner shall never be hailed as the symbol of dominion? [The annexation of Canada!] * * * It cannot be disguised that the idea is gathering strength among us, that the territorial mission of this nation is to obtain and hold at least all that lies north of Panama. * * * Whether the millions that are to dwell on the great Pacific slope of our continent are to acknowledge our banner, or rally to standards of their own; whether Mexico is to become ours by sudden conquest or gradual absorption; whether the British provinces, when they pass from beneath the sceptre of England, shall be incorporated with us, or retain an independent dominion;—are perhaps questions which a not distant future may decide. However they may be settled, the great fact will remain essentially the same, that the two continents of this Western Hemisphere shall yet bear up a stupendous social, political, and religious structure, wrought by the American mind, moulded and coloured by the hues of American thought, and animated and united by an American soul. It seems equally certain that, whatever the divisions of territory may be, these United States are the living centre, from which already flows the resistless stream which will ultimately absorb in its own channel, and bear on its own current, the whole thought of the two Americas. * * * If, then, I have not over-rated the moral and intellectual vigour of the people of this nation, and of the policy lately avowed to be acted upon—that the further occupation of American soil by the Governments of Europe is not to be suffered,—then the inference is a direct one, that the stronger elements will control and absorb the lesser, so that the same causes which melted the red races away will send the influence of the United States not only over the territory north of Panama, but across the Isthmus, and southward to Magellan."

The "New Era" of which America is the "Herald" is, he tells us, to be marked by three grand characteristics,—

"First. A new theory and practice in government and in social life, such as the world has never seen, of which we only perceive the germ as yet." Already have you indeed presented before the world your "peculiar institution" of slavery in a light new and striking. Already have you a "theory and practice" in the government of slaves such as the world never beheld!

"Second. A literature which shall not only be the proper outgrowth of the American mind, but which shall form a distinctive school, as clearly so as the literature of Greece!" Under this head he says, "Very much would I prefer that our literature should appear even in the guise of the awkward, speculating, guessing, but still original, strong-minded *American* Yankee, than to see it mincing in the costume of a London dandy. I would rather see it, if need be, showing the wild rough strength, the naturalness and fervour of the extreme West, equally prepared to liquor with a stranger or to fight with him, than to see it clad in the gay but filthy garments of the saloons of Paris. Nay more, much as every right mind abhors and detests such things, I would sooner behold our literature holding in one hand the murderous Bowie knife, and in the other the pistol of the duellist, than to see her laden with the foul secrets of a London hell, or the gaming-houses of Paris. * * * If we must meet with vice in our literature, let it be the growth of our own soil; for I think our own rascality has yet the healthier aspect."

"Third. A new era in the fine arts, from which future ages shall derive their models and their inspirations, as we do from Greece and Italy. * * * So far as scenery is concerned in the moulding of character, we may safely expect that a country where vastness and beauty are so wonderfully blended will stamp upon the national soul its own magestic and glorious image. It must be so. The mind will expand itself to the measure of things about it. Deep in the wide American soul there shall be Lake Superiors, inland oceans of thought; and the streams of her eloquence shall be like the sweep of the Mississippi in his strength. The rugged strength of the New England hills, the luxuriance of the sunny South, the measureless expanse of the prairie, the broad flow of our rivers, the dashing of our cataracts, the huge battlements of the everlasting mountains,—these are *American*. On the face of the globe there is nothing like to them. When therefore these various influences have been thoroughly wrought into the national soul, there will be such a correspondence between man and the works of God about him, that our music, our poetry, our eloquence, our all, shall be our own, individual and peculiar, like the Amazon and the Andes, the Mississippi and Niagara, alone in their strength and glory."

Now, mark you! amidst all these splendid visions of the future, there is no vision of liberty for 3,000,000 of slaves. That idea was too small to find a place among conceptions so vast. The lecture contains not a syllable of reference to them. On the contrary, the empty boast of freedom is heard in the following words of solemn mockery : " *The soul of man* here no longer sits *bound* and blind amid the despotic forms of the past ; it walks abroad *without a shackle,* and with an uncovered eye." It follows then that there is an essential difference between "the soul of man" and the soul of " nigger," or rather that " niggers" have no soul at all. How *can* men of sense, and especially ministers of the Gospel, sit down to pen such fustian ? These extracts show how intensely national the Americans are, and consequently how futile the apology for the existence of slavery so often presented, that one State can no more interfere with the affairs of another State than the people of England can with France and the other countries of the European continent. The Americans are to all intents and purposes *one* people. In short, the identity of feeling among the *States* of the Union is more complete than among the *counties* of Great Britain.

On the morning of the 4th of March, Dr. Stowe called to invite me to address the students at Lane Seminary, on the following Sabbath evening, on the subject of missions and the working of freedom in the West Indies. I readily promised to comply, glad of an opportunity to address so many of the future pastors of the American Churches, who will occupy the field when emancipation is sure to be the great question of the day. In fact, it is so already.

LETTER XXI.

In the afternoon we went with Mrs. Judge B—— to see an Orphan Asylum, in which she took a deep interest. Requested to address the children, I took the opportunity of delivering an anti-slavery and anti-colour-hating speech. The building, large and substantial, is capable of accommodating 300 children; but the number of inmates was at that time not more than 70. While the lady was showing us from one apartment to another, and pointing out to us the comforts and conveniences of the institution, the following colloquy took place.

Myself.—" Now, Mrs. B——, this place is very beautiful : I admire it exceedingly. Would you refuse a little *coloured* orphan admission into this asylum ? "

The Lady (stretching herself up to her full height, and with a look of horror and indignation).—" Indeed, we would ! "

Myself.—" Oh, shocking ! shocking ! "

The Lady.—" Oh ! there is another asylum for the coloured children; they are not neglected."

Myself.—"Ay, but why should they not be together?—why should there be such a distinction between
the children of our common Father?"

The Lady (in a tone of triumph).—"Why has God
made such a distinction between them?"

Myself.—"And why has he made such a distinction
between me and Tom Thumb? Or (for I am not very
tall) why has he made me a man of 5 feet 6 inches instead of 6 feet high? A man may as well be excluded
from society on account of his stature as his colour."

At this moment my wife, seeing I was waxing warm,
pulled me by the coat-tail, and I said no more. The
lady, however, went on to say that she was opposed to
slavery—was a colonizationist, and heartily wished all
the coloured people were back again in their own country. "In their own country, indeed!" I was going to
say,—"why, this is their country as much as it is
yours;" but I remembered my wife's admonition, and
held my peace. These were the sentiments of a lady
first and foremost in the charitable movements of the
day, and regarded by those around her as a pattern of
piety and benevolence. She was shocked at the notion
of the poor coloured orphan mingling with fellow-
orphans of a fairer hue.

In the evening we went to take tea at the house of
an English Quaker. About half-a-dozen friends had
been invited to meet us. These were kindred spirits,
anti-slavery out-and-out, and we spent the evening very
pleasantly. One of the company, in speaking of the
American prejudice against colour, mentioned a remark-

able circumstance. Some time ago, at an hotel in one of the Eastern States, a highly respectable coloured gentleman, well known to the host and to his guests, was about to sit down at the dinner table. A military officer—a conceited puppy—asked the landlord if that " nigger" was going to sit down? The landlord replied in the affirmative. "Then," said the fop, " *I* cannot sit down with a nigger." The rest of the company, understanding what was going forward, rose as one man from their seats, ordered another table to be spread, and presented a respectful invitation to the coloured gentleman to take a seat with them. The military dandy was left at the first table, "alone in his glory." When thus humbled, and when he also understood who the coloured man was, he went up to him to apologize in the best way he could, and to beg that the offence might be forgotten. The coloured gentleman's reply was beautiful and touching,—" Favours I write on marble, insults on sand."

On the morning of the 5th of March, the sun shining pleasantly, we were tempted to cross over to Covington, on the Kentucky or slave side of the river. Ferry-steamers ran every five or ten minutes, and the fare was only 5 cents. At this place the Baptists have a large and important college. Why did they erect it on the slave rather than on the free side of the Ohio? This institution I was anxious to see; but I found it too far off, and the roads too bad. Feeling weary and faint, we called at a house of refreshment, where we had a genuine specimen of American inquisitiveness.

In five minutes the daughter of the house had asked us where we came from—what sort of a place it was—how long we had been in the United States—how long it took us to come—how far we were going—how long we should stay—and if we did not like that part of America so well that we would come and settle in it altogether ! and in five minutes more our answers to all these important questions had been duly reported to the rest of the family in an adjoining room.　This inquisitiveness prevails more in the slave than in the free States, and originates, I believe, in the fidgetty anxiety they feel about their slaves.　The stranger must be well catechised, lest he should prove to be an Abolitionist come to give the slaves a sly lesson in geography.

In the afternoon I went to see the school of the coloured children in Cincinnati.　This was established about four years ago by a Mr. Gilmore, a white gentleman, who is also a minister of the Gospel.　He is a man of some property, and all connected with this school has been done at his own risk and responsibility. On my venturing to inquire what sacrifice of property he had made in the undertaking, he seemed hurt at the question, and replied, " No sacrifice whatever, sir." " But what, may I ask, have these operations cost beyond what you have received in the way of school-fees ?" I continued.　" About 7,000 dollars," (1,500*l.*) said he.　Including two or three branches, there are about 300 coloured children thus educated.　Mr. Gilmore was at first much opposed and ridiculed ; but that state of feeling was beginning to wear away. Several of the children were so fair that, accustomed as I am to shades of colour, I could not distinguish them from the Anglo-Saxon race; and yet Mr. Gilmore told me even they would not have been admitted to the other public schools! How discerning the Americans are! How proud of their skin-deep aristocracy! And the author of "Cincinnati in 1841," in speaking of those very schools from which these fair children were excluded, says, "These schools are founded not merely on the principle that all men are free and equal, but that all men's children are so likewise; and that, as it is our duty to love our neighbour as ourselves, it is our duty to provide the same benefits and blessings to his children as to our own. These establishments result from the recognition of the fact also, that we have all a common interest—moral, political, and pecuniary— in the education of the whole community." Those gloriously exclusive schools I had no wish to visit. But I felt a peculiar pleasure in visiting this humbler yet well-conducted institution, for the benefit of those who are despised and degraded on account of their colour. As I entered, a music-master was teaching them, with the aid of a piano, to sing some select pieces for an approaching examination, both the instrument and the master having been provided by the generous Gilmore. Even the music-master, notwithstanding his first-rate ability, suffers considerable loss of patronage on account of his services in this branded school. Among the pieces sung, and sung exceedingly well, was the following touching appeal, headed " The Fugitive Slave to the Christian "—Air, " Cracovienne."

" The fetters galled my weary soul,—
    A soul that seemed but thrown away:
I spurned the tyrant's base control,
    Resolved at last the man to play:
        The hounds are baying on my track;
        O Christian ! will you send me back ?

" I felt the stripes,—the lash I saw,
    Red dripping with a father's gore;
And, worst of all their lawless law,
    The insults that my mother bore !
        The hounds are baying on my track;
        O Christian ! will you send me back ?

" Where human law o'errules Divine,
    Beneath the sheriff's hammer fell
My wife and babes,—I call them mine,—
    And where they suffer who can tell ?
        The hounds are baying on my track;
        O Christian ! will you send me back ?

" I seek a home where man is man,
    If such there be upon this earth,—
To draw my kindred, if I can,
    Around its free though humble hearth:
        The hounds are baying on my track;
        O Christian ! will you send me back ?"

March 7.—This being the Sabbath, we went in the morning to worship at Mr. Boynton's church. The day was very wet, and the congregation small. His text was, " Go ye into all the world, and preach the Gospel to every creature. He that believeth and is baptized shall be saved; but he that believeth not shall be damned." The sermon, though read, and composed

I

too much in the essay style, indicated considerable powers of mind and fidelity of ministerial character. Although from incessant rain the day was very dark, the Venetian blinds were down over all the windows! The Americans, I have since observed, are particularly fond of the "dim religious light." Among the announcements from the pulpit were several funerals, which it is there customary thus to advertise.

In the afternoon I heard Dr. Beecher. Here, again, I found the blinds down. The Doctor's text was, "Let me first go and bury my father," &c. Without at all noticing the context,—an omission which I regretted,— he proceeded at once to state the doctrine of the text to be, that nothing can excuse the putting off of religion—that it is every man's duty to follow Christ immediately. This subject, notwithstanding the heaviness of the day, the infirmities of more than threescore years and ten (74), and the frequent necessity of adjusting his spectacles to consult his notes, he handled with much vigour and zeal. Some of his pronunciations were rather antiquated; but they were the elegant New England pronunciations of his youthful days. The sermon was marked by that close and faithful dealing with the conscience in which so many American ministers excel.

Professor Allen called to take me up to Lane Seminary, where I was to address the students in the evening. The service was public, and held in the chapel of the institution; but the evening being wet, the congregation was small. I had, however, before me the future pastors of about fifty churches, and two of the professors. I was domiciled at Mr. Allen's. Both he and his intelligent wife are sound on the subject of slavery. They are also quite above the contemptible prejudice against colour. But I was sorry to hear Mrs. Allen say, that, in her domestic arrangements, she had often had a great deal of trouble with her *European* servants, who would refuse to take their meals with black ones, though the latter were in every respect superior to the former ! I have heard similar remarks in other parts of America. Mr. Allen's system of domestic training appeared excellent. His children, of whom he has as many as the patriarch Jacob, were among the loveliest I had ever seen.

At 8 o'clock in the morning of the 8th of March I left Lane Seminary, with a heavy heart at the thought that in all probability I should never see it again. There was a sharp frost. Dr. Stowe accompanied me to the omnibus. " All right !"—" *Pax vobiscum !*"— the vehicle moved on, and directly the Doctor was at a distance of a hundred yards waving a farewell. It was the last look.

At 11 A.M. myself, wife, baggage,—all were setting off from the " Queen City" for Pittsburgh, a distance of 496 miles, in the Clipper No. 2, a fine boat, and in good hands.

LETTER XXII.

BEFORE proceeding with our trip to Pittsburg, I will bring together all the material points of information I have gathered relative to Cincinnati.

1. *Its History and Progress.*—The first year of the present century found here but 750 inhabitants. In 1810 there were 2,540; in 1820, 9,602; in 1830, 24,381; in 1840, 46,382. At present the population is estimated at 80,000. The coloured population forms one twenty-fifth, or 4 per cent., of the whole. The native Europeans form one-fifth of the white population.

2. *Its Trade and Commerce.*—The principal trade is in pork. Hence the nickname of *Porkapolis.* The yearly value of pork packed and exported is about five millions of dollars, or one million of guineas! As a proof of the amazing activity which characterizes all the details of cutting, curing, packing, &c., I have been credibly informed that two men, in one of the pork-houses, cut up in less than thirteen hours 850 hogs, averaging 300 lbs. each,—two others placing

them on the block for the purpose. All these hogs were weighed singly on scales in the course of eleven hours. Another hand trimmed the hams, 1,700 pieces, in " Cincinnati style," as fast as they were separated from the carcases. The hogs were thus cut up and disposed of at the rate of more than one per minute! And this, I was told, was not much beyond the ordinary day's work at the pork-houses.

Steam-boat building is another important branch of trade in this place.

DOLLARS.

In 1840 there were built here	33	boats of	15,341	tons, costing	592,500
1844	„	„	37	„	7,838	„	542,500
1845	„	„	27	„	6,609	„	505,500

3. *Its Periodical Press.* — There are sixteen daily papers! Of these, thirteen issue also a weekly number. Besides these, there are seventeen weekly papers unconnected with daily issues. But Cincinnati is liberal in her patronage of eastern publications. During the year 1845 one house, that of Robinson and Jones, the principal periodical depôt in the city, and through which the great body of the people are supplied with this sort of literature, sold of

Magazines and Periodicals	. . .	29,822 numbers.
Newspapers	. . . . .	25,390*	„
Serial Publications	. . . .	30,826	„
Works of Fiction	. . . .	48,961	„ !

It is estimated that the people of the United States, at the present time, support 1,200 newspapers. There being no stamp-duty, no duty on paper, and none on

* Besides an immense quantity sent direct per mail!

advertisements, the yearly cost of a daily paper, such as the *New York Tribune* for instance, is only 5 dollars, or one guinea.   The price of a single copy of such papers is only 2 cents, or one penny; and many papers are only one cent, or a half-penny per copy.

4. *Its Church Accommodation.*—By the close of the year 1845 the voluntary principle, without any governmental or municipal aid whatever, had provided the following places of worship :—

Presbyterian . . . 12	New Jerusalem . . . 1	
Methodist Episcopal . . 12	Universalist . . . 1	
Roman Catholic . . 7	Second Advent . . . 1	
Baptist 5	Mormons 1	
Lutheran 5	Friends 1	
Protestant Episcopal . . 4	Congregational . . . 1	
"Christian Disciples" . 4	Restorationists . . . 1	
Methodist Protestants . 3	United Brethren . . 1	
Jewish 2	"Christians" . . . 1	
Welsh 2	—	
German Reformed . . 2	Total . 67	

This number of places of worship, at an average of 600 persons to each, would afford accommodation for nearly two-thirds of what the entire population was at that time; and surely two-thirds of any community is quite as large a proportion as can, under the most favourable circumstances, be expected to attend places of worship at any given time.   Behold, then, the strength and efficiency of the voluntary principle! This young city, with all its wants, is far better furnished with places of worship than the generality of commercial and manufacturing towns in England.

Dr. Reed visited Cincinnati in 1834.   He gives the

population at that time at 30,000, and the places of worship as follows. I insert them that you may see at a glance what the voluntary principle did in the eleven years that followed.

Presbyterian . . . 6	Campbellite Baptists . . 1
Methodist 4	Jews 1
Baptist 2	—
Episcopalian . . . 2	Total in 1834 . 21
German Lutheran . . 2	Do. in 1845 . 67
Unitarian 1	—
Roman Catholic . . . 1	Increase . . 46
Swedes 1	

5. *Its Future Prospects.*—The author of " Cincinnati in 1841" says, "I venture the prediction that within 100 years from this time Cincinnati will be the greatest city in America, and by the year of our Lord 2,000 the greatest city in the world." Our cousin here uses the superlative degree when the comparative would be more appropriate. Deduct 80 or 90 per cent. from this calculation, and you still leave before this city a bright prospect of future greatness.

We must, however, bid adieu to this " Queen of the West," and pursue our course against the Ohio's current towards Pittsburg. We steam along between freedom and slavery. The contrast is striking. On this subject the remarks of the keen and philosophic M. de Tocqueville are so accurate, and so much to the point, that I cannot do better than transcribe and endorse them.

" A century had scarcely elapsed since the foundation of the colonies, when the attention of the planters was struck by the extraordinary fact that the provinces which were comparatively destitute of slaves increased in population, in wealth, and in prosperity, more rapidly than those which contained the greatest number of negroes. In the former, however, the inhabitants were obliged to cultivate the soil themselves, or by hired labourers; in the latter, they were furnished with hands for which they paid no wages: yet, although labour and expense were on the one side, and ease with economy on the other, the former were in possession of the most advantageous system. * * * The more progress was made, the more was it shown that slavery, which is so cruel to the slave, is prejudicial to the master.

" But this truth was most satisfactorily demonstrated when civilization reached the banks of the Ohio. The stream which the Indians had distinguished by the name of Ohio, or Beautiful River, waters one of the most magnificent valleys which have ever been made the abode of man. Undulating lands extend upon both shores of the Ohio, whose soil affords inexhaustible treasures to the labourer. On either bank the air is wholesome and the climate mild; and each of those banks forms the extreme frontier of a vast State: that which follows the numerous windings of the Ohio on the left is Kentucky [in ascending the river it was on our *right*]; that on the right [our left] bearing the name of the river. These two States differ only in one respect,—Kentucky has admitted slavery, but the State of Ohio has not. * * *

" Upon the left bank of the stream the population is rare; from time to time one descries a troop of slaves loitering in the half-desert fields; the primeval forest recurs at every turn; society seems to be asleep, man to be idle, and nature alone offers a scene of activity and life.

" From the right bank, on the contrary, a confused hum is heard, which proclaims the presence of industry; the fields are covered with abundant harvests; the elegance of the dwellings announces the taste and activity of the labourer; and man appears to be in the enjoyment of that wealth and contentment which are the reward of labour."

The Kentucky and the Ohio States are nearly equal as to their area in square miles. Kentucky was founded in 1775, and Ohio in 1788. In 1840 the population of Kentucky was 779,828, while that of Ohio was 1,519,467—nearly double that of the former. By this time it is far more than double.

" Upon the left bank of the Ohio," continues De Tocqueville, " labour is confounded with the idea of slavery; upon the right bank it is identified with that of prosperity and improvement: on the one side it is degraded, on the other it is honoured. On the former territory no white labourers can be found, for they would be afraid of assimilating themselves to the negroes; on the latter no one is idle, for the white population extends its activity and its intelligence to every kind of improvement. Thus the men whose task it is to cultivate the rich soil of Kentucky are ignorant and lukewarm; while those who are active and enlightened either do nothing or pass over into the State of Ohio, where they may work without dishonour."

March the 9th was a dull day; but the scenery was of surpassing beauty. At night a terrible storm of thunder and lightning, accompanied with rain, compelled us to " lie to." A charming morning succeeded. During the forenoon, we passed a small town on the Virginia side called Elizabeth Town. An Indian mound was pointed out to me, which in size and shape resembled " Tomen y Bala" in North Wales. These artificial mounds are very numerous in the valleys of the Ohio and the Mississippi. The ancient relics they are sometimes found to contain afford abundant proofs that these fertile regions were once peopled by a race of men in a far higher state of civilization than the Indians when first discovered by the white man. The innocent and imaginative speculations of a Christian minister in the State of Ohio on these ancient remains laid the foundation of the curious book of " Mormon."

Nature being now arrayed in her winter dress, we could form but a faint conception of her summer loveliness when clothed in her gayest green. Hills were seen rising up, sometimes almost perpendicularly from the stream, and sometimes skirted with fertile fields extending to the river's edge. Here a house on the brow of a hill, and there another at its base. Here the humble log hut, and there the elegant mansion, and sometimes both in unequal juxta-position. The hills are in parts scolloped in continuous succession, presenting a beautiful display of unity and diversity combined; but often they appear in isolated and distinct grandeur, like a row of semi-globes; while, in other instances, they rise one above another like apples in a fruit-vase. Sometimes the rivulets are seen like silver cords falling perpendicularly into the river; at other times, you discern them only by their musical murmurs as they roll on through deep ravines formed by their own action. These hills, for more than 100 miles before you come to Pittsburg, are literally heaps of coal. In height they vary from 100 to 500 feet, and nothing more is required than to clear off the soil, and then dig away the treasure.

What struck me most was the immense number of children everywhere gazing upon us from the river's banks. At settlements of not more than half-a-dozen houses, I counted a groupe of more than twenty children.

LETTER XXIII.

ARRIVING at Pittsburg in the middle of the night of
the 10th of March, we remained on board till morning.
As we had been accustomed on this "Clipper No. 2"
to breakfast at half-past 7, I thought they surely would
not send us empty away. But no! we had to turn out
at that early hour of a morning piercingly cold, and get
a breakfast where we could, or remain without. This
was "clipping" us rather too closely, after we had paid
seven dollars each for our passage and provisions.

Pittsburg is in the State of Pennsylvania. Its progress has been rapid, and its prospects are bright.
Seventy years ago the ground on which it stands was
a wilderness, the abode of wild beasts and the hunting
ground of Indians. Its manufactures are chiefly those
of glass, iron, and cotton. It is the Birmingham of
America. Indeed one part of it, across the river, is
called "Birmingham," and bids fair to rival its old
namesake. Its advantages and resources are unparal-
leled. It occupies in reference to the United States,
north and south, east and west, a perfectly central

position. It is surrounded with solid mountains of
coal, which—dug out, as I have intimated, with the
greatest ease—is conveyed with equal ease down in-
clined planes to the very furnace mouths of the foun-
dries and factories! This great workshop communicates directly, by means of the Ohio, the Mississippi,
Red River, &c., with immense countries, extending to
Texas, to Mexico, and to the Gulph. Its population,
already 70,000, is (I believe) incomparably more intelligent, more temperate, more religious, and more
steady than that of any manufacturing town in England. In fact, England has not much chance of com-
peting successfully with America, unless her artizans
copy more extensively the example of the American
people in the entire abandonment of intoxicating
liquors. In travelling leisurely from New Orleans to
Boston (the whole length of the United States), and
sitting down at all sorts of tables, on land and on
water, private and public, I have never once seen even
wine brought to the table. Nothing but water was
universally used!

At Pittsburg I bought three good-sized newspapers
for 5 cents, or twopence-halfpenny. One of them,
The Daily Morning Post, was a large sheet, measuring
3 feet by 2, and well filled on both sides with close
letter-press, for 2 cents, or one penny. The absence
of duty on paper and of newspaper stamps is no doubt
one great cause of the advanced intelligence of the
mass of the American people. What an absurd policy
is that of the British Government, first to impose taxes

upon *knowledge,* and then to use the money in promoting *education!*

At Pittsburg the Ohio ends, or rather begins, by the confluence of the Alleghany and the Monongahela rivers. We ascended the latter to Brownsville, about 56 miles. Having booked ourselves at an office, we had to get into a smaller steamer on the other side of the bridge which spans the river. The entire charge to Philadelphia was 12 dollars each. We went by the "Consul," at half-past 8 A.M. of the 11th of March. The water was very high, as had been the case in the Ohio all the way from Cincinnati. We had not proceeded far when I found the passengers a-stir, as if they had got to their journey's end. What was the matter? Why, we had come to falls, which it was very doubtful whether the steamer could get over. The passengers were soon landed, and the steamer, with the crew, left to attempt the ascent. There were locks at hand by which, under ordinary circumstances, boats evaded the difficulty; but the flood was now so great that they could not be used. Our steamer, therefore, stirred up her fires, raised her steam, brought all her powers to bear, faced the difficulty, dashed into it, cut along, and set at defiance the fury of the flood. "There she goes!"— "No!"— "Yes!" — "No!"—"She's at a stand,"—the next moment she was gliding back with the torrent: she had failed! But *nil desperandum.* "Try—try—try again!" An immense volume of smoke issued from her chimney, and soon she seemed again to be fully inflated with her vapoury aliment. I expected every moment an explosion, and, while rejoicing in our own safety on *terra firma*, felt tremblingly anxious for the lives of those on board. Having had sufficient time to "recover strength," she made for the foaming surge once more. "There she goes!"—"No!"—"Yes!"—she paused—but it was only for the twinkling of an eye,—the next moment she was over, and the banks of the Monongahela resounded with the joyful shouts of the gazing passengers. We now breathed more freely, and were soon on board again; but we had not advanced very far before we had to get out once more, in consequence of other falls, which were stemmed with the same inconvenience, the same anxiety, and the same success as in the preceding instance.

But ere long an obstacle more formidable than the falls presented itself—a bridge across the river. This bridge the boats were accustomed to pass under, but the water was now so high that it could not be done; and we had to wait till another boat belonging to the same company, above the bridge, came down from Brownsville, and enabled us to effect an exchange of passengers; for neither of the boats could get under the bridge. The down boat soon made its appearance; and a scene of confusion ensued which I know not how to describe. Imagine two sets of passengers, about 150 persons in each set, exchanging boats! Three hundred travellers jostling against each other, with "plunder" amounting to some thousands of packages, to be removed a distance of 300 or 400 yards, at the risk and responsibility of the owners, without any care or con-

cern on the part of the officers of the boats! Trunks
seemed to run on wheels, carpet-bags to have wings,
and portmanteaus to jump about like grasshoppers.
If you had put down one article while looking for the
rest, in an instant it would be gone.   In this amusing
scuffle were involved several members of Congress, returning in the "down" boat from their legislative
duties.   The celebrated Judge M'Lean was among
them.   But the safety of some box or parcel was just
then—to most of us—of more importance than all the
great men in the world.   The baggage storm being
over, and the great division and trans-shipment effected,
we moved forward in peace.   By-and-by, however, each
one was called upon to show his baggage, that it might
be set apart for the particular coach to which it would
have to be consigned.   This was a most troublesome
affair.   At half-past 6 in the evening we arrived at
Brownsville, having been ten hours in getting over the
56 miles from Pittsburg.

And now for the stage-coaches; for, *nolens volens,*
"a-head" we must go that very night.   About seven
or eight coaches were filled by those of our fellow-
passengers who, like ourselves, were going to cross the
mountains.   Some of the vehicles set off immediately;
but three waited to let their passengers get tea or
supper, meals which in America are identical.   About
8 P.M. we started on our cold and dreary journey of 73
miles across the Alleghany Mountains.   A stage-coach
in America is a very different thing from the beautiful
machine that used to pass by that name in England.

It has no outside accommodation, except for one person on the box along with the driver. The inside, in addition to the fore seat and the hind seat, has also a middle seat across the vehicle. Each of these three seats holds three persons, making nine in all. In our stage we had ten persons ; but the ten, in a pecuniary point of view, were only eight and a half. The night was fearfully dark, and the roads were altogether unworthy of the name. Yet there is an immense traffic on this route, which is the highway from East to West. The Americans, with all their " smartness," have not the knack of making either good roads or good streets.

About 11 P.M. we arrived at Uniontown, 12 miles from Brownsville. There the horses were to be changed, an operation which took about an hour to accomplish. Three coaches were there together. The passengers rushed out of the inn, where we had been warming ourselves, and jumped into the coaches. Crack went the whips, off went the horses, and round went the wheels. But, alas! while we could hear the rattling of the other coaches, our own moved not at all! " Driver, why don't you be off?" No answer. " Driver, push on." No reply. " Go a-head, driver,—don't keep us here all night." No notice taken. We began to thump and stamp. No response. At last I put my head out through the window. There *was* no driver ; and, worse still, there were no horses ! How was this ? There was no "team," we were told, for our coach ! I jumped out, and began to make diligent inquiry : one told me one thing, and another another. At length I learned that there was a "team" in the stable, but there was no driver disposed to go. The one who should have taken us was cursing and swearing in bed, and would not get up. This was provoking enough. " Where is the agent of the stage-coach company ?"— " He lives about 47 miles off." " Where is the landlord of this house ?"—" He is in bed." There we were helpless and deserted on the highroad, between 12 and 1 o'clock, in an extremely cold night, without any redress or any opportunity of appeal! It was nobody's business to care for us. I groped my way, however, to some outbuilding, where about half-a-dozen drivers were snoring in their beds, and, with the promise of making it "worth his while," succeeded in inducing one of them to get up and take us to the next place for changing horses. But before we could get off it was 2 o'clock in the morning. We reached the next station, a distance of 10 miles, at 5 P.M., and paid our driver two dollars. In America drivers are not accustomed to receive gratuities from passengers, but ours was a peculiar case. After a most wearisome day of travel, being tossed about in the coach like balls, expecting every moment to be upset, and feeling bruised all over, we reached Cumberland at 9 P.M., having been 25 hours in getting over 73 miles, at the amazing rate of 3 miles an hour! In Cumberland we had to stay all night.

At 8 A.M. the next day we set off by railway, or (as the Americans would say) " by the cars," to Baltimore. In committing my trunk to the luggage-van, I was struck with the simplicity and suitableness of the check system there adopted. A piece of tin, with a certain number upon it, was fastened by a strap to each article of baggage, and a duplicate piece given to the passenger. I also remarked the size, shape, and fittings-up of the cars. They are from 30 to 50 feet long, having an aisle right through the middle from end to end, and on each side of that aisle rows of seats, each of sufficient length to accommodate two persons. The arrangement reminded me of a little country meeting-house, the congregation amounting to from 50 to 100 persons. Each carriage contained a stove,—at that season a most important article of furniture. The seats, which were very nicely cushioned, had their backs so arranged as that the passengers could easily turn them as they pleased, and sit with either their faces or their backs " towards the horses " as they might feel disposed. This part of the arrangement is indispensable, as these long carriages can never be turned. The hind part in coming is the fore part in going, and *vice versâ*. The distinctions of first, second, and third class carriages are unknown. That would be too aristocratic. But the " niggers" must go into the luggage-van. These republican carriages are very neatly fitted up, being mostly of mahogany with crimson velvet linings; but you often feel annoyed that such dirty people should get in.

LETTER XXIV.

THE railway from Cumberland to Baltimore is 178 miles long, and (like most lines in the States) is single. This fact is important; for our cousins, in boasting of the hundreds or thousands of miles of railway they have constructed, forget to tell us that they are nearly all single. Here and there they have a double set of rails, like our sidings, to enable trains to pass each other.

The ground was covered with snow, otherwise the scenery would have been magnificent. For a long time the Potomac was our companion. More than once we had to cross the stream on wooden bridges; so that we had it sometimes on our right and sometimes on our left, ourselves being alternately in Virginia and in Maryland. When within 14 miles of Baltimore, and already benighted, we were told we could not proceed, on account of some accident to a luggage-train that was coming up. The engine, or (as the Americans invariably say) the "locomotive," had got off the rail, and torn up the ground in a frightful manner; but no one was hurt. We were detained for 7 hours; and instead of getting into Baltimore at 8 P.M., making an average of about 15 miles an hour, which was the utmost we had been led to expect, we did not get there till 3 A.M., bringing our average rate per hour down to about $9\frac{1}{2}$ miles. The tediousness of the delay was considerably relieved by a man sitting beside me avowing himself a thorough Abolitionist, and a hearty friend of the coloured race. He spoke out his sentiments openly and fearlessly, and was quite a match for any one that dared to assail him. His name was Daniel Carmichael, of Brooklyn. He is a great railway and canal contractor, and has generally in his employ from 500 to 800 people. He is also a very zealous "teetotaler." We had also a *Mrs. Malaprop,* from Baltimore, with us, who told us, among other marvellous things, that in that city they took the *senses* (census) of the people every month. She was very anxious to let all around her know that her husband was a medical man : she therefore wondered what " the Doctor" was then doing, what "the Doctor" thought of the non-arrival of the train, whether "the Doctor" would be waiting for her at the station, and whether " the Doctor" would bring his own carriage, or hire one, to meet her, &c.

March 14.—The day on which we arrived at Baltimore was the Sabbath. In a public room in the National Hotel, at which we were stopping, was hung up a nicely-framed announcement of the order of services in one of the Presbyterian Churches. We wished, however, to find a Congregational place of

worship, and set off with that view. It was a beautiful
day, and Baltimore seemed to send forth its inhabitants by streets-full to the various churches. In the
Old World I never saw anything like it, nor elsewhere
in the *New*, except perhaps at Boston. All secular
engagements seemed to be entirely suspended, and the
whole city seemed to enjoy a Sabbath! As we walked
along, I asked a young man if he could direct me to a
Congregational church. He stared at me for a moment, and then said, " Do you mean a church with
pews in it?" I asked another, " Can you tell me
where I shall find a Congregational church in this
city?"—" What congregation do you mean, sir?" was
the reply. They evidently knew nothing at all about
Congregationalism. The fact was, as I afterwards
understood, we had not yet come into its latitude; for
in America Presbyterianism and Congregationalism
have hitherto been matters of latitude and longitude
rather than of earnest conviction and firm adherence.
We now inquired for a *Presbyterian* church, and were
told that there was one not far from where we then
stood, in which Mr. Plummer—a very popular minister
just come into the city — preached. Following the
directions given, we came to a certain church, in front
of which two or three grave men stood talking to each
other. In answer to the question, " What church is
this?" one of these grave men said, with a good broad
Scotch accent, " It's a Presbyterian church." The
accent gave a double confirmation to the answer. " Is
it Mr. Plummer's church?" I continued. With the

same accent, and in a tone of gentle rebuke, I was told,
" Yes, it is *Doctor* Plummer's." We entered. The
congregation were assembling. We were left either to
stand in the aisle or to take a seat as we pleased. We
preferred the latter. The building was new, but built
in the old Gothic style. The pews, the pulpit, the
front of the gallery, the organ, and the framework of
the roof, which was all exposed, were of oak, which had
been made to resemble in colour wood that has stood
the test of 400 or 500 years. The windows also were
darkened. The whole affair was tremendously heavy,
enough to mesmerize any one. The congregation was
large, respectable, and decorous. After a few glances
around, to see if there was a negro pew anywhere, I
observed several coloured faces peeping from a recess in
the gallery, on the left side of the organ,—there was
the " Negro Pew." In due time *Doctor* Plummer
ascended the pulpit. He was a fine tall man, grey-
haired, well dressed, with commanding aspect and a
powerful voice. I ceased to wonder at the emphasis
with which the Scotchman called him *Doctor* Plummer.
He was quite the *ideal* of a *Doctor*. His text was
John iii. 18 : " He that believeth on Him is not condemned, but he that believeth not is condemned
already, because he hath not believed in the name of
the only begotten Son of God." His subject was, that
"man is justly accountable to God for his belief."
This truth he handled in a masterly manner, tossing
about as with a giant's arm Lord Brougham and the
Universalists. Notwithstanding my want of rest on

the previous night, the absurd heaviness of the building, and the fact that the sermon—which occupied a
full hour—was all read, I listened with almost breathless
attention, and was sorry when he had done.

And who was this Dr. Plummer? It was Dr. Plummer late of Richmond, in Virginia. "Richmond,"
says Dr. Reed, "is still the great mart of slavery; and
the interests of morality and religion suffer from this
cause.   Several persons of the greatest wealth, and
therefore of the greatest consideration in the town, are
known slave-dealers; and their influence, in addition to
the actual traffic, is of course unfavourable.   The sale
of slaves is as common, and produces as little sensa-
tion, as that of cattle.   It occurs in the main street,
and before the door of the party who is commissioned
to make the sale."   And what was the conduct of this
Doctor of Divinity in reference to this state of things?
He sanctioned it!   He pleaded for it!   He lived upon
it!   He was once actually supported, either wholly or
in part, by slave labour!   The church of which he was
the pastor was endowed with a number of slaves. These
slaves were hired out, and the proceeds were given in
the way of stipend to the *Doctor!*   Nor is this all.
A few years ago the slave-holders of the South were
greatly alarmed by the vigorous efforts of the Abolitionists of the North.   It was about the time that
the Charleston Post-office was plundered by a mob of
several thousand people, and all the anti-slavery publications there found were made a bonfire of in the
street; and where "the clergy of all denominations

attended in a body, lending their sanction to the proceedings, and adding by their presence to the impressive character of the scene." On that occasion the clergy of the city of Richmond were not less prompt than their brethren of Charleston in responding to the "public sentiment." They resolved *unanimously*,—

"That we earnestly deprecate the unwarrantable and highly improper interference of the people of any other State with the domestic relations of master and slave.

"That the example of our Lord Jesus Christ and his Apostles, in not interfering with the question of slavery, but uniformly recognising the relations of master and servant, and giving full and affectionate instruction to both, is worthy the imitation of all ministers of the Gospel.

"That we will not patronise nor receive any pamphlet or newspaper of the Anti-slavery Societies, and that we will discountenance the circulation of all such papers in the community.

"That the suspicions which have prevailed to a considerable extent against ministers of the Gospel and professors of religion in the State of Virginia, as identified with Abolitionists, are *wholly unmerited;* believing as we do, from extensive acquaintance with our churches and brethren, that they are unanimous in opposing the pernicious schemes of Abolitionists."

After this, are men to be branded as "infidels," because they say the American churches are the "bulwarks of slavery?"

But what has all this to do with our fine-looking and dignified "*Doctor?*" I will tell you. When these resolutions were passed, he was from home; but on his return, he lost no time in communicating to the "Chairman of the Committee of Correspondence" his entire concurrence with what had been done,—and here are extracts from his letter :—

"I have carefully watched this matter from its earliest existence; and everything I have seen or heard of its character, both from its patrons and its enemies, has confirmed me beyond repentance in the belief, that, let the character of the Abolitionists be what it may in the sight of the Judge of all the earth, this is the most meddlesome, impudent, reckless, fierce, and wicked excitement I ever saw.

"If Abolitionists will set the country in a blaze, it is but right that they should receive the *first warming at the fire.*

"Let it be proclaimed throughout the nation, that every movement made by the fanatics (so far as it has any effect in the South) does but rivet every fetter of the bondman, and diminish the probability of anything being successfully undertaken for making him either fit for freedom or likely to obtain it. We have the authority of Montesquieu, Burke, and Coleridge, three eminent masters of the science of human nature, that, of all men, slave-holders are the most jealous of their liberties. One of Pennsylvania's most gifted sons has lately pronounced the South the *cradle of liberty*.

"Lastly. Abolitionists are like infidels, wholly unaddicted to martyrdom for opinion's sake. Let them understand that *they will be caught* [lynched] if they come among us, and they will take good heed to keep out of our way. There is not one man among them who has any more idea of shedding his blood in the cause, than he has of making war on the Grand Turk."

So much for my splendid D. D., on whose lips I hung with such intense interest. I did not know all this at the time, or I should have felt very differently. As he had but recently left Richmond when I saw him, it is not at all unlikely that those fine clothes he had on were the fruit of the slave's unrequited toil. He has always, I believe, stood high among his brethren, and one or two excellent tracts of his are published by the American Tract Society.

All denominations are here alike guilty in reference to their coloured brethren. In this very city the General Conference of the Methodist Episcopal Church for 1840 passed the following resolution :—

" That it is inexpedient and unjustifiable for any preacher to permit coloured persons to give testimony against white persons in any State where they are denied that privilege by law."

Against this iniquitous resolution the official members of two of the coloured Methodist Episcopal Churches in Baltimore immediately remonstrated and petitioned. The following powerful and pathetic passages are from their address :—

" The adoption of such a resolution by our highest

K 2

ecclesiastical judicatory,—a judicatory composed of the most experienced and the wisest brethren in the Church, the choice selection of twenty-eight Annual Conferences, —has inflicted, we fear, an irreparable injury upon eighty thousand souls for whom Christ died,— souls who, by this act of your body, have been stripped of the dignity of Christians, degraded in the scale of humanity, and treated as criminals, for no other reason than the colour of their skin! Your resolution has, in our humble opinion, *virtually* declared that a mere physical peculiarity, the handiwork of our all-wise and benevolent Creator, is *primá facie* evidence of incompetency to tell the truth, or is an unerring indication of unworthiness to bear testimony against a fellow-being whose skin is denominated white. * * *

" Brethren, out of the abundance of the heart we have spoken. *Our grievance is before you !* If you have any regard for the salvation of the eighty thousand immortal souls committed to your care,—if you would not *thrust* beyond the pale of the Church *twenty-five thousand souls in this city,* who have felt determined never to leave the Church that has nourished and brought them up,—if you regard us as children of one Common Father, and can upon reflection sympathize with us as members of the body of Christ,—if you would not incur the fearful, the tremendous responsibility of offending not only one, but many thousands of his ' little ones,'—we conjure you to wipe from your journal the odious resolution which is ruining our people."

This address was presented to one of the Secretaries, a delegate of the Baltimore Conference, and subsequently given by him to the Bishops. How many of the members of Conference saw it, is unknown. One thing is certain, *it was never read to the Conference.*

LETTER XXV.

In the afternoon of my first Sabbath at Baltimore I found, after much inquiry, a congregation of coloured people, who were some sort of Methodists. My wife and I were the only white people in the place. We were treated with great politeness, and put, not in a pew apart by ourselves, but in one of the best places they could find, in the very midst of the congregation. A serious-looking coloured man opened the service, with great propriety of manner and expression. He was the regular pastor. A black man, a stranger as I understood, preached. His text (he said) was, "Behold, I come quickly;" and they would find it in the Book of Revelation. But chapter and verse were not given, nor had he the Bible open in Revelation at all. I suspected that he could not read; and that suspicion was confirmed by the amount of nonsense which he soon uttered. At first his words were "few and far between," uttered in a tone of voice scarcely audible. Soon, however, he worked both himself and his audience into a tremendous phrenzy. The burden of his song was— how John had lived to a very great age, in spite of all attempts to put him to death; how his enemies had at last decided to try the plan of throwing him into a "kittle of biling ile;" how God had said to him, "Never mind, John,—if they throw thee into that kittle, I'll go there with thee,—they shall bile me too ;" how John was therefore taken up alive ; and how his persecutors, baffled in all their efforts to despatch him, ultimately determined to throw their victim upon a desolate island, and leave him there to live or perish as he might. During the delivery of all this nonsense, the laughing, the shouting, the groaning, and the jumping were positively terrific. It was Methodism gone mad. How disgraceful, that American Christians, so called, with all their schools and colleges, and with all their efforts to send the Gospel to Africa, should leave these people at their very doors thus to feed upon " husks" and " ashes!" Between 500 and 600 people were listening to this ignorant man, giving as the pure and positive word of God what was of very doubtful authority, intermingled with the crudities of his own brain. I wished to stay through the service, and perhaps at the close express my fraternal feelings ; but I was so shocked and grieved at this ranting exhibition that I felt it unwarrantable to remain.

Leaving these unfortunate people, we peeped into two cathedral churches, — that of the Church of England, or (as it is here called) the Protestant Episcopal

Church, and that of the Church of Rome.   Both buildings are very splendid.   We had been in the former
some time before we felt quite sure that we were not in
a Popish place of worship, so papistical were its aspect
and arrangements.   It was evident that Puseyism, or
Popery in some form, had there its throne and its
sceptre.   The avowedly Popish cathedral was crowded
with worshippers ; and, to the shame of Protestantism
be it spoken, black and coloured people were *there* seen
intermingled with the whites in the performance of
their religious ceremonies !   The State of Maryland, of
which Baltimore is the capital, having been first settled
by a colony of Roman Catholics, might be expected to
be a stronghold of Popery.   Yet, it is not so.   The
adherents of that system are but a small minority of
the population.

Baltimore is, however, a stronghold of slavery.   Here
Garrison's indignation against the system was first
kindled—here Frederick Douglas tasted some of its
bitter draughts—and here Torrey died its victim.   The
following are specimens of the manner in which the
trade in human flesh is carried on in this city :—

"NEGROES WANTED.—I have removed from my
former residence, West Pratt-street, to my new establishment on Camden-street, immediately in the rear of
the Railroad Depôt, where I am permanently located.
Persons bringing Negroes by the cars will find it very
convenient, as it is only a few yards from where the
passengers get out.   Those having Negroes for sale

will find it to their advantage to call and see me, as I
am at all times paying the highest prices in cash.

" J. S. Donovan, Balt. Md."

" o28—6m*."

" Cash for Five Hundred Negroes.—At the old
establishment of Slatter's, No. 244, Pratt-street, Baltimore, between Sharp and Howard Streets, where the
highest prices are paid, which is well known. We
have large accommodations for Negroes, and always
buying. Being regular shippers to New Orleans, persons should bring their property where no commissions
are paid, as the owners lose it. All communications
attended to promptly by addressing

" H. F. Slatter."

" j5—6m*."

Before and since my arrival in the United States, I
had thought much of seeing Washington, and, if possible, Congress in session. But such was the severity
of the weather that we could not cross the Alleghanies
before that assembly had risen and dispersed. At
Baltimore I was within two hours' journey of the capital. Should I go and see it? No; for what can *there*
be found to gratify the friend of freedom and of man?
The Missouri compromise, the annexation of Texas,
and the Mexican War, are all associated with Washington. The capital itself is but a great slave-mart, with
its baracoons and manacles, its handcuffs and auction-
stands! Ay, and all this in full view of the national

K 5

edifice, wherein is deposited that instrument which bears on its head and front the noble sentiment—" That all men are created equal; that they are endowed by their Creator with certain inalienable rights; that among these are life, liberty, and the pursuit of happiness." Under the influence of these recollections, I abandoned the idea of visiting Washington.

At 9 o'clock on Monday morning we set off by railway for Philadelphia. While I was taking a last glance at my trunks in the luggage-van, at the Baltimore station, about half-a-dozen very clean and respectable coloured ladies came up, and made for the said van as a matter of course. It was the only accommodation that would be allowed them, though they paid the same fare as other people! They were ladies to whom any gentleman in England would have been proud to resign a seat. But in the land of equality, they were consigned to the cold, dark, and dirty regions of the luggage-van. I noticed one important difference between the railway economy of England and that of America. In the former, as you know, the railway is haughty, exclusive, and aristocratic. It scorns all fellowship with common roads, and dashes on, either under or over the houses, with arbitrary indifference. In America, it generally condescends to pass along the public streets to the very centre of the city, the engine being taken off or put to in the suburbs, and its place *intra muros*, if I may so say, supplied by horses. In leaving Baltimore, the engine was attached *before* we got quite out of the city; and we were going for some time along the common road, meeting in one place a horse and cart, in another a man on horseback, in another a pair of oxen fastened to each other, and so on. Dangerous enough, apparently! yet railway accidents are much less frequent in America than in England. It is, besides, an immense saving of capital.

In our progress, we had to cross several arms of the Chesapeak Bay. These arms were from one to two miles wide, and the railway is carried over them upon posts driven into the ground. It seemed like crossing the sea in a railway carriage. At Havre de Grace we had to cross the Susquehannah River. This word Susquehannah is Indian, and means literally, I am told, " the rolling thunder." In crossing it, however, we heard no thunder, except that of the luggage-van over our heads, on the top of the steamer. Here we changed carriages. We soon got sight of the Delaware, which kept us company nearly all the way to Philadelphia. Delaware, the smallest of all the States except Rhode Island, we entirely crossed. A few days before, Delaware had well nigh done herself great honour. Her House of Representatives carried, by a majority, a vote for the abolition of slavery within her boundaries; but the measure was lost in her Senate by a majority of one or two. The State legislature will not meet again for two years. All parties are confident that the measure will then be triumphantly carried through. In America, however, the abolition of slavery in any State does not always mean freedom to the slaves. Too often it is a mere transportation of them to the Southern States. Had Delaware passed a law that all slaves should be free at the expiration of five years, or that all children born after a certain period should be free, the owners of slaves would have had an obvious interest in disposing of their human property to the Southern traders *before* that period arrived. Mothers, too, would have been hastened Southward to give birth to their offspring; so that the " peculiar institution" might lose none of its prey. Measures for the abolition of slavery in any part of America do not arise from sympathy with the negro, and from a wish to improve his condition and promote his happiness, but from aversion to his presence, or perhaps from a conviction that the system of slavery is expensive and impolitic. Those who feel kindly towards their coloured brother, and act towards him under the impulse of pure and lofty philanthropy, are, I am sorry to say, very few indeed.

These views may appear severe and uncharitable towards the American people, but they are confirmed by M. de Tocqueville. " When a Northern State declared that the son of the slave should be born free," observes that impartial writer, " the slave lost a large portion of his market value, since his posterity was no longer included in the bargain, and the owner had then a strong interest in transporting him to the South. Thus the same law prevents the slaves of the South from coming to the Northern States, and drives those of the North to the South. The want of free hands is felt in a State in proportion as the number of slaves decreases. But, in proportion as labour is performed by free hands, slave labour becomes less productive; and the slave is then a useless or an onerous possession, whom it is important to export to those Southern States where the same competition is not to be feared. *Thus the abolition of slavery does not set the slave free: it merely transfers him from one master to another, and from the North to the South.*" M. de Tocqueville adds, in a note, " The States in which slavery is abolished usually do what they can to render their territory disagreeable to the negroes as a place of residence; and as a kind of emulation exists between the different States in this respect, the unhappy blacks can only choose the least of the evils which beset them." This is perfectly true.

Crossing the Schuilkyl, we arrived about 3 o'clock P. M. in Philadelphia, " the city of brotherly love," having performed the journey of 97 miles in six hours, a rate of only 16 miles an hour !

In Philadelphia were many men and things that I wished to see. First and foremost, in my professional curiosity, was Albert Barnes; but being anxious to push on to New York that night, I had but an hour and a half to stay. Of a sight of the famous author of the " Notes," I was therefore compelled to deny myself. My regret was diminished, when I learned from an English minister of high standing, who, under the influence of the best feelings, and with an excellent introduction, had called upon the Commentator, that he received him with a degree of indifference bordering on rudeness.

In Philadelphia there is no Congregational Church. A few years ago John Todd, the well-known author of "The Student's Guide," attempted to raise one. He was but little countenanced, however, by Albert Barnes and the Presbyterians, and failed.

In passing through this city, I had a distant glimpse of a most remarkable institution. M. Girard, an old bachelor, a native of France, who had accumulated immense wealth, died a few years ago, leaving by will the enormous sum of two millions of dollars, or upwards of four hundred thousand pounds sterling, to erect and endow a college for the accommodation and education of three hundred orphan boys. The ground on which it was to be built, consisting of no less than 45 acres, he ordered to be enclosed with a high solid wall, capped with marble, and lined upon the top with long iron spikes. He also inserted in his will the following extraordinary clause: " I enjoin and require that no ecclesiastic, missionary, or minister of any sect whatever, shall ever hold or exercise any station or duty whatever in said college; nor shall any such person ever be admitted for any purpose, or as a visitor, within the premises appropriated to the purpose of said college." An attempt was made before the Supreme Court of the United States to set aside this will, and Daniel Webster, the great New England barrister, delivered a powerful " plea" against it; but the attempt was overruled. For some years the building has been slowly proceeding, and is not yet ready for occupation. Had I had time, I could not, being a minister, have entered the premises. To me, and to all like me, "*Procul, procul, este, profani*" is chiselled on every stone! —a singular monument of the priest-hating propensities of the old French Revolutionists.

LETTER XXVI.

AT half-past 4 in the afternoon of March 15 we left
Philadelphia by railway for New York, which we
reached at 10 P.M., an average again of about 16 miles
an hour. In this journey I met with a very communi-
cative Yankee, who, though not a religious man, was
proud to trace his genealogy to the "Pilgrim Fathers,"
and, through them, to the Normans. Intercourse, he
said, had been maintained for the last two centuries
between the English and American branches of the
family. He also took care to inform me that the head
of the English branch was a baronet. This was but
one of many instances in which I found among our
Transatlantic friends a deep idolatry of rank and titles.
In talking of their own political institutions, he declared their last two Presidents to have been—the one a
fool, and the other a knave,—Polk the fool, and Tyler
the knave. He entertained an insane and cruel prejudice against those whose skin was not exactly of the

same colour with his own, and "thanked God" that he had no African blood in his veins.

We passed through Trenton, celebrated as the scene of a bloody conflict between the British and the American forces. The Americans, I am sorry to say, dwell too fondly on the remembrance of those deadly struggles. They cherish the spirit of war. The influence of Elihu Burritt and his "bond of brotherhood" is indeed greatly needed on both sides of the Atlantic.

We also passed what once was the residence of ex-royalty—the princely mansion which Joseph Bonaparte erected for himself after he lost the throne of Spain. It is surrounded with about 900 acres of land, his own private property; and was still in the family, though about to be sold. What a home has America proved both to fallen greatness and to struggling poverty! Princes and peasants alike find shelter here.

This journey conducted us through New Brunswick, Elizabeth Town, Newark,—places associated with the name of David Brainerd, and often (a hundred years ago) the scenes of his toils and travels. But where are the descendants of those Indians on whose behalf he felt such intense solicitude? Alas! not a vestige of them is to be seen.

Having thus crossed New Jersey State, we came to New Jersey city, where we crossed a ferry to New York. After rather more than the usual amount of anxiety about baggage, &c., we reached the Planter's Hotel a little after 10 at night.

Next morning I sallied forth to gaze, for the first time, at the wonders of New York. The state of the streets impressed me unfavourably. The pigs were in the enjoyment of the same unstinted liberty as at Cincinnati. Merchants and storekeepers spread their goods over the entire breadth of the causeway, and some even to the very middle of the street. Slops of all sorts, and from all parts of the houses, were emptied into the street before the front doors! The ashes were disposed of in a very peculiar manner. Each house had, on the edge of the parapet opposite, an old flour-barrel, or something of the sort, into which were thrown ashes, sweepings, fish-bones, dead rats, and all kinds of refuse. A dead rat very frequently garnished the top of the barrel. This was the order of things, not in small by-streets only, but also in the very best streets, and before the very best houses. The pavement too, even in Broadway, was in a very wretched state.

I made for No. 150, Nassau-street, where the Tract Society, the Home Missionary Society, and the Foreign Missionary Society have their rooms. To some parties in that house I had introductions. The brethren connected with those societies treated me with great kindness and cordiality, and made me feel as though I had been in our own missionary rooms in Blomfield-street. By their aid I obtained private lodgings, in a good situation and in good society.

The landlady was a Quaker, with half-a-dozen grown-up daughters. Our fellow-lodgers consisted of the

Rev. A. E. Lawrence, Assistant-Secretary of the American Home Missionary Society (who had a few months before become the landlady's son-in-law); the Rev. Mr. Martyn, and his wife, a woman of fine talents, and editor of "The Ladies' Wreath;" the Rev. Mr. Brace, an editor in the employ of the Tract Society; Mr. Daniel Breed, M.D., a Quaker, and principal of a private academy for young gentlemen (also the landlady's son-in-law); Mr. Oliver Johnson, a sub-editor of the *Daily Tribune,* and a well-known Abolitionist; and Mr. Lockwood, a retired grocer, — who, having gained a small independence, was thus enjoying it with his youthful wife and child in lodgings.

Into society better adapted to my taste and purposes I could not have gone. This mode of life is very extensively adopted in America,—married couples, with families, living in this manner for years, without the least loss of respectability. They seldom have sitting-rooms distinct from their bed-rooms, which are made to answer both purposes; and as to meals, all meet to eat the same things, at the same table, and at the same time. The custom is economical; but it has an injurious effect upon character, especially in the case of the women. The young wife, not being called upon to exercise herself in domestic economy, is apt to become idle, slovenly, and—in a certain sense—worthless. The softening associations and influences, and even the endearments, of "home," are lost. There is no *domesticity.*

In the evening of the 17th I went to the Broadway

Tabernacle, to hear a lecture on Astronomy from Professor Mitchell of Cincinnati, no ordinary man. Although the admission fee was half-a-dollar, upwards of a thousand persons were present. Without either diagrams or notes, the accomplished lecturer kept his audience in breathless attention for upwards of an hour. He seemed to be a devout, unassuming man, and threw a flood of light on every subject he touched. His theme was the recent discovery of the Leverrier planet; and perhaps you will not be displeased if I give you a summary of his lucid observations. In observing how the fluctuations of the planet Herschel had ultimately led to this discovery, he said:

"For a long time no mind dared to touch the problem. At length a young astronomer rises, unknown to fame, but with a mind capable of grasping all the difficulties involved in any of these questions. I refer of course to LEVERRIER. He began by taking up the movements of Mercury. He was dissatisfied with the old computations and the old tables; and he ventured to begin anew, and to compute an entirely new set of tables. With these new tables, he predicted the *precise instant* when the planet Mercury, on the 18th of May, 1845, would touch the sun, and sweep across it. The time rolls round when the planet is to be seen, and his prediction verified or confuted. The day arrives, but, alas! for the computer, the clouds let down their dark curtains, and veil the sun from his sight. Our own Observatory had just been finished; and if the audience will permit, I will state briefly my own observations upon the planet. I had ten long years been toiling. I had commenced what appeared to be a hopeless enterprise. But finally I saw the building finished. I saw this mighty telescope erected,—I had adjusted it with my own hands,—I had computed the precise time when the planet would come in contact with the sun's disk, and the precise point where the contact would take place; but when it is remembered that only about the thousandth part of the sun's disk enters upon the field of the telescope, the importance of directing the instrument to the right point will be realized. Five minutes before the computed time of the contact, I took my place at the instrument. The beautiful machinery that carries the telescope with the sun was set in motion, and the instrument directed to that part of the sun's disk at which it was anticipated the contact would take place. And there I sat, with feelings which no one in this audience can realize. It was my first effort. All had been done by myself. After remaining there for what seemed to be long hours, I inquired of my assistant how much longer I would have to wait. I was answered *four minutes*. I kept my place for what seemed an age, and again inquired as before. He told me that but one minute had rolled by. It seemed as if time had folded his wings, so slowly did the moments crawl on. I watched on till I was told that but one minute remained; and, within sixteen seconds of the time, I had the almost bewildering gratification of seeing the planet break the contact, and slowly move on till it buried itself round and deep and sharp in the sun.

" I refer to this fact for two reasons,—first, to verify
Leverrier; and, second, to impress upon your minds the
desirableness of locating our observatories in different
parts of the earth.   No European astronomer could
have made this observation, because in their longi-
tudes the sun would have set previous to the contact
of the planet with its disk.   I had the gratification
of furnishing these observations to Leverrier himself,
who reported upon them to the Academy of Sciences.
The triumph of Leverrier was complete.   It was after
this that Arago, seeing the characteristics of his mind,
said to him, ' Take up the movements of the planet
Herschel,—watch them, analyze them, and tell us what
it is that causes them.'   Leverrier throws aside all
other employments, and gives his mind to the investi-
gation of this subject.   He begins entirely back.   He
takes up the movements of the planets Jupiter and
Saturn, and investigates them anew : he leaves nothing
untouched.   Finally, after having in the most absolute
manner computed all the influence they exercise upon
the planet Herschel, he says, ' I now know positively
all existing causes that disturb the planet; but there is
an outstanding power that disturbs it not yet accounted
for, and now let me rise to a knowledge of that outstanding cause.'   He did what no other man ever had
attempted.   He cleared up all difficulties;—he made
all daylight before his gaze.   And now, how shall I
give to you an account of the train of reasoning by
which he reached out into unknown space, and evoked
from its bosom a mighty world ?   If you will give me

the time, I will attempt to give you an idea of his mighty workings in the field of science.

" In the first place, let it be remembered that the planets circulate through the heavens in nearly the same plane. If I were to locate the sun in the centre of the floor, in locating the planets around it, I should place them upon the floor in the same plane. The first thing that occurred to Leverrier, in looking for the planet, was this,—he need not look out of the plane of the ecliptic. Here, then, was one quarter in which the unknown body was to be found. The next thing was this,—where is it located, and what is its distance from the sun? The law of Bode gave to him the approximate distance. He found the distance of Saturn was about double that of Jupiter, and the distance of Herschel twice that of Saturn; and the probability was that the new planet would be twice the distance of Herschel,—and as Herschel's distance is 1,800,000 miles, the new planet's would be 3,600,000. Having approximated its distance, what is its periodic time ?— for if he can once get its periodic time, he can trace it out without difficulty. According to the third of Kepler's laws, as the square of the period of Herschel is to the square of the period of the unknown planet, so is the cube of the distance of Herschel to the cube of the distance of the unknown planet. There is only one term unknown. The periodic time of Herschel we will call 1, and its distance 1; and by resolving the equation, we find the periodic time of the new planet to be a fraction less than three times that of Herschel,

or about 220 years. Now, if it be required to perform
360 degrees in 220 years, it will perform about a degree
and a half in one year. Only one thing more remains
to be accomplished. If it is possible to get the position
of the unknown body at *any time*, we can trace it up to
where it should be in 1847.

"First, then, let us suppose the sun, Herschel, and
the new planet in certain fixed positions, which we
will represent as follows,—

☼   ♅   ♑
Sun.   Herschel.   Unknown, or
                                          Leverrier Planet.

"It will be observed that a line drawn out from the
sun to the right will pass through Herschel, and if
continued will intersect the new planet. It is very
apparent that, when these three orbs occupy the position assigned them above, the influence of the unknown
planet upon Herschel will be exercised in the highest
degree, and consequently that Herschel will be drawn
farther from the sun at that juncture than at any other;
and if we know where *Herschel* is, when this effect is
produced, by prolonging the line through Herschel
outward, it must pass through the new planet. The
delicate observations upon Herschel gave this result,
and showed when it was that it was swayed farthest
from the sun. By taking the place occupied by the
planet at that time, and increasing it onward one degree
and a half per annum, we can point out the place it
must occupy at any given period. In September last
we find Leverrier communicating these results to his

friends in Berlin. They are provided with charts, on which every observed star is mapped down; and if any new object presents itself in the heavens, it is immediately subjected to a rigid scrutiny. On the very night on which Leverrier's letter had been received, we find the telescope directed to the designated point in the heavens. A stranger appears, but has only the aspect of a fixed star. Long did the eye watch that night, but no motion was found. When twenty-four hours rolled round, and it was once more possible to fix the instrument upon this strange body, it had moved in the precise degree and direction computed. The new planet was found. The news spread with the utmost rapidity throughout the world,—all Europe was electrified, and soon the intelligence crossed the waters. Our telescope was directed to this object. All had hitherto failed,—no eye had ever seen it round and planet-like from its disk. The evening finally came round for the examination. Time moved on its leaden wings; but twilight faded away at length, and I took my seat, with my assistant, at the instrument. I directed the telescope to that point of the heavens. I found four stars in the field of view. The first was brought to the field of view of the instrument, and pronounced to be a fixed star; and so with the second. The third was brought forward; and before it had reached the centre of the field, I heard the exclamation, ' There it is !' and there it was, as bright and beautiful as Jupiter himself. Here was a result not attained by any other instrument in the world. When we know that a body is a planet, then, and not till then, do we find the disk. The great rival of our instrument had seen it, but did not recognise it.

"Before five minutes had elapsed, the micrometical wires pronounced its diameter to be 40,000 miles. Here were results such as no previous one had attained. I mention it, because I think it is right that our own country, which has but just commenced its career in this science, should know what is her due; and I trust the day is not far distant when we shall become as distinguished for our proficiency, for our learning, for our researches, and for our efforts in behalf of Astronomy, as we have hitherto been for our profound neglect of everything belonging to this sublime science."

So much had been recently said in England about the "Negro Pew" in Dr. Patton's Church that I naturally felt curious to see it for myself, resolving (if possible) to sit in it. On Sabbath morning the 21st of March I set off with my wife on this errand, taking for our guide as to the precise position of the "locality" Mr. Page's "Letter of Apology,"—in which it was stated that in that church they treated the coloured people well; that they were elevated above the rest of the congregation, and nearer heaven; and, finally, that they occupied a position of honour, being on the right hand of the minister, as Jesus Christ was on the right hand of God! We found two coloured people—an old man and an old woman—seated in the front pew close to the minister's right hand; and at once concluded that the section of pews at the end wall must be the favoured spot, the terrestrio-celestial elevation commonly called the " Negro Pew." We advanced, and installed our white faces in the pew immediately behind the sable couple. The old lady seemed really alarmed, and, with amusing earnestness, motioned us to take a seat elsewhere. Remonstrance was all in vain,—we were determined to sit among the happy favourites. At this time but few persons were present. By-and-by the children of the Sunday-school were marched into the neighbouring pews on the other side of the aisle, and one of the lady teachers made eager signs for us to come away from our strange position. I nodded an intimation that we were all right, and perfectly comfortable. After the lapse of a few moments, another polite and compassionate lady actually rose and came to the pew-door to remonstrate with us.

In a serious yet coaxing tone, she said, " Won't you take a seat here on this side of the aisle ?"

" No, thank you, madam," I replied; " we are quite comfortable."

" But," she continued, in a voice of deep commiseration, " this is the place allotted to the coloured people."

" Thank you," I rejoined; " we have made no mistake."

" Well, just as you please, sir !" (as though she had said *De gustibus non disputandum*) and with that she retreated.

The eyes of all in the synagogue were upon us.

The little people whispered, and the big people stared, and all the people marvelled.

The morning was dark and wet, and yet (as usual) the Venetian blinds were all down. The gallery was occupied by three classes of persons : the black people —about a dozen in number—on the "right hand," the singing people in front, and the Sunday-school children everywhere else. The regular congregation, amounting perhaps to 300, were all downstairs.

Dr. Patton ascended the pulpit-stairs with his cloak on, placed a manuscript "fresh from the mint" under the cushion, sat down, took out his pocket-handker-chief, applied it vigorously, and then gazed leisurely around.

The pulpit service commenced with a short prayer ; then followed singing by the choir, all else sitting silent. The tenth chapter of Romans was read ; then came the long prayer, in which the Doctor prayed for the abolition of slavery, and for the spread of the Gospel. The text, which succeeded, was Rom. x. 3, 4. Having noticed the context, the preacher proposed—

I. To explain the text. (Here he examined very critically the meaning of the Greek word δικαι-οσύνης, quoting Moses Stuart and others.)

II. To designate those who go about to establish their own righteousness.

III. To remonstrate against such conduct, as being unnecessary, criminal, and dangerous.

The discourse was sound and good, but every word

read. The disorderly conduct of the children in the gallery proved a great annoyance; and for all the solicitude of the ladies to get us away from the vicinity of coloured skins, not one of them had the politeness to offer us either Bible or hymn-book.

This visit of ours to the "Negro Pew" was immediately laid hold of by the Abolitionists, and made to go the whole round of their papers as a "testimony against caste." This provoked into action the prolix pen of the celebrated Mr. Page, who wasted on the subject an immense quantity of ink and paper. "Page" after page did he pen; continued to do so, to my certain knowledge, for about three months after; and, for aught I know to the contrary, he may be *paging* away to this very day. This commotion answered my purpose exceedingly well,—my object being to bear testimony against the impiousness of such a distinction and separation in the house of God. It is, however, but justice to Dr. Patton to observe that the case is not singular, the peculiar celebrity of his "Negro Pew" arising entirely from the imbecile and somewhat profane apology volunteered by Mr. Page. In point of fact, Dr. Patton and his people, as I ascertained in conversation with him on the subject, are rather in advance of their neighbours in kind feeling towards the coloured people.

LETTER XXVII.

A Presbyterian Church in New York, and its Pastor—The Abbotts and
their Institution — Union Theological Seminary — Dr. Skinner's
Church—New York University—A threatening "Necessity"—
Prejudice against Colour — A Fact connected with Mr. ————'s
Church — Another Fact in Pennsylvania— State of Public Opinion
in New York — An Interview with Dr. Spring — A Missionary
Meeting in Dr. Adams's Church.

In the evening I preached by engagement for
the Rev. — ————, in the —— Presbyterian Church.
It was pouring with rain, and not more than 150
persons were present. The pastor, who had visited
me in a very fraternal manner, kindly proposed to
devote part of the next day to showing me some
of the "lions" of the city. The first place we
visited was Mount Vernon, the institution of the
Abbotts. It is a seminary for young ladies, with 200
pupils. The first of the brothers to whom we were
introduced was John Abbott, the author of "The
Mother at Home." He is apparently 40 years of age.
He introduced us to the room of the senior class, which
consisted of 30 or 40 young ladies, from 14 to 25
years of age. They were engaged in a French exercise
with Jacob Abbott, the author of "The Young Christian," "The Corner Stone," "The Way for a Child,"
&c., &c. The exercise over, we were introduced to

Mr. Jacob Abbott, and were requested to accompany him to a private sitting-room. I found him an exceedingly pleasant and unassuming man. He is 43 years of age, but looks younger. He wrote both "The Young Christian" and "The Corner Stone" when he was only 25. John is two years younger than Jacob; Charles, to whom also I was introduced, is younger still; and Gorham, whom I did not then see, is the youngest of the four. All are ministers, though not pastors,—all highly intellectual men, and connected more or less with this seminary, which is one of the best conducted I have ever seen. The pupils are not boarders, but they pay from 10*l.* to 15*l.* a year for their tuition alone. I subsequently made another visit to this institution in company with my wife, upon whom Mr. Jacob Abbott had very politely called.

Mr. ——— intended to introduce me to Dr. Spring, but he was not at home. He then took me to the Union Theological Seminary. In that institution about 120 young men are preparing for the Christian ministry. The library contains *twenty thousand* volumes on theology alone—musty and prosy tomes! What a punishment it would be to be compelled to wade through the whole! We saw neither professors nor students. My principal recollection of the place is that of feeling intensely hungry, and smelling at the same time the roast beef on which, in some of the lower regions of the buildings, the young divines were regaling themselves. In vain I wished to join them in that exercise.

When we came out, my guide proposed to take me to see Dr. Robinson. Much as I wanted to see the author of the " Greek Lexicon," and the Traveller in Palestine, there were other claims that then more urgently pressed themselves. I had breakfasted at 7, and it was now near 1. I gave my friend a hint to that effect. But he overruled it by saying, " It is close by, and won't take us many minutes." We went, but the Doctor was not in. We were now opposite Dr. Skinner's Church, and my friend insisted on my going to see it. It will hold about 1,000 people. All the pews are cushioned and lined, and the place has a decided air of aristocracy about it. The school-room, the lecture-room, the vestry, &c., were very complete and convenient. " How strange," I observed to my friend, "that you should so far exceed us in the comfort of your places of worship, and at the same time be so far behind us in domestic comforts." " *That*," said he, " was the principle of the Puritans,—the house of God first, their own after." I ventured to ask him what salaries ministers in New York generally received. He told me from 1,000 to 4,000 dollars, or from 200*l.* to 800*l.* " My own," he added, " is 2,000 dollars." We were now not far from the New York University. " You must go and see that," said he. I went, but saw nothing particular except the library, empty lecture-rooms, and chapel,—no professors. My friendly guide pointed to a portrait of Lord Lyndhurst, told me with evident pride that he was a Yankee, and marvelled at my ignorance of the fact.

From time to time I had given him hints that I was afraid of being too late for dinner at my lodgings; and when the sight-seeing was at last ended, he very coolly and complacently said, "Now, if you really think you are too late for dinner at your place, I shall be under the *necessity* of asking you to go and take a plate with me." Those were the *ipsissima verba*. I could scarcely keep my gravity; but I replied, "Thank you, sir; I want to go to the centre of the city, and I can easily get a dinner at any eating-house." He both nodded and expressed an entire concurrence, and seemed to think it an *admirable* arrangement. In parting, he pressed me to preach for him on the following Thursday, but I declined. The next day I was told, on unquestionable authority, that two or three years ago one of the elders of this gentleman's church, meeting a man from South America whom he took to be a mixture of Spaniard and Indian, requested his company to church. The stranger assented, and sat with him in his pew. He liked the service, became interested, and went again and again. At last it was whispered that he was a "Nigger,"—*i. e.* had a slight mixture of African blood in him. The next week a meeting of the Session was held, at which it was unanimously resolved that the intruder's entrance into the body of the church must be prohibited. Two men were stationed at the door for that purpose. The stranger came. He was stopped, and told that he could not be allowed to enter the body of the church, there being a place up in the gallery for coloured people. The man remonstrated, and said he had been invited to take a seat in Mr. So-and-so's pew. "Yes," they replied, "we are aware of that; but public feeling is against it, and it cannot be allowed." The stranger turned round, burst into tears, and walked home.

Mr. Johnson, of the *Tribune*, told me that two or three years ago he and thirty or forty more were returning from an Anti-slavery Convention held at Harrisburgh in Pennsylvania. They had left by railway for Philadelphia at 3 o'clock in the morning. At a town called Lancaster they stopped to breakfast. In the company were two coloured gentlemen, one of whom was a minister. They all sat down together. Soon the waiters began to whisper, "A nigger at table!" "There is two!" The landlord quickly appeared, seized one of the coloured gentlemen by the shoulder, and asked him how he dared to sit down at table in his house. The company remonstrated, and assured him that those whose presence appeared to be so offensive were very respectable men, friends of theirs, whom they had invited to sit down. It was all in vain. The landlord would hear nothing; "the niggers must go." "Very well," said the rest of the company; "then we shall all go." Away they went, and left the refined landlord to console himself for the loss of a large party to breakfast. They had to travel all the way to Philadelphia before they could break their fast.

The same gentleman told me that he believed if a white man of any standing in society in New York were now to marry a coloured lady, however intelligent and accomplished, his life would be in danger,—he would be lynched for having committed such an outrage upon "public opinion." And yet the boast is ever ringing in our ears, "This is a free country—every one does as he pleases here!"

On the 24th of March I called upon Dr. Spring. He is an Old School Presbyterian, and a supporter of the Colonization Society. In the course of conversation reference was made to State Churches.

Myself.—"You see, Doctor, State Churches are the curse of the British Empire, just as slavery is the curse of your country."

The Doctor.—"Ah! so it is; and yet we can do nothing to remove them. Here is our slavery,—we can't touch it; and you cannot touch your Established Church. Do you think you will ever get rid of it?"

Myself.—"Oh! yes; I hope so."

The Doctor.—"But it will be a *very* long time before it comes to pass."

Myself.—"Perhaps not so very long. We are rapidly hastening towards some great change. The old principle of an Establishment is now being abandoned by all parties; and we shall soon come either to the pay-all or to the pay-none principle. I am much afraid it will be the former."

The Doctor.—"But were it to come to that, and the State would pay you as well as all the rest, you would have no further ground of complaint."

Myself.—"Oh! but we should: we dread that above all other evils. It will be a dark day for evangelical religion in England, if ever that principle be adopted."

The Doctor.—"Why? What harm can it do you to receive the money of the State, provided it does not infringe upon your liberties?"

Myself.—"In the first place, it would be a departure from the law of Jesus Christ, and every departure from his law is sure to be productive of evil."

The Doctor.—"Very true. That's a sound principle—that every departure from his law will be productive of evil; but then, it remains to be proved that it *is* a departure from his law. However, I am glad to see you stick so firmly to your principles."

He then went on to ask if I would preach for him next Sabbath. Now, whether he was only trying me on those points, or whether he had not studied the subject, or whether he was anxious to keep me off from the subject of slavery, I cannot tell. But I came away with my knowledge of Dr. Spring less than it was when I entered. He seemed like a cold, stiff, formal State parson.

In the evening I attended a missionary meeting in Dr. Adams's Church. It was the anniversary of the New York and Brooklyn Auxiliary to the Board of Commissioners for Foreign Missions, and embraced about thirty churches. I expected great things. When I entered they were singing. The place was little more than half-full,—say 500 persons. Three gentlemen were sitting in the pulpit. These were Dr. Adams, Dr. Cox, and Mr. Storrers. I looked around for the negro pew. There it was on the left of the organ, and five sable friends in it. The first speaker was Dr. Adams, who delivered a well-prepared oration of half an hour long. The Rev. Mr. Storrers, a young man, the pastor of the " Church of the Pilgrims" in Brooklyn, was the next speaker. His preparation and delivery were of the same character as those of Dr. Adams. But he possesses great mental power. He occupied exactly half an hour. Both speakers complained bitterly of diminished confidence and contributions. I forget the exact amount announced as the contribution of this auxiliary; but it was small. Dr. Cox, of Brooklyn, was the third speaker. He told us that the last meeting he had attended in England, a few months before, was the missionary meeting in Birmingham. It was held in the town-hall, a magnificent building, and well filled. He pronounced an eloquent eulogy on John Angell James. He described the missionary breakfast in Birmingham; but, in mentioning such a thing as a " missionary breakfast," he felt it necessary to make some apology. He assured them it was not attended with the evils they might be apt to imagine would be inseparably connected with it. The fact is that missionary breakfasts are altogether unknown in America. Dr. Cox stated that he had often been asked in England how they managed missionary meetings in America, that the people of England held them in high estimation, that in England they depended chiefly for the support of the missionary cause upon legacies, stock, &c., while they in America were content to say, " Give us day by day our daily bread." He also mentioned Dr. Chalmers's eulogy upon them. While in England, he (Dr. Cox) and another had waited upon Sir Stratford Canning, to commend their mission at Constantinople to his kind notice, and Sir Stratford had spoken in very high terms of the American people. Thus, even at the missionary meeting, incense must be offered to national vanity.

LETTER XXVIII.

A Visit to Mount Vernon—Dr. Robinson—Welsh Deputation—Queen Anne and New York—The Sabbath—Preaching at Dr. L——'s— Afternoon Service at Mr. C——'s—Tea at Dr. L——'s — Evening Service at Mr. ——'s.

THE next day my wife and I paid our promised visit to the institution of the Abbotts at Mount Vernon. In its government there are neither rewards nor punishments; but each pupil, at the close of the day, has to present a brief report of her own conduct. Her good deeds and her bad deeds must be alike proclaimed— proclaimed by herself,—and that in the presence of her fellow-pupils who were witnesses of the conduct to which she refers. This compels her to be faithful. If she tries to conceal what was faulty, she is surrounded by those who will detect that concealment : if she ostentatiously parades her own excellences, she knows she will sink in the estimation of her friends. The encouragement of self-respect, and of a regard for that which is good for its *own* sake, are the great principles of government in this establishment.

Mr. Abbott's plan of teaching a language is, not at first to weary the pupils with the dry rules of grammar, but to store their memories with words. He read a word or a short sentence in French, for instance, and asked the pupils to translate it into English. Then, with closed books, he would give them the English in like manner to be turned into French. I have since adopted the plan with Latin pupils with pleasure and success.

Mr. Abbott allows a recess of five minutes at the close of every half-hour. The hours of attendance are from 9 A.M. to 2 P.M.; but a rest of half an hour is allowed in the midst of that period. We happened to be there when the said half-hour arrived. All the Abbotts, the pupils, and ourselves went out to the play-ground, which was furnished with seats, and swings, and skipping-ropes, and swinging-boats, and all sorts of machines for exercise and amusement. In these gymnastic performances the Abbotts themselves joined the pupils, with a beautiful combination of freedom and propriety. A happier assemblage I never saw. We retired highly delighted with all we had witnessed.

In the afternoon I had the honour of being intro-duced to Dr. Robinson, whose Greek Lexicon I had often thumbed with advantage. He appeared to be from 45 to 50 years of age. His manners were exceed-ingly simple and unostentatious,—the constant charac-teristics of true greatness. I looked upon him with high respect and veneration. He is a man of whom America may well be proud. He pressed me to go and address the students at Union College, of which he is one of the Professors; but an opportunity of doing so did not occur.

In the evening I was waited upon by two gentlemen

who announced themselves as the "President and Secretary" of a Welsh Temperance Society, and wished me to attend and address one of their meetings at a given time. This I could not do. In conversation with them about slavery, and the oppression of the coloured people, I was surprised and grieved to find how soon the Welsh people imbibed the feelings and aped the conduct of the Americans in those matters. On their pressing me to attend a meeting of their society on some *future* occasion, I told them I was one of the most downright Abolitionists that ever lived, and, if I came, would terrify them all with such an abolition speech as they had never heard. This, of course, was cold water upon their love, and our interview soon terminated.

The weather for the next two days was so unfavourable that we could not go out at all. Among the information I then derived from books were the following precious morsels from the Introduction to the Natural History of New York: "The Governor was directed by Queen Anne to take especial care that the Almighty should be devoutly and duly served according to the rites of the Church of England," and was at the *same time* desired by the Queen "to take especial care that the colony should have a constant and sufficient supply of merchantable negroes at moderate rates." Just what our own West India planters *now* want! Oh! how they would hail the return of the palmy days of Queen Anne!

On Sabbath the 28th of March I was invited to

preach in the morning in the church of Dr. L——, a
Congregational place of worship, capable of accommodating about 500 persons.   The attendance was not
more than 200.   There I was delighted to find no
negro pew.   A few coloured children were intermingled with the white ones in the gallery.   The Doctor,
to whom I had not been introduced, was already in the
pulpit when I arrived.   The ceremony of introduction
to each other had to be duly performed in the rostrum.
He is a fine, tall, clean, and venerable-looking old gentleman.   He began the service, and, before sermon,
announced that they would then " take up" the usual
collection.   That place of worship is what they call a
" Free Church,"—*i.e.* there is no pew-letting; as a
substitute for which, they " take up" a weekly collection.   The Doctor also made the following announcement : " A Missionary of the London Missionary
Society, from Guiana, one of the South American pos-
sessions of Britain,—his name is Mr. Davies,—will
now preach; and in the evening Professor Kellog from
——, a *long* friend of mine, will preach."   At the
close I was introduced to the Doctor's *long* friend,
Professor Kellog; and sure enough he was a " long"
one !   There was present also Professor Whipple, of
the Oberlin Institute, to whom I had before been
introduced.

In the afternoon I preached for a Mr. C——, in a
Presbyterian Church.   The place was beautiful, com-
modious, and nearly full.   The pastor introduced the
service.   In his manner of doing so, I was very much

struck with—what I had before often observed in our Transatlantic brethren—a great apparent want of reverence and fervour. The singing was very good—in the choir. In my address, I urged them to give their legislators, and their brethren in the South, no rest till the guilt and disgrace of slavery were removed from their national character and institutions. I also besought them, as men of intelligence and piety, to frown upon the ridiculous and contemptible prejudice against colour wherever it might appear. To all which they listened with apparent kindness and interest.

We took tea by invitation with Dr. L——, for whom I had preached in the morning. There we met with his nice wife, nice deacon, nice little daughters, and nice nieces,—but a most intolerable nephew. This man professed to be greatly opposed to slavery, and yet was full of contempt for "niggers." He talked and *laughed* over divisions in certain churches, and told the company how he used occasionally to go on Sunday nights to hear a celebrated minister, just "for the sake of hearing him *talk*—ha—ha—ha!" And yet this was a professor of religion !

On the subject of slavery the following conversation took place :—

Nephew.—"If I were in a Slave State, I would not hold slaves."

Aunt.—" Ah ! but you would."

Nephew.—" No ! that I would not."

Aunt.—" You could not live there without."

Dr. L—— (gravely).—"Well, I *guess* we had better pray, 'Lead us not into temptation.'"

Aunt (devoutly).—"I *guess* we had."

By-and-by one of the young ladies said to my wife, "I guess we had better go and fix our things, and get ready for church." This was the signal for the breaking up of our social enjoyment, which would have been one of unmingled pleasure, had it not been for this noisy, conceited, talkative nephew.

In the evening I had to preach again for Mr. ——, the place where the coloured gentleman was refused admission to the body of the church. The building was very fine, and the congregation very large. Professor Fowler, of Amherst College, who happened to be present, read the Scriptures and prayed. My subject was "the woes and wants of the African race." I touched upon American slavery, and gave details of the horrors of the slave traffic as at present carried on. I also bore testimony against the cruel prejudice which so extensively exists against the African colour. All were attentive, except one man, who rose and walked out; and I fancied him saying to himself, "I am not going to sit here to listen to this abolition nonsense any longer." And so ended my Sabbath in New York.

LETTER XXIX.

The Rev. Theodore Sedgwick Wright—His Testimony against Caste—His Funeral—Drs. Cox and Patton—The Service in the House—The Procession—The Church—The Funeral Oration—Mrs. Wright.

DURING my stay at this time in New York, there died in that city the Rev. Theodore Sedgwick Wright, a Presbyterian minister of colour. His attainments and talents were very respectable; and for fifteen years he had been the successful pastor of a church of coloured people in the city.

Before you accompany me to his funeral, listen to his voice. Though " dead, he yet speaketh." He had felt this cruel prejudice against the colour of his skin as iron entering his soul. Here is his touching testimony on the subject, delivered in a speech at Boston eleven years before his death:—

" No man can really understand this prejudice, unless he feels it crushing him to the dust, because it is a matter of feeling. It has bolts, scourges, and bars, wherever the coloured man goes. It has bolts in all the schools and colleges. The coloured parent, with the same soul as a white parent, sends his child to the seats of learning; and he finds the door bolted, and he sits down to weep beside his boy. Prejudice stands at the door, and bars him out. Does the child of the coloured

man show a talent for mechanics, the heart of the
parent beats with hope.   He sees the children of the
white man engaged in employment ; and he trusts that
there is a door open to his boy, to get an honest living,
and become a useful member of society.   But, when he
comes to the workshop with his child, he finds a- bolt
there.   But, even suppose that he can get this first
bolt removed, he finds other bars.   He can't work.
Let him be ever so skilled in mechanics, up starts prejudice, and says, ' I won't work in the shop if you do.'
Here he is scourged by prejudice, and has to go back,
and sink down to some of the employments which white
men leave for the most degraded.   He hears of the
death of a child from home, and he goes in a stage or
a steam-boat.   His money is received, but he is
scourged there by prejudice.   If he is sick, he can
have no bed, he is driven on deck : money will not buy
for him the comforts it gets for all who have not his
complexion.   He turns to some friend among the
white men. Perhaps that white man had sat at his table
at home, but he does not resist prejudice here.   He
says, ' Submit.   'Tis an ordinance of God,—you must
be humble.'   Sir, I have felt this.   As a minister, I
have been called to pass often up and down the North
River in steam-boats.   Many a night I have walked
the deck, and not been allowed to lie down in a bed.
Prejudice would even turn money to dross when it
was offered for these comforts by a coloured man.
Thus prejudice scourges us from the table ; it scourges
us from the cabin, from the stage-coach, from the

bed. Wherever we go, it has for us bolts, bars, and rods."

And now let us attend the speaker's funeral. Professor Whipple will be our guide. As we proceed, crowds of coloured people are hastening in the same direction from all quarters. We are at the house. But so great is the throng that it is impossible to get in. Here, however, comes Dr. Cox. " Make room for Dr. Cox !"—"Make room for Dr. Cox !" is now heard on every hand. A path is opened for the great man, and we little men slip in at his skirt. On reaching the room where the remains of the good man lie, we find Dr. Patton and the Rev. Mr. Hatfield. They and Dr. Cox are there in a semi-official capacity, as representing the Presbytery with which Mr. Wright was connected. Louis Tappan, the long-tried and faithful friend of the coloured race, is there also. I am asked to be a pall-bearer : without at all reflecting on the duties and inconveniences of the office, I goodnaturedly consent. A *white* cotton scarf is instantly thrown over my shoulder. There is the coffin ; and there is a life-like portrait of Mr. Wright hung up against the wall, and looking as it were down upon that coffin. But you can see the face of Mr. Wright himself. The coffin-lid is screwed down ; but there is a square of glass, like a little window, just over the face, as is generally the case in America, and you can have a view of the whole countenance.

A black man reads a hymn, and, in connection with it, begins an address in a very oracular style, and with

very solemn pauses.   A hint is given him not to proceed. They sing.   Mr. Hatfield delivers an appropriate
address.   A coloured minister prays, sometimes using
the first person singular, and sometimes the first person
plural ; also talking about the " meanderings of life,"
and a great deal of other nonsense.

We move down stairs.   The immense procession
starts.   Drs. Cox and Patton, Mr. Hatfield, and about
half-a-dozen more white ministers, are in it.   As we
pass on from street to street, and from crossing to
crossing, all sorts of people seem to regard the procession with the utmost respect.   The cabmen, 'busmen,
and cartmen behave exceedingly well.   But did you
overhear what those three or four low dirty men said as
we approached ?   I am ashamed to tell, because those
men are not Americans, but *Irishmen,*—" Here comes
the dead nigger !"   The boys, now and then, are also
overheard counting how many *white* men there are in
the procession.

We are now at the church.   After much delay and
difficulty we enter.   The place, which is not large, is
crammed.   There must be about 600 people in.   Dr.
Cox urges them to make room for more, and says there
are not more than one-tenth in of those who wish to
enter.   If so, there must be a concourse of 6,000
people, and not more than twenty whites among
them all !

A coloured man gives out a hymn.   Dr. Cox reads
the Scriptures, and makes a few remarks.   Dr. Patton
delivers an oration.   In that oration, while speaking

of Mr. Wright's anti-slavery feelings as being very strong, he adds, with very questionable taste, "But at the same time our brother had no sympathy with those who indulged in *denunciation, wrath, and black-guardism.* He would never touch the missiles which *none but scoundrels use.*" What a selection of words in a funeral oration! In speaking of Mr. Wright's labours in connection with that church for fifteen years, he says, "Our brother had difficulties which other men have not. Two or three years ago he had to trudge about the city, under the *full muzzle* of a July or August sun, to beg money in order to extricate this place from pecuniary difficulties. On one occasion, after walking all the way to the upper part of the city to call upon a gentleman from whom he hoped to receive a donation, he found that he had just left his residence for his office in the city. Our brother, though greatly exhausted, was compelled to walk the same distance down again; for—to the shame, the ever-lasting shame of our city be it spoken—our brother, on account of his colour, could not avail himself of one of the public conveyances. The next week disease laid hold of him, and he never recovered."

What a strong and unexpected testimony against that cruel prejudice! According to this testimony, Theodore Sedgwick Wright fell a *victim* to it. But who would have thought that Dr. Patton, who thus denounced the cabmen and 'busmen of New York, had at the very time the "Negro Pew" in his own church!

While on this subject, let me tell you another fact

M

respecting poor Mr. Wright.   The life of his first wife
was sacrificed to this heartless and unmanly feeling.
He was travelling with her by steam-boat between New
York and Boston.   They had to be out all night, and
a bitter cold winter's night it was.   Being coloured
people, their only accommodation was the "hurricane-
deck."   Mrs. Wright was delicate.   Her husband
offered to pay any money, if they would only let her be
in the kitchen or the pantry.   No,—she was a "nigger,"
and could not be admitted.   Mr. Wright wrapped her
in his own cloak, and placed her against the chimney
to try to obtain for her a little warmth.   But she took
a severe cold, and soon died.   *His* colour, it would
seem, hastened his own exit to rejoin her in that world
where such absurd and inhuman distinctions are unknown.

Dr. Patton's oration is now ended.   But—did you
ever hear such a thing at a funeral?—that minister in
the table pew is actually giving out—

"Praise God, from whom all blessings flow!"

and they sing it to a funeral tune!

We start for the place of burial.   But it is a long
way off, and I had better spare you the journey.   The
great men fell off one after another; but my pall-
bearing office compelled me to remain to the last.   It
was 4 o'clock P.M. before the solemnities were closed.

LETTER XXX.

Now for an excursion to New Haven. We leave
by the steamer " Traveller," Captain Stone, at 6½ A.M.
Wrap yourself up well; it is piercing cold, being the
30th of March. This boat is altogether different from
the boats on the Mississippi. It seems to belong to
quite another species. It is, however, admirably
adapted for its purpose,—that of running along a
stormy coast. In the gentlemen's cabin are three tiers
of berths, one above another like so many book-shelves.
The engine works outside, like a top-sawyer. We
shall pass " Hell Gate" directly; but don't be alarmed.
You would not have known it, had I not told you.
The Hog's Back, the Frying Pan, and other places of
Knickerbocker celebrity, are in this neighbourhood.

Let us go to the ladies' saloon. Well! I declare!
There is a coloured woman, and allowed to remain
unmolested! Things improve as we approach New
England, and are much better even there than they
were a few years ago.

But here comes the captain muffled up. He brings

with him a poor sickly-looking woman, begs the ladies'
pardon, and bids her sit down by the stove and warm
herself.　He then tells the passengers her painful
story.　The night before, in New York, this woman
came on board, from one of the Philadelphia boats,
bringing with her a bed and a child.　On being spoken
to by the captain, she informed him that she was on
her way from St. Louis to her home in Massachusetts,
—that she had been fifteen days upon the journey, and
had two children with her.　On being asked where the
other was, she replied, "There it is," pointing to the
bed, where, clad in its usual dress, the little sufferer,
released from the trials of life, lay extended in death.
It had caught cold, and died in her arms in New York.
She was friendless and penniless, and wanted a passage
to New Haven.　The captain had obtained a coroner's
inquest over the body, purchased for it a little coffin,
had it decently laid out, and gratified her maternal
feelings by allowing her to bring it with her, that it
might be buried in her village-home in Massachusetts.
All this he had done without money and without price,
had also given her a free passage to New Haven, and
was about to forward her home by railway at his own
expense!　Captain *Stone*—"what's in a name?"—at
the close of this statement had to take out his pocket-
handkerchief, and wipe away a few manly tears from
his weather-beaten cheeks, as he added, "I have met
in my life with many cases of distress, but with none
that came so much to my heart as this."　His object,
in introducing the woman and her case, was to make an

appeal to the passengers on her behalf. He did so; and the result was a subscription amounting to about five pounds sterling, which was handed over to her. Captain Stone's was a deed worthy of a golden inscription!

It is half-past 11 A.M., and we are now at the landing-place in the harbour of New Haven, having accomplished the distance from New York, about 80 miles, in five hours! We have a long wharf of 3,943 feet to travel; and then we set foot for the first time on the soil of New England. We have been invited to make our abode here with the Rev. Leicester Sawyer, who makes his abode at Deacon Wilcoxon's, corner of Sherman-avenue and Park-street. Thither, therefore, let us go. Mr. Sawyer, whom we had before met in New York, is the author of several books, comprising two on Mental and Moral Philosophy, and was also lately the President of the Central College of Ohio. Deacon Wilcoxon and his wife are plain, homely, kind Christian people. They make you feel at home as soon as you have crossed their threshold.

Soon after our arrival the Rev. Dr. Bacon and the Rev. Mr. Dutton, the pastors of the " first " and " second " Congregational Churches in this city, honour us with a call. This is brotherly, and more than we could have expected. Dr. Bacon regrets that he is going from home, and cannot have us to spend a few days at his house. Mr. Dutton, however, presses us to accept of his hospitality. We promise to do so in a day or two. Dr. Bacon is one of the great men of New England. He is a living encyclopædia,— a walking library. He keeps fully up with the literature and sciences of the day. I have not met a man, either in the Old World or in the New, that so thoroughly understood the state of the British West Indies at the present time as he does. He might have spent years in that part of the world, and devoted himself to its exclusive study. His position at home is high, and his influence great. The estimation in which he is held in New England may be judged of by the fact, that when, in August 1846, Dr. Theodore Dwight Woolsey had to be installed as President of Yale College, Dr. Bacon, living within a stone's throw of that institution, was the man chosen to preach the inauguration sermon.

In the middle of the afternoon, my friend Mr. Sawyer presses me to preach in his place of worship— the Howe-street Church — this evening. I consent. By-and-by I observe him very busy with some slips of paper; and I ask him what he is doing? "I am sending," he says, "notices to the evening papers, to make it known that you are going to preach this evening!" What a people the Americans are for newspapers! New Haven has only a population of about 18,000; and yet it has six daily papers—all having a weekly issue besides, two monthly periodicals, and two quarterly ones! The daily papers are, I believe, none of them more than 5 dollars (a guinea) a year, or 2 cents (one penny) per number. No paper duty, and no stamp. At the service in the evening several ministers and students were present.

The next day snow to the depth of six inches cover the ground. Let us, however, turn out in the afternoon. We will go and see the central square,—or the Green, as it is commonly called. This is a large open space like a park, surrounded on all sides with rows of stately elms, and is considered one of the most beautiful spots in the United States. And now we are in a position to take a full view. Three churches, arranged side by side on this open space, at a few rods from each other, stand before us. The central one has the most imposing aspect. It is a large Grecian building, having a portico, supported by four massive columns, from which rises a lofty bell-tower, ending in a spire. The combination of the belfry or spire with the Grecian style is a violation of propriety; but *I like it*. This is the "first" Congregational Church—that in which Dr. Bacon ministers. That church—not the building—is coeval with the colony, and can trace back its history for more than 200 years. It was formerly a State Church. Congregationalism was for ages the "standing order," or the established religion, in Connecticut! All the people were taxed for its support; and no man could have any share in the administration of the civil government, or give his vote in any election, unless he was a member of one of the churches. It was not till forty years after the separation of Church and State in Virginia, where the establishment was Episcopal, that the example was followed in Connecticut. Happily, however, in 1816 all parties that differed from it— Episcopalians, Baptists, Methodists, Universalists, &c.,

combined together, gained a majority in the legislature, and severed the connection between Congregationalism and the State! There are old men now
living who then anxiously and piously "trembled for
the Ark of the Lord." They have, however, lived to
see that the dissolution of the union between Church
and State in Connecticut, as in Virginia, was to the
favoured sect as "life from the dead." The Congre-
gatibnalist of the one, and the Episcopalian of the
other, would alike deprecate being placed in the same
position again. But this is a digression.

We are still looking at these churches. The church
on our right, which is about the same size and of the
same architectural character as the other, though not
quite so showy, is the " second" Congregational Church,
commonly called the North Church — that in which
Mr. Dutton now ministers. This church originated in
the "great awakening" in 1740, was formed in 1742,
and has a history of more than a century in duration.
It arose from dissatisfaction with the ministry of a
Mr. Noyes, a contemporary of Jonathan Edwards, but
one who had no sympathy in Edwards's views and
spirit. This man was, indeed, greatly opposed to the
" awakening," and refused George Whitfield admission
to his pulpit. The originators of this second church,
therefore, separated from the original parent, availed
themselves of the Act of Toleration, and became Congregational Dissenters from a Congregational Establishment! They had of course no State support, nor were
they " free from taxation by the society from which

they dissented." "The foundations of this church, my brethren," said its present gifted pastor, in a sermon preached at the centenary of its formation, "are love of evangelical doctrine, of ecclesiastical liberty, of revivals of religion. Such ever be its super-structure."

Here, for a quarter of a century, lived and laboured Jonathan Edwards the younger. Perhaps you have never before heard of him; neither had I till I came to New Haven. If you won't think it too long to be detained here standing in front of the church, I will tell you a few facts respecting him. He was the second son and ninth child of the celebrated Jonathan Edwards of Northampton. His mother, too, was an extraordinary woman. You will smile at the impression she made on the mind of good old George Whit-field. He had spent two days at Mr. Edwards's house in Northampton; and he says, "I felt wonderful satis-faction in being at the house of Mr. Edwards. He is a son himself, and hath a daughter of Abraham for his wife. A sweeter couple I have not yet seen. She is a woman adorned with a meek and quiet spirit, and talked so feelingly and solidly of the things of God, and seemed to be such a helpmeet to her husband, that she caused me to renew those prayers which for some months I have put up to God, that he would send me a daughter of Abraham to be my wife. I find, upon many accounts, it is my duty to marry. Lord, I desire to have no choice of my own. Thou knowest my circumstances."

In quoting this, an American writer adds, " He had not yet learned, if he ever did, that God is not pleased to make such ' sweet couples' out of persons who have no choice of their own."

Mr. Edwards, junior, or rather Dr. Edwards, was (like his father) a great scholar and a profound divine. He was frequently invited to assist at the examinations in Yale College. On those occasions he used frequently to display his strictness and accuracy by calling out, " *Haud recté*" (not right). This procured him the *sobriquet* of " Old Haud Recté," by which he was afterwards known among the students. Some time after his resignation of the pastorate of this church he became the President of Union College. His works have recently been published in two large octavo volumes. There is a striking parallel between the father and the son. They were alike in the character of their minds and in their intellectual developments. The name, education, and early employments of the two were alike. Both were pious in their youth; both were distinguished scholars; both were tutors for equal periods in the colleges where they were respectively educated; both were settled in the ministry as successors to their maternal grandfathers; both were dismissed, and again settled in retired places, where they had leisure to prepare and publish their works; both were removed from those stations to become presidents of colleges; both died shortly after their respective inaugurations, the one in the 56th and the other in the 57th year of their age; and each of them preached on the first Sabbath of the year of his death from the same text—" This year thou shalt die!"

But we must not dwell too long on these historical incidents. I have told you something about the Centre Church and the North Church. That Gothic building on our left is an episcopal church. That white building immediately in the rear of the Centre Church is the State House, completed in 1831. It is constructed of stone and marble, and forms a prominent ornament of the city. It presents one of the best copies of a Grecian temple I have seen in the States. In the rear of the North Church, quite at the remote corner of the Green, stands a plain barn-like Methodist chapel. And, behind the whole, peeping through the elm-trees, you see the long range of buildings which constitutes Yale College. Take it all in all, a view more interesting than that from the spot on which we now stand I have never beheld.

LETTER XXXI.

BEFORE I take you to " Yale," let me show you the spot on the Green on which, in 1745, Whitfield, being refused admission to the Congregational church, preached in the open air, under a tree, to an immense congregation,—so great at that time was the dislike to a fervid evangelical ministry. But more than a century has rolled away; and how changed is the scene !

But, observe you that feeble, tottering old gentleman coming along the avenue ? It is the Hon. David Daggett, LL.D., late Chief Justice of the Supreme Court of Connecticut. He is a member, and, I believe, a deacon of one of the Congregational churches in this city. Twelve or thirteen years ago that very man, sitting on the judicial bench, condemned Miss Randall to be punished for — teaching a coloured child to read !

Now for Yale. The Rev. Samuel W. S. Dutton, the minister of the North Church, will accompany us. This institution was founded in the year 1700. It

derived its name from the Hon. Elihu Yale, a gentleman, I am proud to say, descended from an ancient
and respectable family in Wales. His father, Thomas
Yale, Esq., came over with the first settlers of New
Haven. His son Elihu went to England at ten years
of age, and to the East Indies at thirty. In the latter
country he resided about twenty years, was made
Governor of Madras, acquired a large fortune, returned
to England, was chosen Governor of the East India
Company, and died at Wrexham in Denbighshire in
1721. On several occasions he made munificent dona-
tions to the new institution during the years of its
infancy and weakness, on account of which the trustees
by a solemn act named it " Yale College."

The college buildings—which, like Rome, were not all
erected in a day—consist of four plain spacious edifices,
built of brick, each four stories high, and presenting
a front, including passage-ways, of about 600 feet.
That neat white house on your right, as you stand
before these buildings, is the President's dwelling—
the very house in which resided Dr. Timothy Dwight.
But you are not looking at it. Ah! I see your attention is attracted by that student sitting on the sill of
the open window of his study, having in his hand a
book, and in his mouth a pipe of clay; by which, with
the aid of fire, he is reducing a certain tropical weed
into its original chemical elements. Perhaps you think
that rather undignified; and so it is. I wish you had
not seen it; but worse is done at Oxford and Cambridge.

Behind this range of buildings is another, a more modern and more imposing pile. This extends in front 151 feet, is built of red sandstone, is in the Gothic style, and contains the libraries of the institution. The central building, called the College Hall, containing the College Library properly so called, measures in front 51 feet, and in depth from front to rear 95 feet, having at each corner a tower of the extreme height of 91 feet. The interior is one room, whose measurement is 83 feet by 41, resembling in form a Gothic chapel, with its nave and aisles. The nave is 51 feet high, and its breadth 17 feet. Between its clustered pillars on either side are alcoves, each 10 feet by 12, fitted up with shelves for books. The number of volumes it now contains is about 20,000. The extreme wings and the connecting wings on either side ′ are very elegant, and fitted up for various libraries connected with the institution, such as the Students' Library, the Reading Room, the Calliopean Library, and the Livonian Library. The Students' Library contains 9,000 volumes. This beautiful range of buildings probably contains not fewer than 40,000 volumes; and ere long the number will be doubled! Little did the ten ministers who, in 1700, met together to establish this seminary, each laying down his donation of books with these words, " I give these books for the founding of a college in this colony," and who found that their joint-contribution amounted to only *forty volumes*,— little did they think what that small beginning would come to !

You are looking out for literary curiosities. Here is one—Elliot's Indian Bible! You have heard of Elliot, "the Apostle of the North American Indians." Here is a translation of the entire sacred volume into one of the languages of those people. The New Testament was published in 1661, and the Old Testament in 1663. The book before us is a copy of the second edition of the New Testament in 1680, and of the Old Testament in 1685. But where are those Indians, or their descendants? They are extinct; and there is not now a man on the whole continent of America that speaks their language!

Time will not permit me to describe the Picture Gallery, the Anatomical Museum, the Cabinet of the Materia Medica, the Museum of Natural History, and many other objects of interest. You must, however, take a peep at the Mineral Cabinet, or Geological Museum. It has been collected and arranged, with great industry and taste, by Professor Silliman. Look at this meteoric iron-stone. It fell a few years ago in Texas, and weighs 1,635 lbs.!

Our guide, Mr. Dutton, insists upon our calling at the college-room of Dr. Goodrich, one of the Theological Professors. We do so; and find him engaged in revising Webster's Large Dictionary, about a dozen volumes, for a new edition. But what a polite man! Talk of American rudeness! A reception more kind and courteous than this you have never received from any man.

Yale College is a noble institution. Oh that we had

a few like it in England! The Faculty consists of
25 Professors—men who would be an honour to any
country, 7 "Tutors," and 6 "Instructors." At the
time of our visit there are 584 students thus classi-
fied :—

Theological Students		53
Law　　　　"		52
Medical　　　"		52
Resident Graduates		5
Undergraduates,—		
Seniors	121	
Juniors	90	
Sophomores (wise fools) . . .	112	
Freshmen	99	
	——	422
Total . .		584

Candidates for admission to the Freshmen Class are
examined in Cicero's Select Orations, the whole of
Virgil and Sallust, and the first three books of Xeno-
phon's Anabasis, together with various "Readers,"
"Exercises," and Grammars.

The whole course of instruction occupies four years,
each year being divided into three terms or sessions.

With regard to expense, the annual charges made by
the Treasurer are—

	DOLLS.	CENTS.
For instruction	33	00
For rent of chamber in college (average) . .	12	00
For ordinary repairs and contingencies . .	2	40
For general damages, sweeping, &c. . .	3	60
For expenses of recitation-rooms . . .	3	00
	54	00 = £11. 5s.

Board is obtained at prices varying from a dollar and a quarter to 3 dollars a week. To a majority of the students, the cost of board is less than 2 dollars a week, or, reckoning the dollar at 4s. 2d., less than 8s. 4d. Fuel is procured by the College Corporation, and sold to the students at cost-price. The students provide for themselves bed and bedding, furniture for their rooms, candles, books, stationery, and washing. In the several classes and literary societies subscriptions to a small amount are required. If books and furniture are sold when the student completes his course, the expense incurred by their use will not be great. The following is an approximate estimate of the *necessary* expenses, without including apparel, pocket-money, travelling, and board during vacations:—

	DOLLARS.		
Treasurer's account as above	54	...	54
Board for forty weeks	from 60	to	90
Fuel and lights	„ 6	„	15
Use of books recited, and stationery .	„ 5	„	15
Use of furniture, bed and bedding . .	„ 5	„	15
Washing	„ 5	„	15
Contributions in the classes . . .	„ 5	„	6

140 to 210

or from 29l. to 43l. No students are permitted to take lodgings in town, except when the rooms in college are all occupied.

In addition to the regular college course of four years, those who study for the ministry go through a theological course, which occupies three years more. No charges are made for tuition or lectures. For the accommodation of students of this order a building has been erected, in which the rooms are free of charge. The law department, in like manner, occupies two years, and the medical two or three.

Let us now go and see the graves of the Regicides. They are at the rear of the Centre Church. Soon after the restoration of Charles II., many of the judges who had condemned to death his father were apprehended; of whom thirty were condemned, and ten executed as traitors. Three, however, made their escape to New England,—Generals Goffe and Whalley, and Colonel Dixwell. A cave is shown in the neighbourhood, still called the "Judges' Cave," in which a great part of their time was spent in concealment. Many were their hair-breadth 'scapes from their pursuers—the Royalist party. The colonists, however, gave them all the sympathy and protection that they deserved. On one occasion, knowing that the pursuers were coming to New Haven, the Rev. Mr. Davenport preached on the text, "Hide the outcasts; betray not him that wandereth. Let mine outcasts dwell with thee, Moab; be thou a covert to them from the face of the spoiler." This, doubtless, had its effect, putting the whole town on their guard, and uniting the people in caution and concealment.

Do you see that rudely-shaped, dark blue stone, about 2 feet in width, the same in height, and 8 inches thick? Do you see the inscription upon it— E W in coarsely-carved letters, and the figures 1658 over them? That is, doubtless, the headstone of

Whalley's grave. The footstone is similar, having the same letters; but above them you see figures that may be read either sixteen hundred and fifty-eight, or sixteen hundred and seventy-eight—1657̸8. The latter was the date of the General's death; and the figures, perhaps, were thus tampered with to baffle the Royalists.

The other stone, about a foot broad and ten inches high, bearing the letters ⋀. G. and the number 80, is supposed to indicate the resting-place of Goffe. He died about the year 1680. The ⋀, with a deep-drawn stroke under its limbs, may be taken for an inverted W; and thus, with the G, stand for William Goffe, in harmony with the designed concealment that pervades the whole. Colonel John Dixwell lived here, for seventeen years or more, under the assumed name of James Davids, and died here after an exile of twenty-nine years from his native country. He, as well as the other two judges, lived and died in the firm expectation of another revolution in England. That revolution had actually taken place in the November before his death; but, as those were the days of slow and tedious voyages, the news did not arrive till about a month after his death. A little before his decease he revealed to the people his real name and character, which had long been known to the Rev. Mr. Pierpont the minister, but requested that no monument should be erected at his grave, " lest his enemies might dishonour his ashes," but only a plain stone inscribed with his initials J. D., Esq., his age, and time of death. And here it is—that piece of red stone, about 2 feet in height and breadth, and 5 inches thick, inscribed—

" I. D. Esq^R
DECEASED MARCH y^e
18th IN ye 82^d YEAR OF
HIS AGE 1688⁹."

President Stiles, in his " History of the Judges," says, " So late as the last French war, 1760, some British officers passing through New Haven, and hearing of Dixwell's grave, visited it, and declared, with rancorous and malicious vengeance, that if the British ministry knew it, they would even then cause their bodies to be dug up and vilified. Often have we heard the crown officers aspersing and vilifying them; and some so late as 1775 visited and treated the graves with marks of indignity too indecent to be detailed."

By those who can make a due allowance for difference of time and circumstances, the graves of these exiles will be visited with sentiments of veneration. It would have been grand to spare the presumptuous monarch; but we cannot feel surprised that he was sacrificed to the indignation of an outraged people. In these days, happily, kings and nations have learned that to take away the life of tyrannical rulers, or of resisting subjects, is but to sow the seeds of future troubles, and not to lay the foundation of permanent peace.

LETTER XXXII.

GOOD FRIDAY was observed by the people of New England as an annual fast-day, to humble themselves on account of their national sins. It seemed, somewhat to our inconvenience, to be literally and very rigidly observed in the circle in which we moved. On that day all ministers are at liberty to preach upon politics. Accordingly, my friend Mr. Sawyer took for his text Isaiah lviii. 6: "Is not this the fast that I have chosen? to loose the bands of wickedness, to undo the heavy burdens, and to let the oppressed go free, and that ye break every yoke?" He touched upon the war with Mexico, but dwelt chiefly on the subject of slavery in America. His remarks were, however, too much mingled with party politics to make the church uncomfortable.

In the afternoon I heard Mr. Dutton, in the North Church. His text was Neh. ii. 3, and his subject *Patriotism*. The existing war occupied much of his attention, and was strongly and unsparingly denounced. The maxim—too frequently heard at that time in the United States—"Our country, right or wrong," he shattered to atoms. Defensive war, however, he justified. He dwelt powerfully on the responsibility connected with the exercise of the elective franchise, and urged the duty of voting, at all times, not blindly and for party purposes, but intelligently, honestly, and piously. Exceptions might perhaps be taken by some to his views on defensive war; otherwise the discourse was excellent and seasonable. At the close of the service, we went, in accordance with previous arrangements, to be his guests for a few days.

In the evening I attended a Congregational church of coloured people. The place was exceedingly neat and clean. The minister, the Rev. Mr. Beman (himself a coloured man), gave out the well-known hymn—

> "Come we that love the Lord,
> And let our joys be known," &c.,

which was sung beautifully. He then offered up a very judicious, sensible, and pious prayer. The meeting was one of a series of revival meetings. A large number professed to have been converted; but, such were the care and caution exercised, none of them had been admitted into the fellowship of the church. Mr. Beman was so prudent, unassuming, and devout, that I could not resist the inclination to go up, introduce myself, and give a short address. Most cordial was my reception, and great my enjoyment. At the close, one and another were introduced to me as having

made their escape from Southern slavery, under circumstances painfully affecting; and they would not
let me go without a promise that I would preach to
them on the following Sabbath morning.

I did so, and enjoyed the service very much. As in
the evening there was to be a service in the North
Church, in which all the other churches were to unite,
for the purpose of hearing from me a statement with
regard to the history and operations of the London
Missionary Society, together with some special reference to British Guiana, I said to Mr. Beman, " Brother Beman, won't you and your people go to the
North Church to-night?" He hesitatingly said, " No,
—he thought not." " Why not?" said I,—" you
know my statements will in a great measure refer to
those who are your brethren—your kindred according
to the flesh." " Yes," he replied,—" we should be
glad to come; but the fact is they would pack us—
myself and all—into some negro pew, and we should
feel it keenly."

In the afternoon I preached for Mr. Dutton, in the
North Church. Dr. Bacon had that day exchanged
pulpits with Dr. Hawes of Hartford. My service
closing a little sooner than his, I reached the Centre
Church in time to hear the latter part of his sermon.
Dr. Hawes is a fine, tall man, of about 55 years of
age. In personal appearance, and in tones of voice,
he struck me as greatly resembling some of the sons of
Caledonia. His sermon, which was read, seemed to
be very good; but the delivery, even in the applica-

tion, was slow and heavy.   Both churches were even
more beautiful inside than out, and were filled with
very large congregations.

Shortly after, Mr. Dutton took me to attend the
afternoon worship at the College Chapel, where a church
is formed, and public services are conducted every
Sabbath.   It was here that Dr. Dwight delivered his
well-known Lectures.   There are prayers morning and
afternoon every day, which the students are expected
to attend.   Such was the present engagement.   One of
the professors read a chapter; gave out a hymn, which
was magnificently sung; and then offered an extempore
prayer.   There were between 300 and 400 students
present.

In the evening Dr. Hawes accompanied me into the
pulpit, and took the introductory part of the service.
Most of the professors and students were present.   It
was a fine, though formidable, opportunity to plead the
cause of the despised and oppressed sons of Afric before an audience of so much learning and intelligence.
What a contrast!   In 1742 the students were forbidden
to attend the meetings of this church; and it was
partly for once disobeying this prohibition, in order to
hear the Rev. Gilbert Tennent, that David Brainerd
was expelled from the college.

Nor were the sentiments I uttered new in this place.
Nearly 60 years have rolled away since Jonathan Edwards the younger preached here a sermon, afterwards
published by *request,* on the injustice and impolicy of
the slave-trade and slavery,—a sermon which in these

days would be called by many not merely abolitionism but incendiarism.

On Monday morning we were taken to see the cemetery, outside of the city. Formerly the Green was used as a burying-ground; but in the latter part of last century this field of ten acres was levelled and inclosed for the purpose; and in 1821 the monuments, with the exception of the humble stones of the three judges, were removed hither. The broken tablets and half-legible inscriptions, which constituted the memorials of the fathers and founders of this colony, were peculiarly interesting. On the 18th of April, 1638, those men kept their first Sabbath here. The people assembled under a large spreading oak, and Mr. Davenport, their pastor, preached to them from Matt. iv. 1: "Then was Jesus led up of the Spirit into the wilderness to be tempted of the devil." His subject was the temptations of the wilderness; and he recorded the remark, that he had enjoyed "a good day." The following year they met in a large barn, and in a very solemn manner proceeded to lay the foundation of their civil and religious polity. Mr. Davenport introduced the business with a sermon on "Wisdom hath builded her house; she hath hewn out her seven pillars." The most ancient record of this event is a curiosity in the history of civil government. It thus begins:—"The 4th day of the 6th moneth, called June, all the free planters assembled together in a general meetinge, to consult about settling civil government according to God, and about the nomination of persons that may be found by consent of all fittest in all respects for the foundation work of a church, which was to be gathered in Quinipiack [the Indian name of the place]. After sollemne invocation of the name of God in prayer," &c., they resolved—Alas! for that resolve! it admitted a wrong principle, and was productive, for more than 150 years, of the most withering and blighting effect upon that religion which they aimed to foster—they resolved among other things, "That church members only shall be free burgesses; and that they only shall chuse magistrates and officers among themselves, to have the power of transacting all publique civil affairs of this plantation," &c.

But why record their errors while standing over their tombs? *De mortuis nil nisi bonum.* Take them for all in all, they were men whom we delight to honour. Here are some of their memorials, dated so far back as 1657. Here too is the resting-place of Dr. Dwight.

As we return from this necropolis, the Rev. Mr. Sawyer points out to us the house of Professor Gibbs. "Gibbs—Gibbs," said I; "what! Gibbs's Gesenius?" "Yes," said he. "I should like to see him," I replied, "for I used at college his editions of Gesenius's Hebrew Lexicon." "Let us then call by all means," said Mr. Sawyer. We did so; and a thin, spare, sallow, sickly, withered, little old gentleman made his appearance. This was the Professor. He seemed as if all the juice and sap of his constitution had been pressed out to nourish the Hebrew roots. I expressed my pleasure in seeing him, and acknowledged the advantages I had derived from his labours. The conversation soon touched upon the Established Church of England, of which he seemed to have a great horror. "You ought to put down," said he, "that Establishment. You might very easily do it." "We should be very happy, sir, to know how," I replied. "I will tell you. Make thorough Hebrew scholars of your ministers. Let them be with regard to Biblical learning quite on a par with those of the Establishment, and it will soon fall." I answered, that upon the whole I thought they were in that respect quite in advance of those of the Establishment. But I was amused at the good Professor's simplicity. He little understood the mighty bulwarks by which that institution is defended. A little more of the article in which *he* dealt would be just the thing to accomplish wonders! It was his nostrum.

To-day the annual election of the State of Connecticut is held. All the officers of state are to be chosen, and New Haven is one of the principal polling-places. But how quiet the town! The only thing that indicates an election is the presence of a larger number of people than usual; and the only display you can see is that little bit of a flag, about 18 inches square, stuck on the top of a cab, having on the word "Democracy!" Let us go into the State House, and see how it is done. Men leave their stores or their studies,—enter by one door, drop their vote into a box,

and quietly return to their avocations. The students
at Yale who are 21 years of age do the same, and go
back to their exercises. The whole affair is managed
with as much propriety as the election of deacons in
the church at New Amsterdam. *This* is the working
of universal suffrage in New England. Oh that all
America, and all the world, were in this respect like
the land of the Pilgrim Fathers!

And now we must bid adieu to New Haven. Many
are the warm hearts and clear heads it contains. The
population is about 18,000. There are in it—

5 Congregational Churches, and 1 Coloured ditto.
2 Episcopal ditto   .   .   1   „
2 Methodist Episcopal ditto   1   „
2 Baptist ditto.
1 Primitive Methodist ditto.   1 Bethel ditto.
1 Catholic ditto.   —
———   4
13 + 4 = 17 total of places of worship.

		DOLLARS.
The Salary of the Governor of Connecticut is	.	1,100
„ Lieutenant „ .	.	300
„ Rev. Dr. Bacon . .	.	1,500
„ Rev. Mr. Dutton . .	.	1,250

In the middle of the day, we leave by railway for
Hartford, 36 miles off. Dr. Hawes is our fellow-traveller. Coloured people are here allowed to travel in
the same carriages with others. It was not so, even
on this line, three or four years ago, when the Rev.
Mr. Pennington was setting off from Hartford for England. He told me himself that he was obliged on that
occasion to travel in the luggage-van. On our arri-

val, we are met by Charles Hosmer, Esq., (a cousin of Elihu Burritt,) an old and valued correspondent of mine, and of my predecessor Mr. Wray. To both of us he had occasionally sent presents of excellent American publications. We must be his guests during the few days we remain at Hartford. Dr. Hawes and Chief Justice Williams came in a homely way to spend the evening with us. The Chief Justice is a deacon of the Doctor's church, and a teacher in the Sabbath-school.

The next day we were taken to see the Deaf and Dumb Institution. This asylum was founded by the Rev. Mr. Gallaudet, who, becoming deeply interested in this class of afflicted humanity, visited England and the Continent with a view to obtain information as to the best mode of communicating instruction to them. I may also observe that he himself married a deaf and dumb lady, by whom he has a large family of children, now grown up, none of whom however inherit the maternal affliction. His son also has married a lady who, like his mother, is deaf and dumb. We were highly delighted with the success of the undertaking as seen in the comfort, cheerfulness, and proficiency of the pupils. In coming out, we met at the door a respectable well-dressed man and a woman, both of them deaf and dumb, who had formerly been pupils here, had formed an attachment to each other, married, settled comfortably in life, and were now coming to pay a visit to their former home.

On our return we saw the celebrated Charter Oak.

The early settlers of this place had obtained from the second Charles, and that in the very year in which 2,000 ministers were ejected from the Church of England, a most favourable charter—far more so than the Colonial Office in the present day would grant. Charles, however, repented having granted it, and in 1687 sent over Sir Edmund Andross, under some pretence or other, to demand it back. It was night, and the Legislative Assembly were convened on the subject, when suddenly the lights were extinguished, and the charter was missing. For a long time it was not known, except to the initiated, what had become of it. When, however, the danger was past, the Charter was forthcoming. It had been concealed in the hollow of this old oak, which still survives. I was gratified in seeing the document carefully preserved in the office of the Secretary of State. It is dated 1662, and "in the fourteenth year of our reign," though in reality Charles had then reigned but two years.

LETTER XXXIII.

The "Retreat"—Introductions to the Insane—Piety and Profanity—Service in the Fourth Church—Memorials of the Pilgrims—Dr. Bushnell and his Opinions—The Mother Church and its Burying-Ground—The New Cemetery—Prejudice against Colour—Mrs. Sigourney—Departure from Hartford—Worcester and Elihu Burritt—Boston—The Rev. Seth Bliss—The Cradle of Liberty—Mr. Garrison—Bunker's Hill.

HAVING seen the Charter Oak, let us proceed in company with the Rev. Mr. Gallaudet to the "Retreat for the Insane," of which he is chaplain. The place is delightfully situated, and severity of treatment carefully avoided. As we pass from room to room, we are very gravely and formally introduced, as strangers in the country, to the inmates Here we are introduced to a tall muscular old lady, who has her cap fantastically trimmed with bits of ribbon of various gaudy colours. With an air of assumed politeness and dignity, she asks me if I have been to Washington. On receiving a reply in the negative, she expresses great regret, and inquires if I have seen "Dan Webster," and, without waiting for an answer, hurries on, "Fine fellow Dan,—some solid timbers about Dan,—indeed, the Yankees altogether are not to be sniffed at." I nodded the most entire assent to all she said.

We enter another room, and are introduced to a curious groupe. One woman has tied her mouth up with a handkerchief, to prevent her talking too much. She tells us that at first she had tied it over her ears, to prevent her hearing another woman's voice, who is constantly talking to herself, and making her head ache; but that she found her own tongue then going faster than anybody else's. She had therefore adopted the *wise* plan of tying her own mouth. She is eloquent in the praises of the institution, and calls it "A blessed Retreat—a blessed Retreat."

We move on, and are introduced to a fine-looking woman—the wife of a respectable merchant in New York. She looks wild, and shakes her head violently. She pours upon us a flood of questions, most of which relate to her own husband, such as—When did we see him last?—How was he?—What message did he send to her? &c. Turning to my wife, she said, " You had better have staid at home, and never come to this country. This country *was* once a great country: it is so no longer, and all through that man,"—pointing to Mr. Gallaudet. " Oh that man! what a villain he is! People out of doors don't know him; and," looking at myself, "you can't do this country better service than to make known everywhere the real character of that man. Here he keeps me a prisoner in this place for nothing at all; but I hope the State will take up the matter, and punish him well for it." I promised to make known Mr. Gallaudet's character, and bade her adieu.

We are next introduced to a student of theology, who asks very sensible and pious questions in reference to the missionary cause and the progress of the Gospel in British Guiana. This man is perfectly sane except on one point. He thinks there is a conspiracy to poison him, and that slow poison is administered to him continually in his food. Mr. Gallaudet, even by dining at the same table and eating out of the same dish, has failed to convince him to the contrary.

Now we are taken to the chapel in which Mr. Gallaudet officiates among them. On the desk is an elegantly-bound Bible, which has been presented by a former patient, who had experienced in his restoration the value of this "Retreat." The hymn-book is a collection made on purpose for the insane, everything gloomy and terrific being excluded. Mr. Gallaudet, a most intelligent and accomplished man, describes many remarkable developments of human nature which have come under his observation, comprising strange combinations of piety and profanity in the same persons. A patient, who was really a very religious man, in enumerating the many advantages they there enjoyed said, "We have a good house to live in; good rooms to occupy; good food to eat; a good doctor to attend us; a good chaplain to give us religious instruction; and" (waxing warm) "what the devil do we want more?"

In the afternoon we meet with Dr. Hawes, at the house of Chief Justice Williams to tea.

In the evening there is a united service in the "Fourth Church"—that of which Dr. Patton's son is minister,—to hear from me an address on the subject of

N 5

missions.   After which Dr. Bushnell puts to me pub-
licly some very close and intelligent questions with
regard to the working of freedom in our West India
Colonies.   He is evidently anxious to elicit from me
that kind of information which would enable them to
contradict the statements of the pro-slavery party.
Young Patton is also an anti-slavery man, and will not
tolerate the distinction of colour in his own church.

The next day Mr. Gallaudet and Mr. Patton call and
accompany us to the Historical Room.   There we see
carefully kept an old chest that had come over in
the "May Flower," and also the three-legged pot in
which the "Pilgrims" had first boiled their food
after landing on Plymouth Rock.   These and many
other memorials of the "Fathers" we are happy to find
are very piously preserved.   Then we go to a Gallery
of Pictures.   The admission fee is 25 cents, or one
shilling; but from us, being strangers, they will accept
of nothing!   In the collection there was much to admire; but I could not help regretting that the canvas
was made to preserve the memory of so many conflicts
between England and her Transatlantic sons.

We dined at Dr. Bushnell's house.   The Doctor is
a very unassuming man, and a very original but somewhat eccentric thinker.   He had lately published a
sermon on Roads, a sermon on the Moral Uses of the
Sea, a sermon on Stormy Sabbaths, and a sermon on
Unconscious Influence,—all treated in a very striking
manner.   He had recently visited England and the
continent of Europe, and had also contributed an

article to the *New Englander*, a quarterly review, on the Evangelical Alliance. The views of a keen thinker from another land on that and kindred topics deserve to be pondered. "The Church of God in England," says the Doctor, "can never be settled upon any proper basis, whether of truth or of practical harmony, until the Established Church, as such, is separated from the State." His estimate of "a large class of English Christians" is not very flattering. "They are good men, but not thinking men. Their piety gurgles in a warm flood through their heart, but it has not yet mounted to their head. * * * In the ordinary, *i. e.* in their preaching and piety, they show a style of goodishness fitly represented by Henry's Commentary; in the extraordinary, they rise into sublimity by inflation and the swell of the occasion." Towards slavery and slaveholders he manifests a tenderness of feeling at which we are surprised and pained. The proposed exclusion of slaveholders from the Alliance he characterizes as "absurd and fanatical," speaking of the subject as having been "so unhandsomely forced upon" the American brethren in London. Again, "There is too much good sense among the Christians of this country (America) to think of constituting an Alliance on the basis which denies Christian character to all slaveholders. At a future time, when slavery has been discussed long enough, we shall do so. We cannot do it now,—least of all can we do it at the dictation of brethren beyond the sea, who do not understand the question," &c.

And yet in the same article the Doctor proposes that

the Christians of England and America should unite
their efforts for the promotion of religious liberty in
Italy, and says, " If we lift our testimony against all
church dungeons and tortures, and against all suppres-
sion of argument by penalties, as cruel, absurd, anti-
christian, and impious, there is no prince or priesthood
in Italy or anywhere else that can long venture to per-
petrate such enormities." Will they yield, Doctor, to the
"dictation of brethren beyond the sea ?" But this subject of American slavery is always represented by our
Transatlantic friends as a thing so *profound* that none
but themselves can understand it ; and yet it is evident
that they understand it least of all. Hear the Doctor :—

" We do not propose, however, in this movement for
religious liberty, to invite the efforts of our English
brethren here against slavery. We have too little confidence in their knowledge of our condition, and the
correctness of their opinions generally on the subject of
American slavery. They must consent to let us manage the question in our own way," &c. How strikingly
is it here seen that this slavery is the weak point and
the wicked point in the American character ! We liked
Dr. Bushnell's company, his hospitality, his wife, his
children, his domestic discipline, his church, his other
writings,—everything better than the article in question,
though even it contained much that we admired.

The next day we went to see the " First Congregational Church" in this place—that in which Dr. Hawes
ministers, together with the old burying-ground attached to it. This was the original church formed by

the first settlers, who in 1636 came from Braintree in Essex, bringing their pastor the Rev. Thos. Hooker along with them. Of him it is said, that he appeared in the pulpit with such dignity and independence as if "while engaged in his Master's work he could put a king in his pocket." Here is his tomb, dated 1647. Two eventful centuries have rolled away, during which this church has had only nine pastors; all of whom, except the last, Dr. Hawes, who still survives, died in their charge, and were interred in this place. Interments here are no longer continued; but an old bachelor, of independent means, a descendant of the Pilgrims, spends nearly the whole of his time "among the tombs" of the fathers and prophets, and, *con amore*, keeps the ground and the graves in the most beautiful order.

Our host Mr. Hosmer took us to see the new burying-ground outside of the city. Here the Catholics and the coloured people had each a parcel of ground allotted for themselves,—the former because they *would* not, and the latter because they *should* not, mingle their dust with that of other people!

On our way back I said to my friend, "How was it that neither Mr. Pennington nor any of his people (coloured congregation) were at the meeting last night? I should have thought they would have come to hear about their own brethren in Guiana." "Why," he replied, "the fact was I did not send a notice to them on Sunday: I knew that in the 'Fourth' Church they would have been scattered all over the place; it would

have been so unpleasant, and talked of for months."
Here then was a man of a large heart, a friend of missions and of all that is good, one who seemed as if he
could embrace the whole world in his sympathies,
under the dominion of a prejudice you would have
expected him to scorn!

At Hartford lives Mrs. Sigourney, the graceful
American poetess. She is a pious member of one of
the Congregational Churches. Mr. Hosmer kindly took
us to call upon her; and we were greatly pleased with
our brief visit.

At 2 P.M. we left with regret this delightful little
city, and shall always cherish a grateful remembrance
of the Christian kindness and hospitality with which we
were treated. In all the States we met with nothing to
be compared, in all that was pleasing, to the two cities
of Connecticut—New Haven and Hartford.

In passing, on our way to Boston, through Worcester
in Massachusetts, I cast a hurried glance at every place
that looked like a smithy, wondering whether it was
there that Elihu Burritt had wielded his forge-hammer
and scattered his "sparks from the anvil."

We reached Boston at 9 P.M., and stopped at the
United States Hotel. The next day I called to deliver
notes of introduction to several of the Boston divines.
Among them was one to the Rev. Seth Bliss, at the
Tract Depository. Having glanced at the note, he
very hurriedly said to me, "Ah, how do you do?—
very glad to see you!—where are you stopping at?"—
"At the United States Hotel, sir." "Oh," he replied

all in a breath, "you had better come to my house,—
it'll be cheaper for you,—they'll charge you 2 dollars a
day at the United States Hotel,—I only charge a dollar
and a half,—I have a room at liberty now. Besides, if
you want to get acquainted with ministers, you can't
do better than come to my house. In fact, the wags
call my house the 'Saints' Rest,'—because, I suppose,
they see I sell the book here." The conjuncture of
"Bliss" and "Saints' Rest!" Who could refuse? We
went. But I will not tell how far the accommodation
tended to realize our conceptions of those beatitudes.

On the morrow we went to see Faneuil Hall, the
"Cradle of Liberty." A notice was up at the door to
say the key was to be found at such a store in the
neighbourhood. I asked for the key; had it without
a single question being put; went, opened the door
myself, and staid as long as we pleased. There was
no hanger-on, to try to squeeze a fee out of us, as
would have been the case in a country I know.

I then went and called without any introduction
upon William Lloyd Garrison, from whom I received
the most kind attentions. He accompanied me to the
celebrated Bunker's Hill, a scene of dreadful encounter
between those who ought never to have been foes. A
column of 200 feet high now stands upon the spot.
It is unfortunate that the Americans have so many
mementos, both natural and artificial, of their struggles with us. They tend to perpetuate an undesirable
feeling.

LETTER XXXIV.

Boston (continued)—The Old South—Unitarianism, and Connection between Church and State—A Welsh Service in an "Upper Room" —Laura Bridgman and the Wedding Ring—Oliver Caswell—Departure from Boston—John Todd and his Family—His Congregationalism — Albany and the Delevan House — Journey to Utica — Remsen and the Welsh People—Dogs made to churn, and Horses to saw Wood.

On Sabbath morning the 11th of April I preached for the Rev. Mr. Blagden, in the Old South Church. This is a large old-fashioned square building, having two galleries, one above the other, on three of its sides. It is rich in historical recollections. Here Whitfield preached. Here patriotic meetings were held even before Faneuil Hall was built; and here the British troops were quartered at the time of the Revolutionary War. Here, too, the lamp of truth was kept feebly burning when all around had sunk into darkness and heresy. At the commencement of this century, the ministry in all the other Congregational Churches in Boston had become Unitarian. In the Old South, however, there were a few people, eight in number, who formed a "Society for Religious Improvement." They could not at first *pray* together; they only read the Scriptures and conversed on religious subjects. But they grew in wisdom, fervour, and zeal, and were eventually the means, not only of reviving religion in the Old South, but also of giving an impulse in Boston which is felt to this day. Church after church on orthodox principles has been instituted, till there are in Boston more than a dozen large and vigorous churches of the Congregational order; and the Old South, the honoured "mother of churches," has had her "youth renewed like the eagles."

But how came Congregationalism to be so deteriorated? It was owing to its having been made the State religion. All were at first taxed for its exclusive support. This was felt to be unjust and oppressive, and it brought the favoured system into bad repute. Then a modification of the law was adopted, and the citizens had their choice of systems, but were taxed for the support of some system or other. This provision, likewise, began ere long to be felt as unjust towards those who did not wish to maintain *any* system, or at least not by taxation. This law, moreover, gave a virtual support to Unitarianism. "This," says the Rev. Mr. Dutton of New Haven, "has been more fully illustrated in Massachusetts than in Connecticut. The repeal of the law for the compulsory support of religion in that commonwealth has proved a severe blow to Unitarianism."

After the morning service at the Old South, we turned in to see Park-street Church, another Congregational place of worship, which for the following reason I was curious to enter. A few years ago a coloured gentleman of respectability instructed a friend to purchase for him a pew in that church. That no objection to the sale might arise from any neglect of decorations, the new proprietor had it beautifully lined and cushioned. It was made to look as handsome as any other pew in the church ; and, when it was finished, the gentleman and his family one Sabbath morning took possession. This gave rise to great anxiety and alarm. Niggers in the body of the church! What was to be done ? In the course of the following week a meeting was held, and a deputation appointed to wait upon the gentleman, and to tell him that it was against " public feeling" for him to occupy the pew in question. The gentleman remonstrated, and pointed out the injustice, after he had purchased the pew, and incurred the expense of fitting it up, of not being allowed to enjoy it. To this the deputation replied that they were sorry for any inconvenience or loss he might sustain, but public feeling *must* be respected, and the pew *must* be given up. Against this decision there was no appeal ; and the gentleman was obliged to let the pew be resold for such a price as the white aristocracy thought fit to give. On the principle that " prevention is better than cure," they have, I am told, in Boston introduced into every new trust-deed a clause that will effectually guard against the recurrence of such a calamity. But so " smartly" has it been done that, were you to examine those deeds, you would look in vain for a single syllable having the remotest apparent bearing on either black or coloured people, and you would be ready to suspect that the whole was a mere invention of the Abolitionists. Indeed, Mrs. " Bliss," at the " Saints'

Rest," assured me in the most positive manner that
such was the case, and that the whole of the story
I have related had not the shadow of a foundation in
truth. But she might as well have attempted to deny
the existence of Bunker's Hill or Boston Bay. This
was only a specimen of the manner in which the colour-
hating party attempt to throw dust in the eyes of
strangers, and deny the existence of the most palpable
facts. But how runs the conservative clause which led
to this digression? It is expressed in words to this
effect,—That no sale of any pew is valid if two-thirds
or three-fourths (I forget which) of the congregation
should object to the purchaser! This was quite enough.
Those against whom it was directed need not be even
mentioned. It was well known that with this clause
no coloured man could ever own a pew. Public feeling
would piously take hold of this key, and turn it against
him.

In the afternoon I heard the Rev. E. N. Kirk. The
church was new and beautiful, the congregation large,
and the sermon good.

In the evening I preached in Welsh to about 70
people, in a small "upper room." It was my first
attempt for many years to deliver a *sermon* in that
language. Nor should I have made it, but for the
peculiarity of the case. The parties were representatives of four different denominations in Wales, had
formed themselves into a kind of Evangelical Alliance,
and had no stated minister, but gladly availed themselves of the occasional services of any minister of

evangelical views who might be passing through ! Poor and few as they were, they insisted upon my receiving towards travelling expenses four dollars and a half. This was not done at the Old South, though the pastor told me they were "burdened with wealth;" nor was it done in any other instance in the *American* churches.

The next day the Rev. Mr. Blagden accompanied us to see the Massachusetts Asylum for the Blind.   Here we were introduced to Laura Bridgman, who since she was about two years of age has been deaf, dumb, and blind.   Her senses of taste and smell are also impaired. She is 18 years of age, and has been in the institution ten years.   Every avenue of communication with the soul was closed—but one.   The sense of touch remained ; and by means of that they have contrived to reach the mind, to inform it, to instruct it, to refine and elevate it.   We found her exactly corresponding to the beautiful description given of her by Dr. Howe, who is at the head of the institution.   That description has so often been published in England that I will not transcribe it.   Her figure is genteel, slender, and well-proportioned.   She appears to be lively, sensitive, and benevolent.   The place where the bright blue eyes once sparkled that are now quenched in darkness is covered with a piece of green ribbon.   Conversation with her is carried on by means of the " speaker's" rapid fingering on her right hand.   It was in this manner that we were introduced.   She shook hands with us very affectionately,—taking hold of both hands of Mrs. Davies, and feeling all about her head, her dress, and her arms. In doing so she felt the wedding-ring, and wanted to know by means of her interpreter—her governess—why the English ladies wore a ring on that finger. (The American ladies do not observe the custom.) On my wife telling her it was to show they were married, she seemed very much amused and astonished. Here it was very interesting to observe the progress of a thought from ourselves to the governess, and from her to that "little, white, whispering, loving, listening" hand that received and communicated all ideas, until the brightened countenance and the lovely smile showed it had reached the soul. She felt a deep sympathy for Ireland, and wished to know what the English were doing for the starving inhabitants. We told her; and soon after we saw by the public papers that, subsequently to our visit, she had done some needle-work, which was sold, and the proceeds appropriated at her request to purchase a barrel of flour for that unhappy land. "How," exclaims Elihu Burritt, "she plied at morning, noon, and night, those fingers! wonderful fingers! It seemed that the very finger of God had touched them with miraculous susceptibilities of fellowship with the spirit world and that around her. She put them upon the face of His written word, and felt them thrilled to her heart with the pulsation of His great thoughts of love to man. And then she *felt* for other's woe. Poor child! God bless her richly! She reached out her short arms to feel after some more unhappy than she in the condition of this life; some whose fingers' ends had not

read such sweet paragraphs of heaven's mercy as her's
had done; some who had not seen, heard, and felt
what her dumb, silent, deaf fingers had brought into
her heart of joy, hope, and love. Think of that, ye
young eyes and ears that daily feast upon the beauty
and melody of this outer world! Within the atmosphere of her quick sensibilities, she felt the presence of
those whose cup was full of affliction. She put her
fingers, with their throbbing sympathies, upon the lean
bloodless faces of the famishing children in Ireland,
and her sightless eyes filled with the tears that the
blind may shed for griefs they cannot see. And then
she plied the needle and those fingers, and quickened
their industry by placing them anon upon the slow
sickly pulse of want that wasted her kind at noonday
across the ocean. Days, and nights too—for day and
night were alike to her wakeful sympathies—and
weeks she wrought on with her needle. And then the
embroidery of those fingers was sold to the merchants.
Would it had been sold to England's Queen, to be
worn by the young princesses on days of state! It was
sold; and its purchase price was *a barrel of flour*,
instead of a country's harvest, which it was well worth.
And that barrel of flour was stowed away without other
private mark than that the recording Angel put upon
it, among the thousands that freighted the *Jamestown*
on her recent mission of brotherly love to Ireland.
Laura Bridgman and her barrel of flour should teach
the world a lesson worth the woes of one year's
famine." Laura favoured us with her autograph on

a slip of paper, which we shall always carefully preserve as a memorial of a visit to one of the greatest
wonders of the age.

In another room we were introduced to Oliver Caswell. He is about the same age as Laura, and similarly
afflicted, but has been in the institution only six years.
His teacher told him, in the same finger-language
which was used with Laura, that we came from British
Guiana, and desired him to find out the place on the
large globe before him. This globe was made for the
use of the blind, having upon it the countries and their
names in relievo. Oliver turned it round, and felt
with his fingers until they soon rested on the required
spot, when he seemed greatly delighted. His attainments are not so remarkable as those of Laura, for he
has not been so long under tuition; but his progress is
highly encouraging.

At 4 p.m. we left Boston by railway for Albany,—fare
5 dollars each. We rested, however, at Springfield for
the night, and that in the most comfortable hotel we
had met with in the States. The next day we moved
on to Pittsfield, where we arrived at half-past 11.
Finding that we might get off from that train, and go
by another in three or four hours' time, we availed
ourselves of the opportunity of calling upon the Rev.
Dr. Todd, the author of " Lectures to Children,"
" The Student's Guide," &c. Instead of the prim,
neat, little man we had always imagined him to be,
we found him tall, coarse, slovenly, and unshaven ; a
man of 46 years of age; hair of an iron-grey, rough

and uncombed; features large; cheek-bones prominent; and the straps of his trowsers unbuttoned, and flapping about his slippers. But, under this unpromising exterior, we discerned a soul of great intelligence, frankness, and brotherly kindness. Mrs. Todd has been a woman of great beauty, and, though she has brought up a large family of children, is still fresh and comely. Their eldest daughter is 19 years of age; and John, to whom the "Lectures to Children" were dedicated, is now 14 years of age. The Doctor's insane mother, for whose sake he was first led to employ his pen, has been dead for some years. His desire to visit England is very strong. He had been appointed by the churches of Massachusetts to visit those of England last year in the character of a delegate; but the means of meeting the expenses of such a delegation were not provided, and consequently the visit was not paid. It is worthy of observation that the Doctor's books have been sold in England far more extensively than in America; but from the English editions he receives no profit, and even from the American ones very little. As it may be the first time that English readers hear of John Todd as *Doctor* Todd, and as there is an impression that our American friends bestow their literary honours too freely and indiscriminately,—which, indeed, is true in reference to some scores of institutions,—nothing being easier than to obtain a D. D.,—I would just observe that this applies not to the New England Colleges. They are very chary of such honours, and only confer that of D. D. on ministers of long standing and high attainments. In the case of Mr. Todd it was most deservedly bestowed.

Pittsfield is but a small town, of about 5,000 inhabitants. The Governor of Massachusetts resided there, and was a deacon of a Baptist Church. Dr. Todd presides over a Congregational Church. To the principles of Congregationalism he is devoutly attached. While others regard Presbyterianism and Congregationalism as matters of mere geographical boundary, Todd could never be prevailed upon, even by the most advantageous offers, to do the same. He said he had nailed his flag to the mast, and would never abandon it. " I regard Congregationalism," said he to me, "as a sort of a working-jacket : with it on I can work with anybody, in any place, and in any way." With this great and good man we exceedingly enjoyed a homely dinner and a few hours' converse. In coming out, I observed before the door, half-covered with snow, a beautiful model of the Temple of Theseus. This was the work of the Doctor's own hands.

At 3½ P.M. we left for Albany. At the station, before crossing the Hudson, we observed in large letters the ominous words "Beware of pickpockets !" On reaching the city we went to the "Delevan House," so called after Mr. Delevan, who has done so much for the advancement of temperance in America. The house is his property, but he does not conduct it. He lives there as a lodger; and I was permitted to spend the evening in conversation with him. The house is the largest temperance hotel in the world. It will accommodate about 400 guests. Those who keep it are religious people, and have a public family-worship every evening, usually conducted by the master of the house; but if a minister of any denomination be present, he is asked to officiate. A bell is rung, and all who feel disposed to unite in the worship assemble in a large room. On this occasion it was my privilege to conduct the service; and in such a place, and under such circumstances, it was to me an exercise of peculiar interest. A hymn too was sung, and well sung,—the tune being led by the master of the house, aided by his family.

The next morning, at half-past 7, we set off by railway to Utica, a distance of 94 miles, which we did not accomplish in less than $6\frac{1}{2}$ hours, making an average of less than 15 miles an hour, and for which we paid $2\frac{1}{2}$ dollars, or 10s. 6d. This journey led us through the valley of the Mohawk, and that river was for the most part our constant companion. The railway and the river seemed to be wedded to each other,—the former conforming to all the whims and windings, and turnings and twistings of the latter.

Utica is a small city, of about 14,000 inhabitants. Its progress has been but slow. The houses are painted white, and appear neat and comfortable. I was struck with the immense number of them that were erected with their gable end to the street, and with a small portico supported by two fluted columns. A large portion of the inhabitants are Welsh, who have here four or five places of worship. The Rev. James Griffiths, a man of great piety and worth, is the minister of the Welsh Independents. At his house we were most kindly entertained during our stay. On the Sabbath I preached for him twice in Welsh. The following week we were taken to Remsen, eighteen miles off, to see the Rev. Mr. Everett, whose farewell sermon on leaving Wales I had heard when quite a boy,—and the Rev. Morris Roberts, to whom I had bidden adieu in Liverpool sixteen years before. It was delightful to meet these honoured brethren in their adopted home, after the lapse of so many years. Remsen is quite a Welsh settlement; and these men both preside over Welsh churches there. Mr. Everett is the editor of a Welsh Monthly Magazine. In that periodical, as well as in his ministrations, he has been unflinching in his denunciations of slavery. This has exposed him to cruel persecutions. There are about 70,000 Welsh people in the United States who worship in their own language. At Remsen I had to deliver two addresses on the results of emancipation in the West Indies. On our return to Utica, the friend who drove us happened incidentally to mention that in that country they make the dogs churn! " The dogs churn !" I said, " Yes," said he ; " and I dare say they have a churning-machine so worked at this house : let us call and see." It was a farm-house. At the door about half-a-dozen chubby little children, with fine rosy cheeks, were assembled to see the strangers. I began to speak in English to the eldest, a boy about 10 years of age ; but the lad stared ! He understood not a word I said.

Though born and so far brought up there, he knew nothing but Welsh! We were gratified with an inspection of the machine for churning. It was worked very much on the same principle as a treadmill, and exceedingly disliked by the poor dog. Goats are sometimes made to perform the same service. In several instances, we saw horses in like manner made to saw wood, and admired the ingenuity of our cousins in turning to account every particle of power they possess. "What is the difference," said Dr. Beecher once to a ship-captain, "between an English sailor and a Yankee one?" The answer was, "An English sailor can do a thing very well in *one* way, but the Yankee can do it in half-a-dozen ways."

LETTER XXXV.

A Peep at the House of Representatives in Albany—"The Chair is but a Man," &c.—Sailing down the Hudson—Dr. Spring—His Morning Sermon — Afternoon Service — Gough the great Lecturer — The Tract House and Steam-presses—May-day in New York—Staten Island—Immigrants—A hurried Glance.

On the 22nd we left Utica at 11 A.M., and reached Albany at 5 P.M. At Schnectady Mr. Delevan got into the same carriage with us; and we had his company to Albany. He had caused to be put into the hand of every passenger by that train a tract on the claims of the Sabbath, a large number of which he had printed at his own expense. He spends an immense fortune in doing good, chiefly by means of the press.

In the evening I strolled out to see a little of Albany, the capital of the State of New York. I gazed with interest on Dr. Sprague's Church, and wandered until I came to a large building brilliantly lighted. It was the State House or Capitol. The legislature was then in session. I marched on, and got in without the least hinderance. There was no crowd and no stir about the doors. A simple rail divided the part allotted to the spectators from that which was used by the members. About a hundred of the latter were present. The Senate, whose hall was in another part of the same building, had been adjourned till next day. This was the House of Representatives; and they seemed to be in the midst of a very angry discussion. Their cheeks swelled with rage, or with—quids of tobacco. A spittoon, constantly used, was placed by the side of each member. They were rebelling against the speaker; and, of all mortals, I never saw one in a more unenviable position than he. All that his little hammer, his tongue, and his hands could do was of no avail. The storm raged. The words "honourable member," "unparliamentary," "order," "chair," and "*in*-quiry," were bandied about in all directions. One of the "honourable members," rushing out past me, said with a loud voice, "I'll go and get a segar," &c. At last the speaker—poor fellow!—in tones of humiliation and despair said, "The *chair* is but a *man*; and, if we err, we are ready to acknowledge our error."

The next day we left by the steam-boat "Roger Williams," and sailed down the majestic Hudson to New York, a distance of 145 miles; fare one dollar each. This river has so often been described by travellers that I need not repeat the attempt.

The following day was Saturday. In the afternoon I met Dr. Spring at the Tract House. After the usual salutation, he said, "Shall we hear your voice at our place to-morrow afternoon?"—"I have no objection, sir,—what time does your service commence?" "At 4 o'clock."—"Very well." "Where shall I find you?" —"Where will you be?" "I shall be in the pulpit five minutes before the time."—"Oh! *very* well, *very* well."

In the morning I went to hear the Doctor. His introductory prayer was long. In it he prayed for Mexico—that it might have a "free and religious government," and that the present war might result in the overthrow there of the "man of sin;" but no reference to American slavery. The Doctor, bear in mind, is an Old School Presbyterian, and a supporter of the Colonization Society. His text was John v. 23 : "That all men should honour the Son, even as they honour the Father," &c. His divisions were—

I. What honours are ascribed to the Father.

1. Appropriate names and titles. Jehovah, &c.

2. Ascription of most glorious attributes. Eternal —Immutable—Omnipotent, &c.

3. Great and glorious works. Creation—Preservation — Redemption — Atonement — Regeneration— Justification—Raising the dead—Judging the world —Destroying it — Glory of the righteous — Punishment of the wicked. (All these were supported by appropriate quotations of Scripture.)

4. Duties enjoined in reference to Him. Confidence—Worship, &c.

II. That the same honours are ascribed to the Son. (He went over each of the above particulars, showing from Scripture their application to the Son.)

III. That, therefore, the Son is properly and truly God.

1. We cannot believe the Scriptures would ascribe the same honours to Him as to the Father, if He were not equal to the Father.

2. If He be not truly God, the Scriptures tempt to idolatry.

3. If He be not truly God, the accounts which the Scriptures give of Him are self-contradictory.

4. If He be not truly God, there is no evidence from Scripture that there is a God at all.

This was a massive and compact argument for the Divinity of Christ. It occupied upwards of an hour in the delivery, and was read.

In the afternoon I took care to be in the pulpit five minutes before the time. The Doctor shortly after came, and took his seat behind me. This to me is always an annoyance,—I would almost as soon have a man with me in bed as in the pulpit;—and in this instance it was peculiarly so, as towards the close, although I had not exceeded forty minutes, I felt quite . persuaded that the Doctor was pulling at my coat-tail, which led me rather abruptly to conclude. In this, however, I was mistaken; and the Doctor assured me it was what he had never done in his life, except in one instance,—and that was when the preacher, having occupied two hours with his sermon, was entering upon a third.

In the evening of the 27th of April I heard, at the Tabernacle, New York, the celebrated Gough deliver a lecture on Temperance. It was to commence at 8 o'clock; but we had to be there an hour before the time, in order to get a comfortable place. That hour was a dreary one. The scraping of throats and the spitting were horrible. It seemed as if some hundreds of guttural organs were uttering the awfully guttural sentence, " *Hwch goch dorchog a chwech o berchill cochion.* "

At last Gough made his appearance on the platform. He is a slender young man of three or four and twenty. He told us he had spoken every night except three for the last thirty nights, and was then very weary, but thought " what a privilege it is to live and labour in the present day." He related his own past experience of *delirium tremens,*—how an iron rod in his hand became a snake,—how a many-bladed knife pierced his flesh,—how a great face on the wall grinned at and threatened him ; " and yet," he added, " I *knew* it was a delusion ! "

A temperance man, pointing to Gough, had once observed to another, " What a miserable-looking fellow that is ! " " But," replied the other, " you would not say so, if you saw how he keeps everybody in a roar of laughter at the public-house till 1 or 2 in the morning." " But I *was* miserable," said Gough ; " I *knew* that the parties who courted and flattered me really *despised* me." He told us some humorous tales,—how he used to mortify some of them by claiming acquaintance with them in the street, and in the presence of their respectable friends. He returned scorn for scorn. " Gough," said a man once to him, " you ought to be ashamed of yourself to be always drinking in this manner." " Do I drink at your expense ? "—" No." " Do I owe you anything ? "—" No." " Do I ever ask you to treat me ? "—" No." " Then mind your own business," &c. He introduced this to show that that mode of dealing with the drunkard was not likely to answer the purpose.

"Six years ago," said he, "a man on the borders of Connecticut, sat night after night on a stool in a low tavern to scrape an old fiddle. Had you seen him, with his old hat drawn over his eyebrows, his swollen lips, and his silly grin, you would have thought him adapted for nothing else. But he signed the pledge, and in two years became a United States senator, and thrilled the House with his eloquence."

In one place, after Gough had delivered a lecture, some ladies gathered around him, and one of them said, "I wish you would ask Joe to sign the pledge,"— referring to a wretched-looking young man that was sauntering near the door. Gough went up to him, spoke *kindly* to him, and got him to sign : the ladies were delighted, and heartily shook hands with Joe. A year after Gough met Joe quite a dandy, walking arm-in-arm with a fine young lady. "Well, Joe, did you stick to the pledge?" said Gough to him. "Yes," said Joe with an exulting smile, "and the lady has stuck to me."

For more than an hour Gough kept the vast audience enchained by his varied and charming talk.

On the 29th I went over the Tract House in New York, and was delighted to see there six steam-presses, —four of which were then at work, pouring forth in rapid succession sheet after sheet impressed with that kind of literature which in my judgment is admirably adapted to meet the wants of this growing country. They were then printing on an average 27,000 publications, including nearly 2,400 of each kind, *per diem!* and employing sixty women in folding and stitching. During the last year they printed 713,000 volumes, and 8,299,000 smaller publications, making a total of 217,499,000 pages, or 58,154,661 pages more than in any previous year! Of the *volumes* issued, I may mention 14,000 sets of four volumes of D'Aubigné's History of the Reformation, 17,000 of Bunyan's Pilgrim, 10,000 of Baxter's Saints' Rest, 9,000 of Doddridge's Rise and Progress, 7,000 of Pike's Persuasives, 13,000 of Alleine's Alarm, and 41,000 of Baxter's Call! The two Secretaries, whose business it is to superintend the publishing department and matters relating to the raising of funds, the Rev. Wm. A. Hallock and the Rev. O. Eastman, are enterprising and plodding men. They told me they were brought up together in the same neighbourhood, and had both worked at the plough till they were 20 years of age!

The 1st of May is the great moving day in New York. Throughout the city one house seems to empty itself into another. Were it to the next door, it might be done with no great inconvenience; but it is not so. Try to walk along the causeway, and you are continually blocked up with tables, chairs, and chests of drawers. Get into an omnibus, and you are beset with fenders, pokers, pans, Dutch ovens, baskets, brushes, &c. Hire a cart, and they charge you double fare.

One day at the water-side, happening to see the steamer for Staten Island about to move off, we stepped on board, and in less than half an hour found ourselves there. The distance is 6 miles, and the island is 18 miles long, 7 miles wide, and 300 feet high. Here are a large hospital for mariners and the quarantine burying-ground. It is also studded with several genteel residences. In 1657 the Indians sold it to the Dutch for 10 shirts, 30 pairs of stockings, 10 guns, 30 bars of lead, 30 lbs. of powder, 12 coats, 2 pieces of duffil, 30 kettles, 30 hatchets, 20 hoes, and one case of knives and awls.

Several emigrant vessels were then in the bay. On our return, we saw with painful interest many of them setting their foot for the first time on the shore of the New World. They were then arriving in New York, chiefly from the United Kingdom, at the rate of one thousand a day. The sight affected me even to tears. It was like a vision of the British Empire crumbling to pieces, and the materials taken to build a new and hostile dominion.

I should draw too largely upon your patience, were I to describe many objects of interest and many scenes of beauty I witnessed in New York and the neighbourhood. The Common Schools; the Croton Water-works, capable of yielding an adequate supply for a million-and-a-half of people; Hoboken, with its sibyl's cave and elysian fields; the spot on which General Hamilton fell in a duel; the Battery and Castle Garden—a covered amphitheatre capable of accommodating 10,000 people; the Park, and the City Hall with its white marble front; Trinity Church; and its wealthy Corporation; Long Island, or Brooklyn, with its delightful cemetery, &c., &c. Suffice it to say that New York has a population of about 400,000; and that it has for that population, without an Established Church, 215 places of worship. Brooklyn has also a population of 60,000, and 30 places of worship.

LETTER XXXVI.

The May Meetings—Dr. Bushnell's Striking Sermon—Two Anti-Slavery
Meetings—A Black Demosthenes—Foreign Evangelical Society—
A New Thing in the New World—The Home-Missionary Society
—Progress and Prospects of the West—Church of Rome—Depar-
ture from New York—What the Author thinks of the Americans.

THE American May Meetings held in New York
do not last a month as in England,—a week suffices.
That week is the second in the month. On the Sabbath preceding, sermons on behalf of many of the
societies are preached in various churches. On the
morning of the Sabbath in question we went to the
Tabernacle, not knowing whom we should hear. To
our surprise and pleasure, my friend Dr. Baird was the
preacher. His text was, "Let thy kingdom come;"
and the object for which he had to plead was the
Foreign Evangelical Society, of which he was the
Secretary. His sermon was exceedingly simple, and
the delivery quite in an off-hand conversational style.
There was no reading.

In the evening we heard Dr. Bushnell preach, on
behalf of the American Home-Missionary Society, at
the "Church of the Pilgrims" in Brooklyn. This is
a fine costly building, named in honour of the Pilgrim
Fathers, and having a fragment of the Plymouth Rock

imbedded in the wall. The sermon was a very ingenious one on Judges xvii. 13 : " Then said Micah,
Now know I that the Lord will do me good, seeing
I have a Levite to my priest." The preacher observed
that Micah lived in the time of the Judges—what
might be called the " emigrant age" of Israel,—that
he was introduced on the stage of history as a thief,—
that he afterwards became in his own way a saint, and
must have a priest. First, he consecrates his own
son; but his son not being a Levite, it was difficult
for so pious a man to be satisfied. Fortunately a young
Levite—a strolling mendicant probably—comes that
way; and he promptly engages the youth to remain
and act the *padre* for him, saying, " Dwell with me,
and be a *father* unto me." Having thus got up a
religion, the thief is content, and his mental troubles
are quieted. Becoming a Romanist before Rome is
founded, he says, " Now know I that the Lord will do
me good, seeing I have a Levite to my priest." Religion to him consisted in a fine silver apparatus of gods,
and a priest in regular succession. In this story of
Micah it was seen that *emigration, or a new settlement
of the social state, involves a tendency to social decline.*
" Our first danger," said the preacher, " is barbarism—
Romanism next."

The tendency to barbarism was illustrated by his-
toric references. The emigration headed by Abraham
soon developed a mass of barbarism,—Lot giving rise to
the Moabites and the Ammonites ; meanwhile, Abraham throwing off upon the world in his son Ishmael

another stock of barbarians—the Arabs,—a name which according to some signifies *Westerners*.　One generation later, and another ferocious race springs from the family of Isaac—the descendants of Esau, or the Edomites.　Then coming down to the time of the Judges we find that violence prevailed, that the roads were destroyed, and that the arts had perished: there was not even a smith left in the land; and they were obliged to go down to the Philistines to get an axe or a mattock sharpened.　Then the preacher came to the great American question itself.　It was often supposed that in New England there had always been an upward tendency.　It was not so.　It had been downward until the "great revival" about the year 1740.　The dangers to which society in the South and "Far West" is now exposed were powerfully described.　The remedies were then pointed out.

"First of all, we must not despair."　"And what next?　We must get rid, if possible, of slavery."　"'We must have peace.'"　Also "Railways and telegraphs."　"Education, too, we must favour and promote."　"Above all, provide a talented and educated body of Christian teachers, and keep them pressing into the wilderness as far as emigration itself can go."　The conclusion of this great sermon was so remarkable that I cannot but give it in the Doctor's own words.

"And now, Jehovah God, thou who, by long ages of watch and discipline, didst make of thy servant Abraham a people, be thou the God also of this great nation. Remember still its holy beginnings, and for the fathers' sakes still cherish and sanctify it. Fill it with thy Light and thy Potent Influence, till the glory of thy Son breaks out on the Western sea as now upon the Eastern, and these uttermost parts, given to Christ for his possession, become the bounds of a new Christian empire, whose name the believing and the good of all people shall hail as a name of hope and blessing."

On the Tuesday I attended two Anti-slavery Meetings in the Tabernacle. The one in the morning was that of Mr. Garrison's party. The chief speakers were Messrs. Garrison, Wendell Phillips, and Frederick Douglass. This party think that the constitution of the United States is so thoroughly pro-slavery that nothing can be done without breaking it up. Another party, at the head of which is Lewis Tappan, think that there are elements in the constitution which may be made to tell powerfully against slavery, and ultimately to effect its overthrow. Both parties mean well; but they unhappily cherish towards each other great bitterness of feeling. Mr. Tappan's party held their meeting in the afternoon. Among the speakers was the Rev. Mr. Patton from Hartford, son of Dr. Patton, who made a very effective speech. The Rev. Samuel Ward also, a black man of great muscular power, and amazing command of language and of himself, astonished and delighted me. I could not but exclaim, " There speaks a black Demosthenes ! " This man, strange to say, is the pastor of a Congregational

church of white people in the State of New York.
As a public speaker he seemed superior to Frederick Douglass. It was pleasing at those anti-slavery
meetings to see how completely intermingled were the
whites and the coloured.

I had been invited in the evening to speak at the
public meeting of the Foreign Evangelical Society,
and to take tea at Dr. Baird's house. While I was
there, Dr. Anderson, one of the Secretaries of the
American Board of Commissioners for Foreign Missions, and Mr. Merwin, called to invite me to address
the public meeting of that society on the Friday. I
promised to do so, if I should not previously have
left for the West Indies. The public meeting of Dr.
Baird's society was held in the Dutch Reformed
Church, Dr. Hutton's, a magnificent Gothic building.
Dr. De Witt took the chair. The attendance was
large and respectable. Dr. Baird, as Secretary, having
recently returned from Europe, where he had conversed
on the subject of his mission with fourteen crowned
heads, read a most interesting report. The writer had
then to address the meeting. After him three other
gentlemen spoke. There was no collection! Strange
to say, that, with all their revivals, our friends in
America seem to be morbidly afraid of doing anything
under the influence of excitement. Hence the addresses on occasions like this are generally stiff and
studied, half-an-hour orations. This feeling prevents
their turning the voluntary principle, in the support
of their religious societies, to so good an account as

they otherwise might. At the close of this meeting, there seemed to be a fine state of feeling for making a collection; and yet no collection was made. This society is one of great value and importance. It is designed to tell in the promotion of evangelical truth on the Catholic countries of Europe and South America. In those countries, it employs a hundred colporteurs in the sale and distribution of religious publications.

The next morning I addressed a breakfast meeting of about 400 people, in a room connected with the Tabernacle. This was a new thing in the New World. It was, moreover, an anti-slavery breakfast, under the presidency of Lewis Tappan. It was charming to see the whites and the coloured so intermingled at this social repast, and that in the very heart of the great metropolis of America.

At 10 the same morning a meeting of the American Tract Society was held at the Tabernacle. I had been engaged to speak on that occasion, but was obliged to go and see about the vessel that was to take us away.

In the evening I was pressed, at half an hour's notice, to speak at the meeting of the American Home-Missionary Society. The Rev. H. W. Beecher of Indianapolis, one of the sons of Dr. Beecher, made a powerful speech on the claims of the West and South-west. In my own address I complimented the Directors on the ground they had recently taken in reference to slavery, and proceeded to say that there was an important sense in which that society should be an anti-slavery society. This elicited the cheers of the few, which were immediately drowned in the hisses of the many. The interruption was but momentary, and I proceeded. The next morning one of the Secretaries endeavoured to persuade me that the hisses were not at myself, but at those who interrupted me with their cheers. I told him his explanation was ingenious and kind; nevertheless I thought I might justly claim the honour of having been hissed for uttering an anti-slavery sentiment at the Tabernacle in New York!

This society has an herculean task to perform; and, in consideration of it, our American friends might well be excused for some years, were it possible, from all foreign operations.

" Westward the star of empire moves."

Ohio welcomed its first permanent settlers in 1788, and now it is occupied by nearly 2,000,000 of people. Michigan obtained its first immigrants but fourteen or fifteen years ago, and now has a population of 300,000. Indiana, admitted into the Union in 1816, has since then received a population of more than half a million, and now numbers nearly a million of inhabitants. Illinois became a State in 1818. From that date its population trebled every ten years till the last census of 1840, and since then has risen from 476,000 to about 900,000. Missouri, which in 1810 had only 20,800 people, has now 600,000, having increased 50 per cent. in six years. Iowa was scarcely heard of a dozen years ago. It is now a State, and about 150,000 people call its land their home. Wisconsin was organized but twelve years ago, and has now a population of not less than 200,000. One portion of its territory, 33 miles by 30, which ten years before was an unbroken wilderness, numbered even in 1846 87,000 inhabitants; and the emigration to the " Far West" is now greater than ever.

A giant is therefore growing up there, who will soon be able and disposed to rule the destinies of the United States. The Church of Rome is straining every nerve to have that giant in her own keeping, and already shouts the song of triumph. Says one of her sanguine sons, " The Church is now firmly established in this country, and persecution will but cause it to thrive. Our countrymen may grieve that it is so; but it is useless for them to kick against the decrees of the Almighty God. They have an open field and fair play for Protestantism. Here she has had free scope, has reigned without a rival, and proved what she could do, and that her best is evil; for the very good she boasts is not hers. A new day is dawning on this chosen land, and the Church is about to assume her rightful position and influence. Ours shall yet become conse-crated ground. *Our hills and valleys shall yet echo to the convent-bell.* The cross shall be planted throughout the length and breadth of our land; and our happy sons and daughters shall drive away fear, shall drive away evil from our borders with the echoes of their matin and vesper hymns. No matter who writes, who declaims, who intrigues, who is alarmed, or what leagues are formed, THIS IS TO BE A CATHOLIC COUNTRY; and from Maine to Georgia, from the broad Atlantic to broader Pacific, the ' clean sacrifice' is to be offered daily for quick and dead." The triumph may be premature; but it conveys a timely warning.

The next day the Anniversary of the Bible Society was held. The Hon. Theodore Frelinghuysen presided. At that meeting I had been requested to speak, but could not. Indeed, we were detained all day on board a vessel by which we expected every hour to sail for Jamaica; though, after all, we had to wait until the following day. On that day, the 14th of May, just at the time the Board of Missions were holding their public meeting, we sailed, and bade adieu to New York and all the delightful engagements of that memorable week.

But, say you, Tell us in a few words what you think of America upon the whole ? I will try to do so. There is a class of things I greatly admire; and there is a class of things I greatly detest. Among the former I may mention—

1. Religious equality — the absence of a State Church.

2. The workings of the voluntary principle in the abundant supply of places of worship, and in the support of religious institutions.

3. General education. With regard to their com-

mon schools, and also to their colleges, they are far in advance of us in England. The existence of universal suffrage has the effect of stimulating educational efforts to a degree which would not otherwise be attained. The more respectable and intelligent of the citizens are made to feel that, with universal suffrage, their dearest institutions are all perilled unless the mass be educated.

As education is the great question of the day, I must not omit to make a few remarks on the Primary Schools of the United States. There is no *national* system of education in America. Congress does not interfere in the matter, except in the "Territories" before they become "States." The States of the Union are so many distinct Republics, and, in the matter of education, as in all their internal affairs, are left entirely to take their own measures. With regard to education, no two States act precisely alike. If we glance at the States of Massachusetts, New York, and Ohio, we shall, however, discover the three great types of what in this respect generally prevails throughout the States.

MASSACHUSETTS. — Scarcely had the "Pilgrims" been half-a-dozen years in their wilderness home before they began to make what they deemed a suitable provision for the instruction of their children. They adopted the same principle in reference to education and religion—that of taxation. A general tax was not imposed; but the people in the various townships were empowered to tax themselves to a certain amount, and to manage the whole affair by means of their own

" select men." But, although this law has continued for 200 years, the people have always done far more than it required. In Boston, for instance, the law demands only 3,000 dollars a year, but not less than 60,000 dollars is raised and applied! So that here we have a noble proof, not so much of the effect of government interference, as of the efficiency of the voluntary principle in providing education for the young. The people of Massachusetts, and indeed of all the New England States, are doubtless the best educated in the world. Not one in a thousand of those born here grows up unable to read and write.

The calumniated "Pilgrims" were thus early attentive to the importance of education; and their system had been in full operation for between thirty and forty years, when, in 1670, Sir William Berkley, Governor of Virginia, the stronghold of the Anglican Church, thus devoutly addressed the " Lords of Plantations in England:"—" I thank God *there are no free schools nor printing,* and I hope we shall not have them these hundred years; for learning has brought *disobedience and heresy and sects* into the world, and printing has divulged them, and libels against the best government. God keep us from both !"

The system of Massachusetts may be regarded as a type of what prevails in the six New England States, except Connecticut, where there is a State fund of upwards of 2,000,000 dollars, yielding an annual dividend of about 120,000 dollars for school purposes.

NEW YORK.—In this State a large fund for schools

has been created by the sale of public land.   The proceeds of this fund are annually distributed in such a way as to secure the raising by local efforts of at least three times the amount for the same object. This fund is thus used as a gentle stimulant to local exertions.   The system described will convey a notion of what exists in the *middle* States.

OHIO.—In this and the Western States every township is divided into so many sections of a mile square; and one of these sections, out of a given number, is devoted to the maintenance of schools.   As a township increases in population, the reserved section advances in value.   These schools are not subject to any central control, but are under the management of a committee chosen by the township.

Still education is not so general in all the States as might be wished.   Miss Beecher, the daughter of Dr. Beecher, having devoted to the subject much time and talent, tells us that there are in the United States " a million adults who cannot read and write, and more than two millions of children utterly illiterate and entirely without schools !"   Of the children in this condition, 130,000 are in Ohio, and 100,000 in Kentucky.

In the working of this system of education, the absence of a State Church affords advantages not enjoyed in England.   Of late, however, an objection to the use of the Bible in these schools has been raised by the Roman Catholics, and the question in some States has been fiercely agitated.   In the city of St. Louis the Bible has been excluded.   In Cincinnati the Catholics, failing to exclude it, have established schools of their own.

This agitation is one of great interest.   It leads thoughtful and devout men to ask, whether, when the State, assuming to be the instructor of its subjects, establishes schools, and puts Protestant Bibles, or any other, or none into them *by law*, they have not thenceforth Protestantism, Popery, or Infidelity so far *by law established;* and whether it is not better that the State should restrict itself to its proper function as the minister of justice, leaving secular instruction, like religious, to the spontaneous resources of the people.

To this, I think, it will come at last.   The Common School economy is a remnant of the old Church-and-State system, which has not been entirely swept away. But for this impression I should feel some uneasiness, lest it should prove the germ of a new order of things leading back to State-Churchism.   It appeared to me quite natural to say, " Here is a State provision for schools,—why not have a similar provision for churches? It works well for the one,—why not for the other ?   Is it not as important that our churches should rely, not alone on the capricious and scanty efforts of the voluntary principle, but also on the more respectable and permanent support of the State, as it is that our Common Schools should adopt this course ?"   To me it seemed that the arguments which recommended the one supported the other ; but when I have mentioned to intelligent men the possibility, not to say probability, of the one step leading to the other, they have invariably been surprised at my apprehensions, and have assured me that nothing was more unlikely to take place.

But, to show the jealousy with which on *other* grounds the system begins to be viewed, I will close by a short quotation from a writer in the *New Englander*, a respectable *Quarterly*, to which I have before referred. " It will, doubtless, be thought strange to say that the systems of public common-school edueation now existing, and sought to be established throughout our country, may yet, while Christians sleep, become one of the greatest, if not *the* greatest, antagonism in the land to all evangelical instruction and piety. But how long before they will be so,—when they shall have become the mere creatures of the State, and, under the plea of no sectarianism, mere naturalism shall be the substance of all the religious, and the basis of all the secular teaching which they shall give? And let it not be forgotten that strong currents of influence, in all parts of the country, acting in no chance concert, are doing their utmost to bring about just this result."

4. I admire their *temperance*.

I confess that I felt humbled and ashamed for my own country, when, so soon as I trod on British ground, or British *planks*, the old absurd drinking usages again saluted my eye. In all the States I met with nothing more truly ludicrous than some of these. For instance, when A. B.'s mouth happens to be well replenished with "flesh, fish, or fowl," potatoes, pudding, or pastry,

at one table, C. D., from another table far away
across the room, at the top of his voice, calls out,
" Mr. A. B., allow me the pleasure to take a glass of
wine with you." A. B. makes a very polite bow,
fills his glass in a great hurry, holds it up with his
right hand, C. D. doing the same thing with his; and
then A. B. and C. D., making another polite bow to
each other, simultaneously swallow their glasses of
wine ! Were we not *accustomed* to the sight, it would
appear as laughable as anything travellers tell us of
the manners and customs of the least enlightened
nations. Surely, if this childish practice is still a
rule in polite society, it is one " more honoured in
the breach than the observance." In no city on the
Eastern side of the Alleghany Mountains did I meet
a single drunken American in the street. The few
whom I did detect in that plight were manifestly recent
importations from Great Britain and Ireland !

5. I also greatly admire their *secular enterprise.*
They afford a fine illustration of the idea conveyed
in their own indigenous phrase, " Go a-head."

LETTER XXXVII.

Slavery—Responsibility of the North—District of Columbia—Preponderance of the Slave Power—Extermination of the Indians—President Taylor and his Blood-hounds—Conclusion.

BUT there is a class of things among them which men of well-regulated minds and habits cannot but detest. These, as they have come under my notice, I have pointed out. The chief of all is *slavery*. This stared me in the face the moment I entered the States; and it presses itself on my notice now that I have retired from the American shore. It is the beginning and the ending of all that is vile and vicious in this confederation of Republics. In England, you have been often told by American visiters that the Northern States of the Union are not at all identified with slavery, and are, in fact, no more responsible for its existence in the South than we are for the existence of a like system in the colonies of some of our European Allies. Than this representation nothing can be further from the truth. There is really no analogy whatever between the two cases. Each State, it is true, has its own distinct and independent legislature; but all the States are united in one federation, which has a thoroughly pro-slavery government. The constitution is pledged to maintain the execrable system,

P 3

and the Northern States are pledged to maintain the hypocritical constitution.

That no preponderance of influence might be given to any one State over the rest, by making it the seat of the central government, a district of 10 miles square was partitioned out, partly from Virginia and partly from Maryland, for that purpose. This district, called the District of Columbia, has no government and no representation of its own, but is under the absolute control and regulation of the United Government or Congress, " exclusive jurisdiction over it in all cases whatsoever" having been given by the constitution. In this absolute government of the "ten miles square," embracing the site of Washington the capital, the Northern States, by their representatives in Congress, have their full share. Now, not merely does slavery exist in that District, but it exists there under statutes so barbarous and cruel that the neighbouring slave States have actually abolished the like within the bounds of their separate jurisdiction, leaving to the *free* States the unenviable responsibility of enforcing laws too horrible for kidnappers. Take a specimen,— " A slave convicted of any petit treason, or murder, or wilful burning of a dwelling-house, to have the right hand cut off, to be hanged in the usual manner, the head severed from the body, the body divided into four quarters, and the head and quarters set up in the most public places of the county where such act was committed." Take another,—" A *free negro* may be arrested, and put in jail for 3 months, on *suspicion* of being a runaway; and if he is not able to *prove* his freedom in 12 months, *he is to be sold as a slave* TO PAY HIS JAIL FEES !" Are there not hundreds of free men, both black and white, who could not *prove* their freedom under such circumstances? Yet, for this *crime,* they are reduced to perpetual bondage *by authority of Congress.* And all this the North upholds !

Washington, the capital, thus governed, is but the great mart of the national man-trade. From the adjoining port of Alexandria, 7 miles off, the victims are shipped for the South. Listen to the *Gazette* of that place,—" Here you may behold fathers and brothers leaving behind them the dearest objects of affection, and moving slowly along in the mute agony of despair,—there the young mother sobbing over the infant, whose innocent smiles seem but to increase her misery. From some you will hear the burst of bitter lamentation; while from others the loud hysteric laugh breaks forth, denoting still deeper agony."

But you will be told that it is not in the power of Northern members to alter this state of things. Why not? In the House of Representatives the free States have a majority of about 50, and in the Senate they have for some years been equal. But have they tried? Have they protested? Have they voted? Have they divided the House? They *have* voted. How? *Eighty-two Northern men,* a few years ago, voted that Congress ought not to interfere *in any way* with slavery in the District of Columbia !

Look at some of the provisions of the Federal Government. See what " SOLEMN GUARANTEES" it gives to the accursed system of slavery, in whatever State it may be found!

Art. I., sect. 2, says, "Representatives and direct taxes shall be apportioned among the several States which may be included within this Union according to their respective numbers, which shall be determined by adding to the whole number of free persons, including those bound to serve for a term of years, and excluding Indians not taxed, *three-fifths of all other persons*," — that is to say, *slaves*, for once called "persons!" Here is a positive premium on slaveholding. This constitutes an aristocracy of the most monstrous character, and introduces into the social fabric an element as absurd as it is perilous. Talk of the aristocracy of England, and the undue influence of landed proprietors! You have nothing half so unjust and vicious as this. Suppose the Southern States have two millions and a half of slaves : for that amount of property they have one million and a half of additional votes; while in the free States there is no property representation whatever. Or look at the question in another aspect. Two citizens have each a capital of 5,000*l.* to invest. The one invests in shipping or commerce in New York, and at the time of the election counts *one;* the other invests in slaves in South Carolina, obtaining for the sum mentioned a whole gang of 100 human beings of both sexes and of all ages, and at the time of the election he counts *sixty-one,* —swamping with his 100 slaves the votes of sixty-one respectable merchants in a free State! This it is which has constituted an aristocracy of about 200,000 slave-holders in the South, the ruling power in the United States. It has made the preservation and extension of slavery the vital and moving principle of the national policy. So that ever since 1830 slavery, slave-holding, slave-breeding, and slave-trading have enjoyed the special and fostering care of the Federal Government. As to the *quid pro quo*—the taxation that was to be connected with the representation of " three-fifths of all other persons," that has been almost entirely evaded. " There has not been," says a New England Reviewer, " if we mistake not, but in one instance, and then in a very light degree, an assessment of direct taxation."

Art. I., sect. 8, says, " Congress shall have power" —among other things—" to suppress *insurrections*." And Art. IV., sect. 4, says, " The United States shall guarantee to every State in this Union a republican form of government; and shall protect each of them against invasion; and on application of the legislature, or of the executive (when the legislature cannot be convened), against *domestic violence*."

These clauses pledge the whole force of the United States' army, and navy too, if needs be, to the maintenance of slavery in any or in all the States and Districts in which it may exist. But for this, the system could not stand a single day. Let the North say to the South, " We will not interfere with your ' peculiar institution,' but we will not defend it; if you cannot keep your slaves in subjection, you must expect no aid from us." Let them only say this, and *do* nothing, and the whole fabric of slavery would instantly crumble and fall. The edifice is rotten, and is propped up only by the buttresses of the North. The South retains the slave, because the free States furnish the sentinels.

Again, Art. IV., sect. 2, says, "No person held to service or labour in one State, under the laws thereof, escaping into another, shall, in consequence of any law or regulation therein, be discharged from such service or labour; but shall be *delivered up* on claim of the party to whom such service or labour may be due."

This clause pledges the North, not only to refuse an asylum to the fugitive slave, but also to deliver him up to his unrighteous and cruel task-master,—a deed which the law of God expressly condemns, and which the best impulses of our nature repudiate with loathing and contempt. The article before us constitutes all the free States of the Union a slave-hunting ground for the Southern aristocracy. Talk of the game laws of England! Here is a game law infinitely more unjust and oppressive. A free country this! A noble government! Hail Columbia!

See how this slave-holding aristocracy have always managed to oppress the North, and to secure to themselves the lion's share of the good things of government.

THE PRESIDENCY.—Out of the 16 presidential elections since the origin of the Confederation, 13 have been in favour of slave-holders, and only 3 in favour of Northern men. By holding the Presidency, slavery rules the cabinet, the diplomacy, the army, and the navy of the Union. The power that controls the Presidency controls the nation. No Northern President has ever been re-elected.

THE VICE-PRESIDENCY.—The individual who holds this office is *ex-officio* President of the Senate, and, as such, has a casting vote in all questions before that body. During the last 20 years, with one exception, this functionary has always been a slave-holder.

THE OFFICE OF SECRETARY OF STATE. — This is second only in importance to the Presidency. It is the duty of this officer to direct correspondence with foreign courts, instruct the foreign ministers, negotiate treaties, &c. Of the 16 who have hitherto filled that office, 10 have been from the slave States, and 6 from the free.

THE SPEAKER OF THE HOUSE OF REPRESENTATIVES.—This officer has the appointment of all committees, and exerts an immense influence on the legislation of the country. During 31 of the 34 years from 1811 to 1845 the Speakers were all slave-holders.

The slave power, having thus the whole machinery of government under its control, can at any time bring all the resources of the nation to bear upon the preservation and extension of the " peculiar institution." While Florida, for instance, belonged to Spain, it furnished an asylum for runaway slaves from the neighbouring States. It must therefore be purchased by the Union, and five millions of dollars were paid for it. Still the native Indians, those children of the forest, afforded a shelter to fugitives from slavery. They must therefore be either exterminated or exiled. A war was waged against them. They were driven from the homes of their fathers, and the negroes among them hunted and shot like wild beasts. At the urgent recommendation of Zachary Taylor—the person who in March next will doubtless mount the presidential chair —blood-hounds were purchased as AUXILIARIES to the army, at a cost of five thousand dollars; and blood-hounds and soldiers and officers marched together under the "star-spangled banner" in pursuit of the panting fugitives from Southern oppression. In this expedition they captured 460 negroes, each one at the cost of the lives of two white men, and at a further expense of at least eighty thousand dollars per head. The whole outlay of the war was *forty millions of dollars,* most of which was drawn from the pockets of Northern people.

The Annexation of Texas and the Mexican War—all for the perpetuation and extension of slavery—are fresh in your remembrance.

And here I quit the land of " The Bond and the Free."

> " Nineveh, Babylon, and ancient Rome
> Speak to the present times, and times to come:
> They cry aloud in every careless ear,
> ' Stop, while you may; suspend your mad career;
> Oh! learn from our example and our fate,—
> Learn wisdom and repentance ere too late.' "